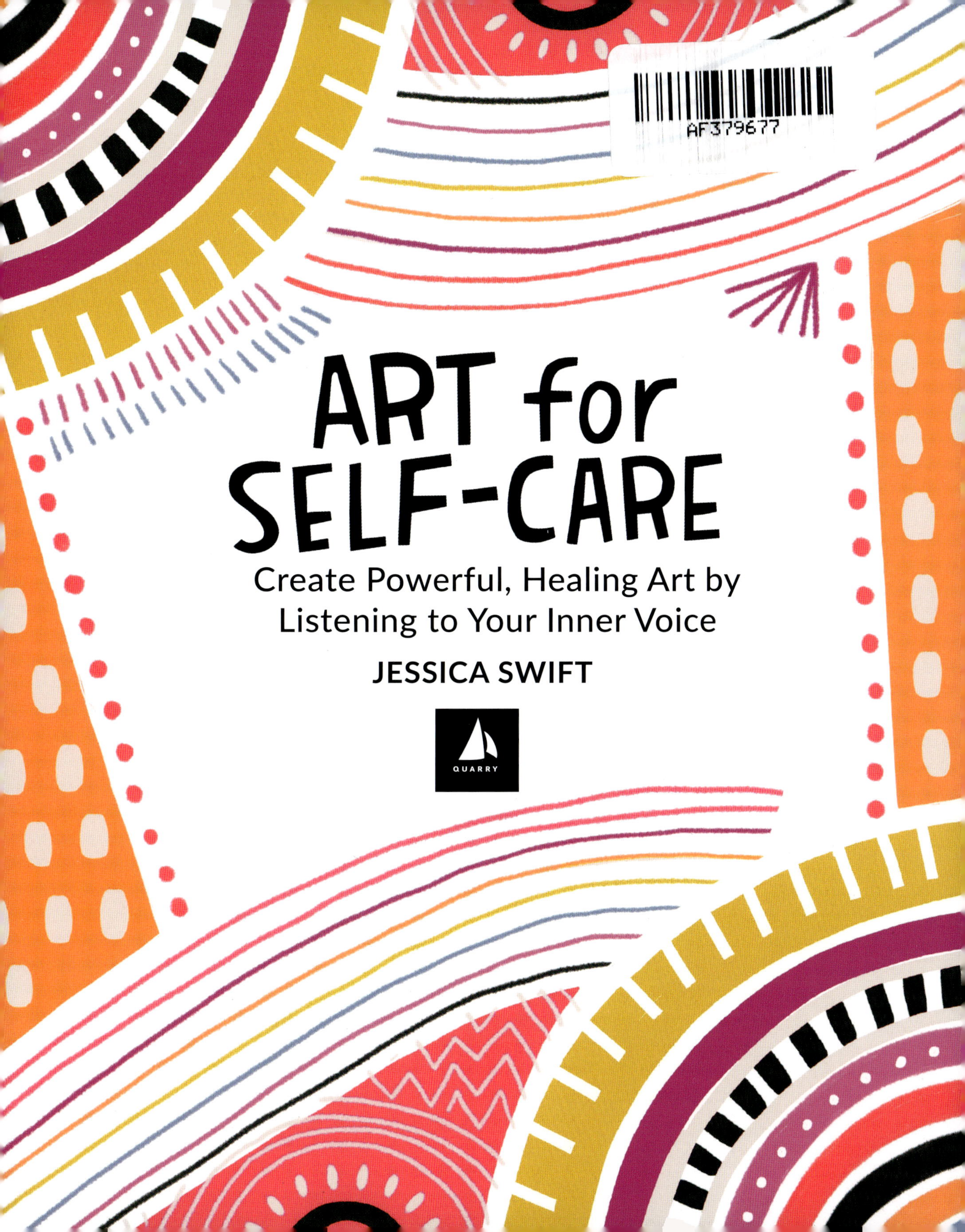

ART for SELF-CARE

Create Powerful, Healing Art by Listening to Your Inner Voice

JESSICA SWIFT

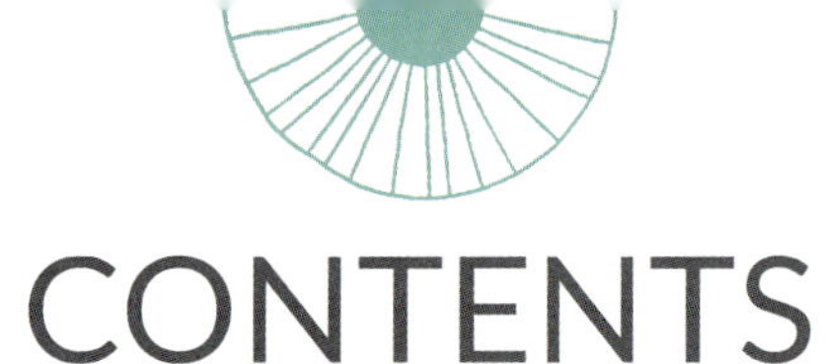

CONTENTS

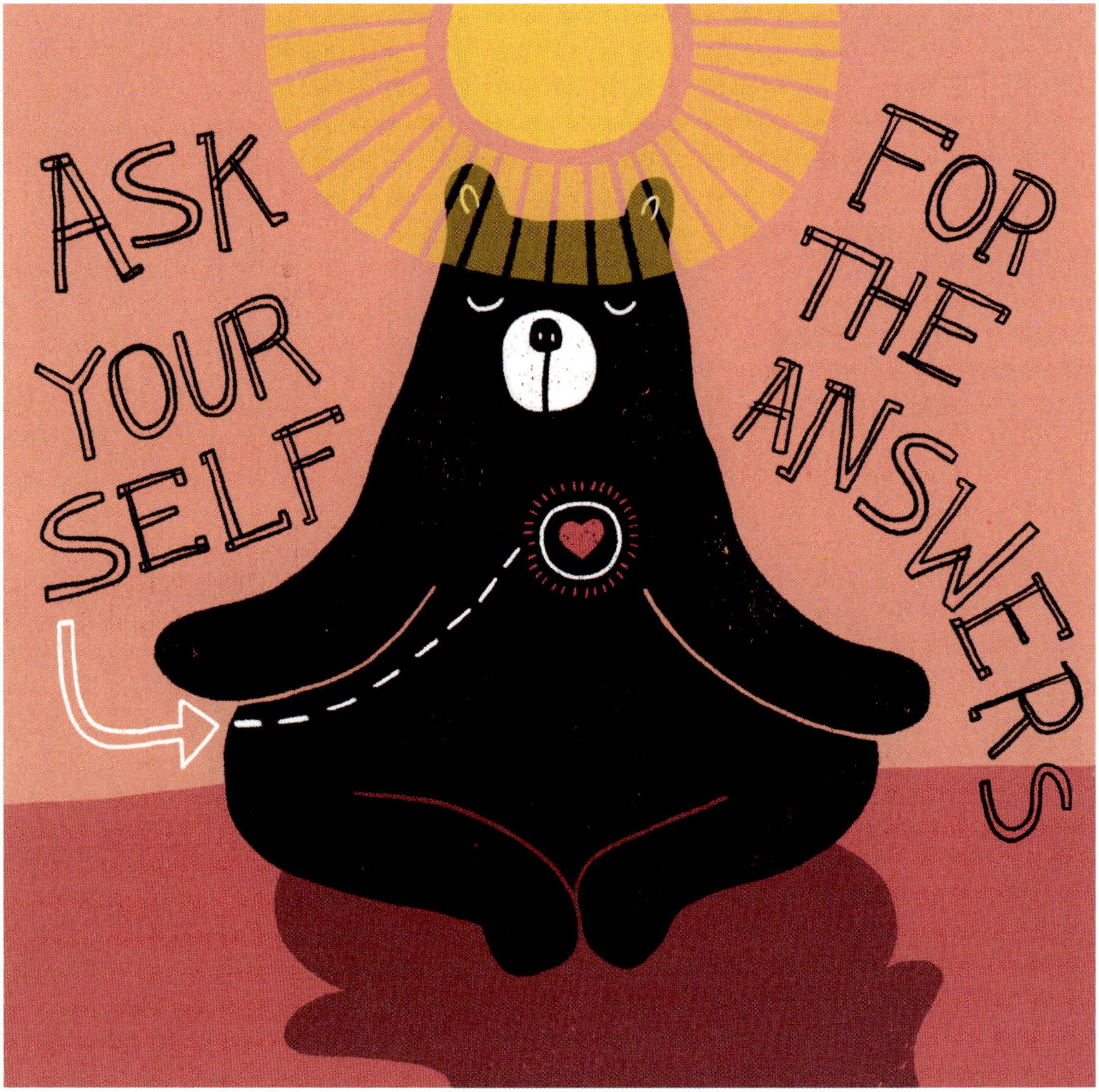

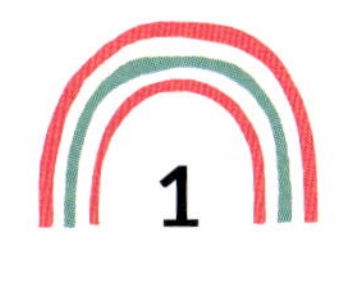

1
GOING INWARD

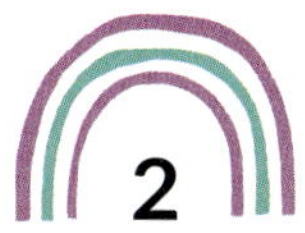

2
INSIDES OUTWARD

3
INTEGRATING + HONORING

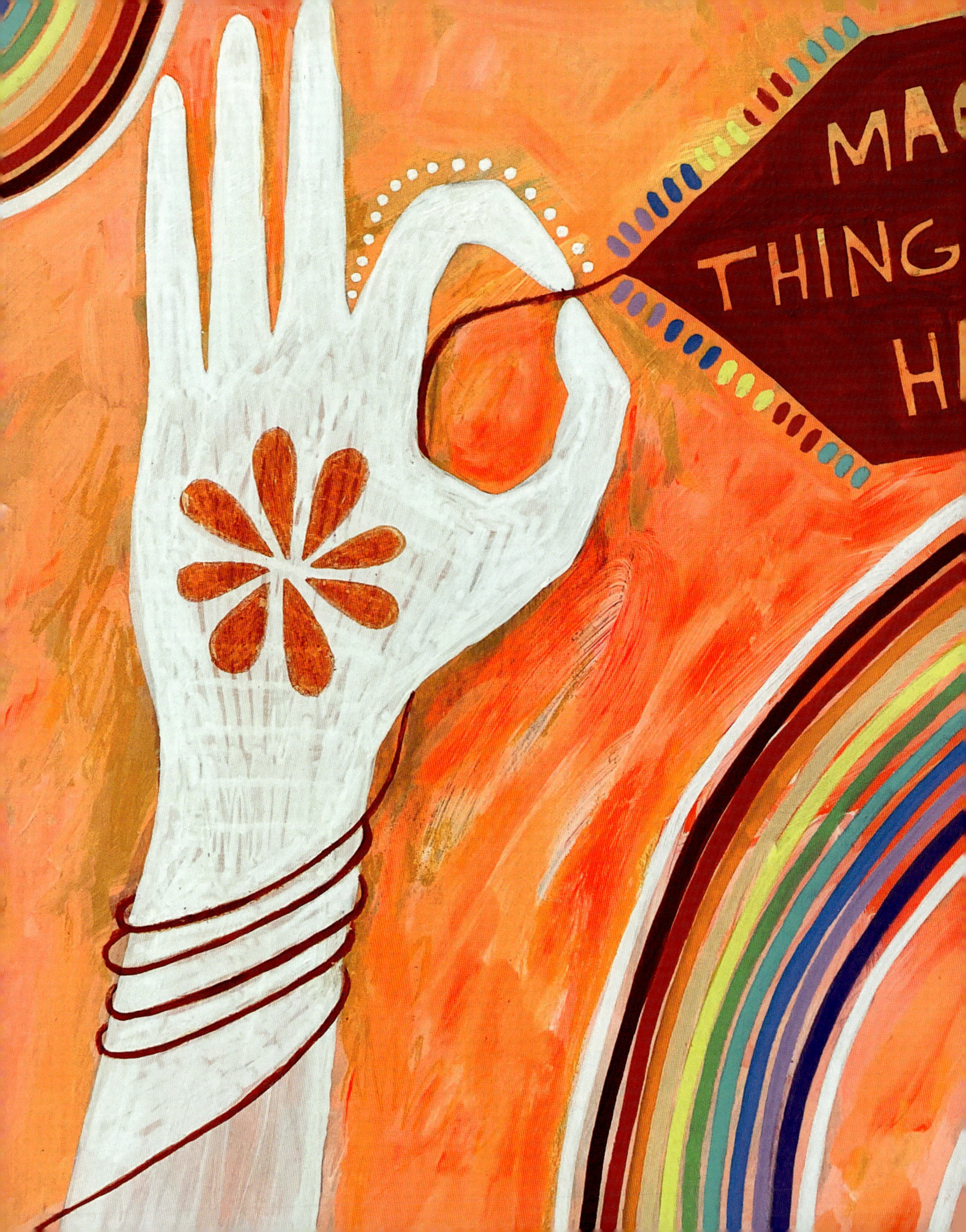
MAG
THING
HA

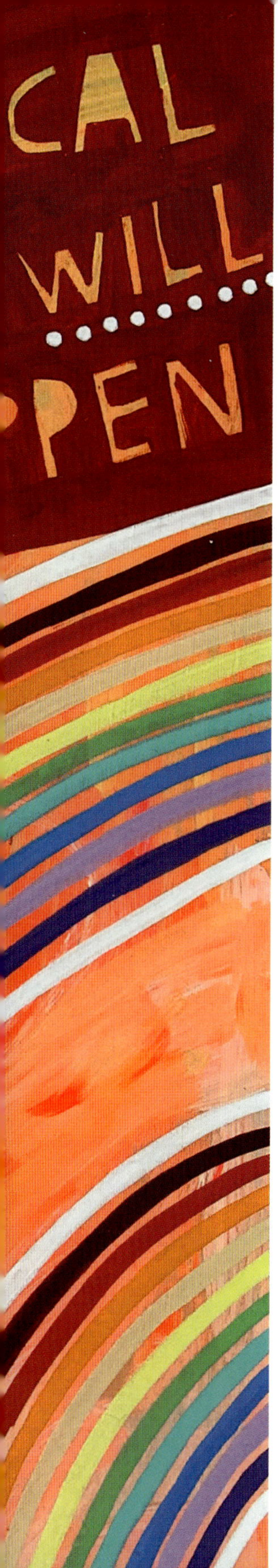

INTRODUCTION

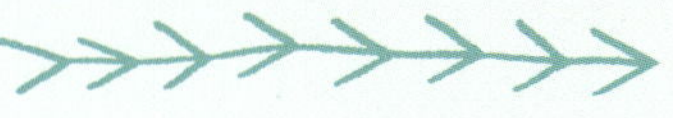

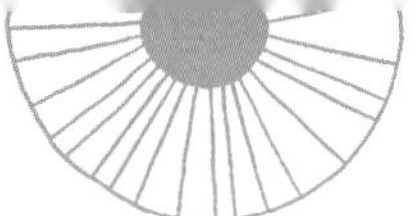

MY STORY, MY PROCESS

*"You will be ok.
This will not stop you.
This will not break you.
This will not end you."*

I HEARD THESE words as I leaned down to scoop a cup of cat food into a bowl, during a quiet and painful moment alone in my kitchen. The voice that delivered them was calm and matter-of-fact and came from somewhere deep within my own mind. I remember standing up quickly, the words reverberating in my mind, surprised and a little shaken by the clarity of the message I'd just received. I didn't know exactly what had just happened, but I just knew somehow that these words were true and real and that I could trust this voice. This deep knowing filled me with a sense of comfort, connection, and strength that I wasn't expecting on the worst morning of my life.

On August 14, 2018, my husband Ryan died. I was a married thirty-seven-year-old woman with a nearly three-year-old son and another baby on the way. A doctor, son, brother, husband, father, uncle, skier, woodworker, friend, animal lover, and so much more, Ryan also struggled with a powerful and consuming addiction that cut his life tragically short and left an ocean of grief in its wake. He was forty. In an instant, my world had turned upside down. It was disorienting, terrifying, heartbreaking, traumatic, and overwhelming. I didn't know how I was going to walk forward through the heart-wrenching pain and fear of my new reality, but I knew I could trust this voice and that what it told me was true. I was going to be okay, and I was going to be able to handle it. I didn't know how, but deep inside myself I knew that I would.

Looking back on this moment in the kitchen, I didn't know what a catalyst that voice would be, but it transformed the way I make art and live my life forever. The dramatic way it communicated with me that morning caught my attention and ignited a curiosity in me. *Where did that voice come from? What else did it have to tell me? What else did it know? Could I intentionally connect with this voice whenever I wanted to?* I had so many questions, and it felt like an incredible gift had just landed in my lap, specifically for me.

This gift, I came to realize, had been with me all along. It wasn't something outside of myself; it *was* myself! The voice I heard was my wise inner voice—the one that's tapped into the universal mystery of life itself. We all have one. No exceptions. It wasn't new; it had always been there. I just hadn't been paying attention.

So I started practicing listening to and paying attention to this voice, and the more I did, the more I saw how much I'd ignored it over the years. I also began to see the enormous amount of stress, anxiety, and fear that had built up in my body and in my mind. I started to realize that my inner world mattered more than anything else and that it would always lead me in the direction of growth, self-love, and my highest good.

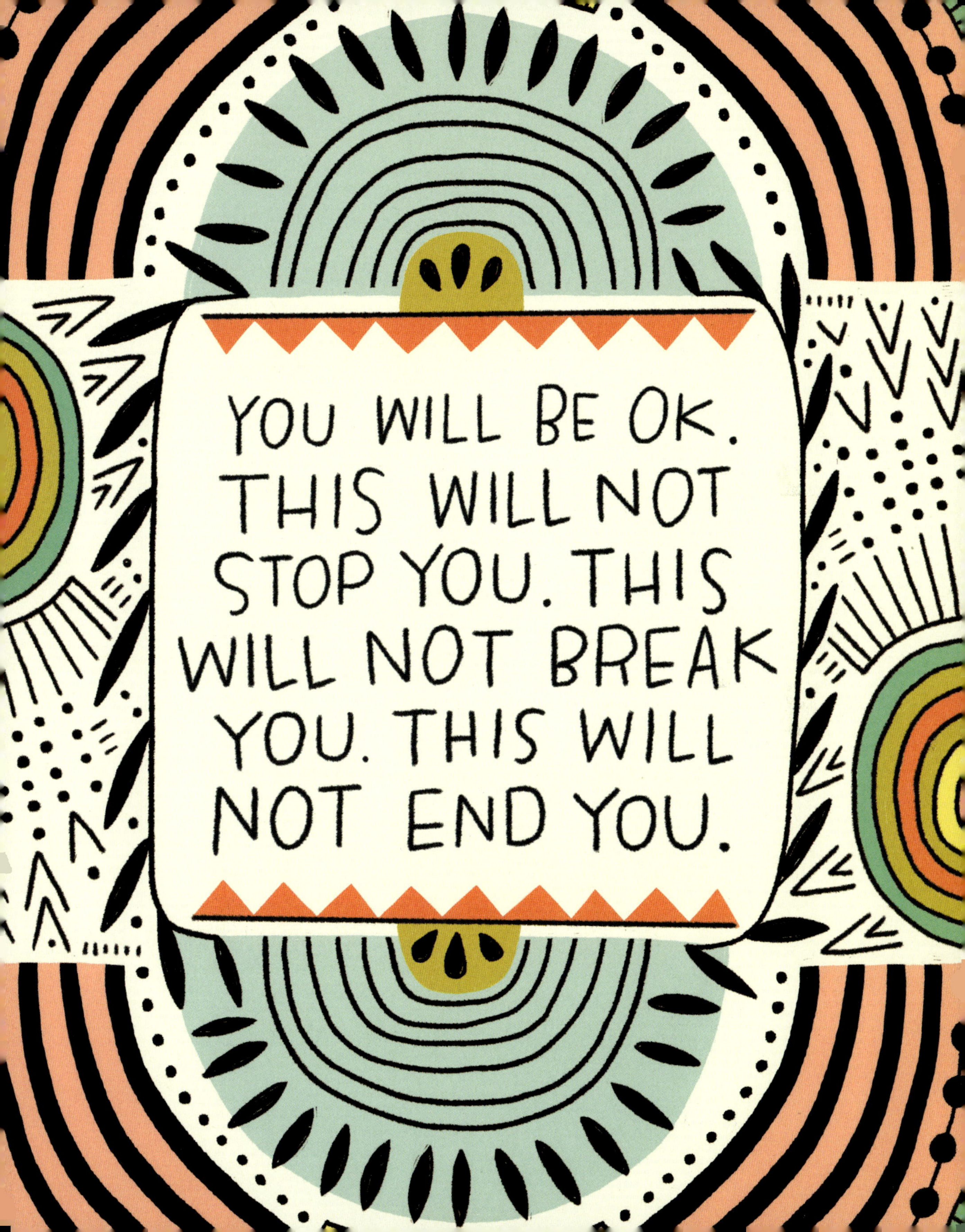

YOU WILL BE OK. THIS WILL NOT STOP YOU. THIS WILL NOT BREAK YOU. THIS WILL NOT END YOU.

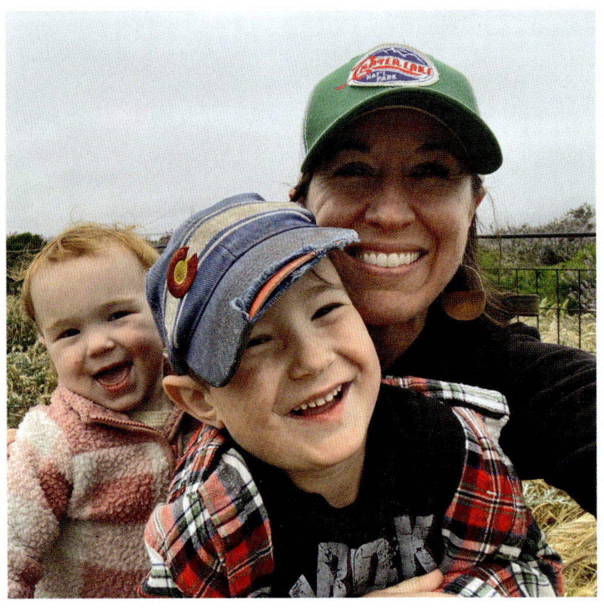

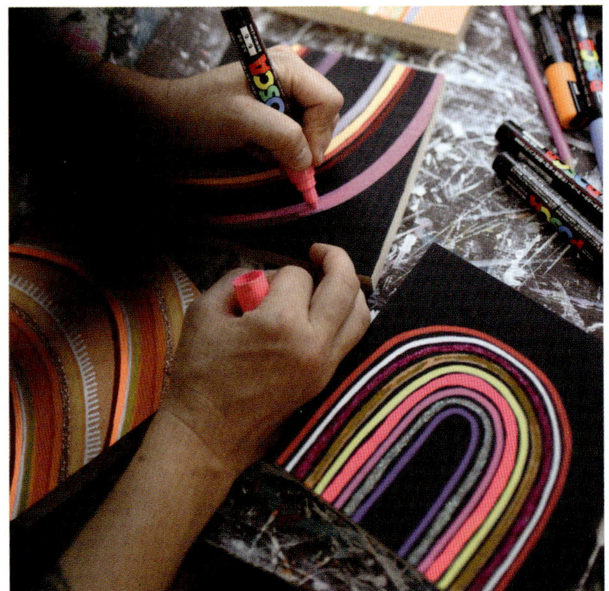

I also began to see ways I *had* trusted and listened to my inner voice over the years, without necessarily realizing that's what I was doing. It was proof that my inner voice had been communicating with me all along, getting through to me more successfully sometimes than others. I learned that I didn't have to wait for big dramatic communications from my inner voice; I could build a relationship with it and intentionally tap into its wisdom and guidance whenever I needed it, night or day.

I didn't have much time alone in the early days following Ryan's death, but when I did I spent time painting in my studio. This quiet time creating helped me care for and tune in to myself as I walked through my grief. Making art has always been a nurturing practice for me and a space where I can process my feelings, and so I intuitively knew that making art would help me heal and move through this painful experience. Since I was already practicing tuning in to my inner voice in general, I naturally began listening for it more intentionally as I painted as well.

These quiet hours in my studio were the times I most looked forward to during the painful early weeks and months following Ryan's death. They were critical for my sanity and for my well-being. In my studio, I was able to give myself the space to quiet my mind and to feel whatever I needed to feel each day. As I listened to my inner voice, my inner world slowly became more peaceful and my artmaking practice deepened. I trusted myself. I followed my intuition, I cried, I painted, I screamed, I felt my feelings, and I began to heal. And my artwork naturally began to reflect it. When I heard my inner voice loud and clear in the kitchen the morning that Ryan died, I didn't realize what an important piece of my artmaking practice it would be in the years to follow. But that voice started a revolution within me—one that's impacted every part of my life, every day since. I realize more and more each day how sacred and vital artmaking is for me in making sense of all my experiences and feelings.

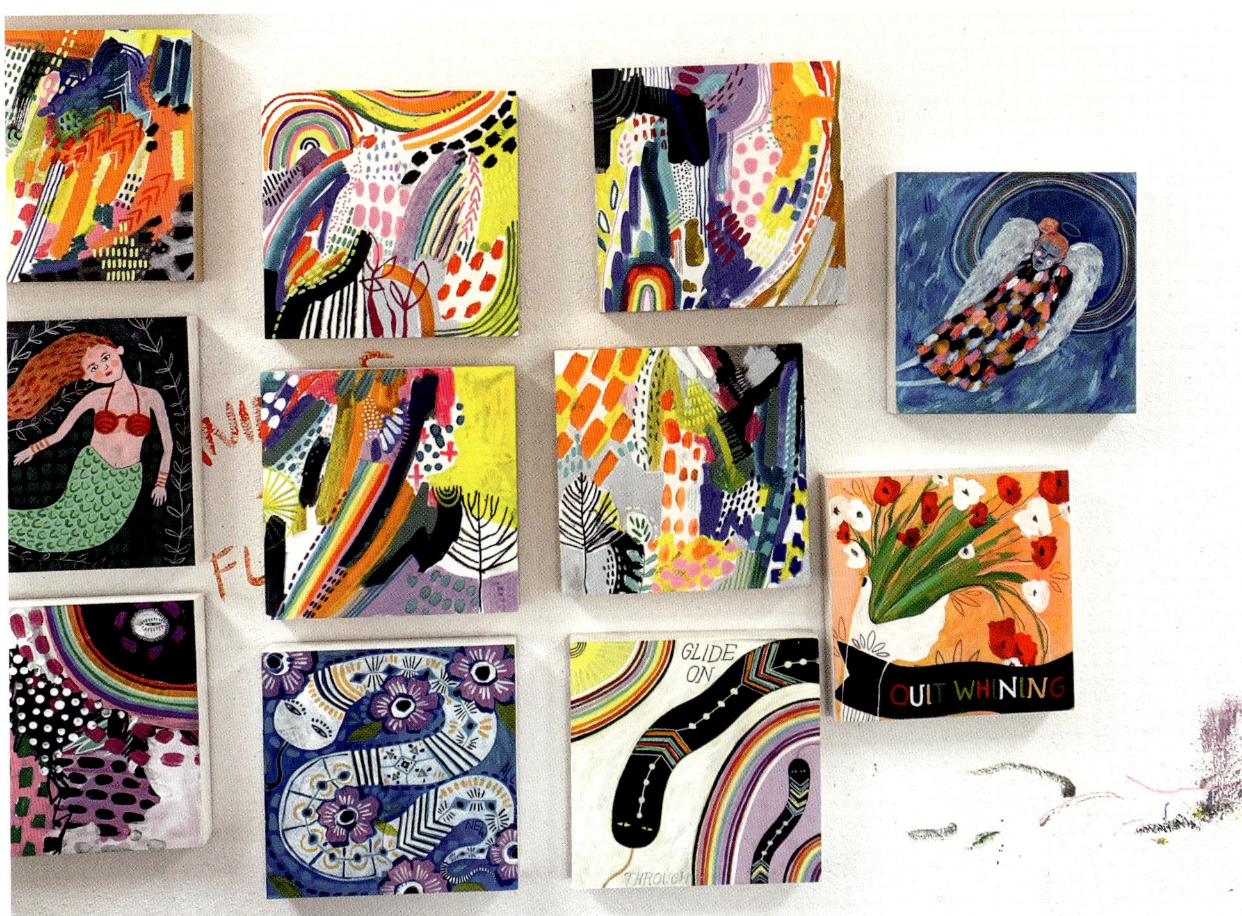

Creativity, I believe, is a powerful tool we can use in learning to take exquisite care of ourselves. Everything in life is intertwined. Life, art, grief, joy, pain, creativity, gratitude, sorrow, ease, disappointment . . . and through it all, our bodies and our wise inner beings know exactly what we need to do in order to return to balance and peace. We just have to be willing to listen.

The journey inward, back home to our truest selves, is a lifelong one, but it's the most important journey of all and absolutely worth taking. Pain is often a catalyst. If you're a human who is going through or who has gone through something hard, know this: creativity as a healing tool is available for you, too. You're in the right place. And you're not alone.

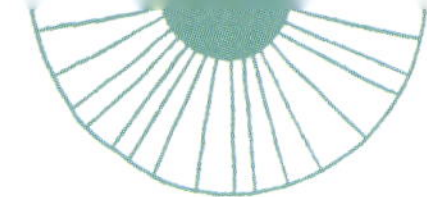

WHOM THIS BOOK IS FOR

THE MOST IMPORTANT thing for you to remember as you work your way through this book is this: **You do not have to be an artist.** Considering yourself "an artist" is absolutely not required here! What *is* required is a sense of curiosity, openness, courage, and a willingness to show up for yourself.

This process will crack you open if you let it. It will change you and it will deepen your relationship with yourself. If you want to learn how to use art as a way to care for yourself and to process feelings and experiences, then this book is for you.

Tuning in to your intuition and making art from the messages you receive will increase your self-confidence and feelings of self-worth. You'll get to know and understand yourself better. It'll help you learn to value yourself, your needs, and your own experiences more wholly. Giving yourself time and space to feel your feelings and express them can be deeply meaningful, powerful, and healing.

This process is less about artmaking and more about using art for self-care in times of stress, change, uncertainty, grief, and fear. It's all about acknowledging and making space for what you're experiencing in your life as it happens each day. Your art may not look the way you want it to or think it should. That's okay! Just keep going. Of course, it feels great to make something that you think is beautiful, but that's not the point here. The point is simply to get your inner self out onto the page and to make something that's meaningful and useful for yourself.

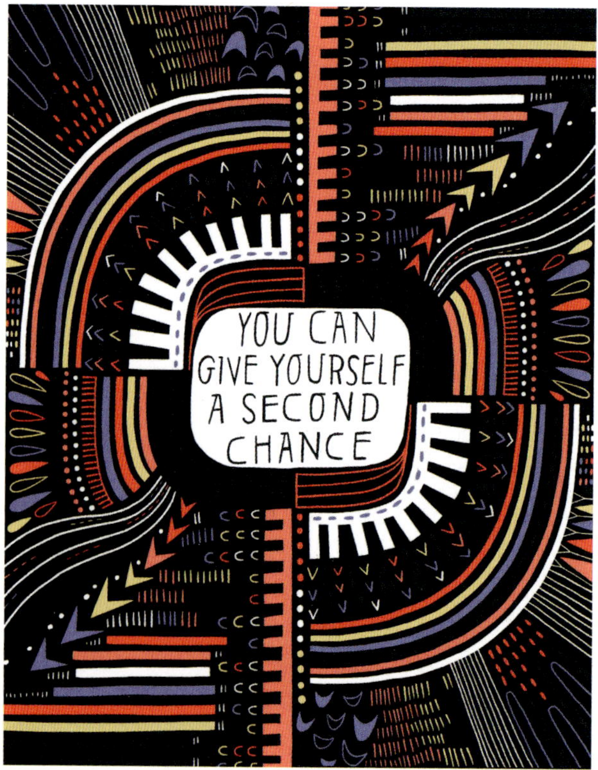

Some days your art might be hopeful. Some days it could be sad. Some days it might be colorful and other days muted. Some days you might love what you create and other days you might want to burn it. Sometimes you may feel proud and other times you may feel embarrassed. Sometimes your art might have words in it, and some days it might be only images or symbols. Sometimes you might not want to show up to tune in and listen and practice. (In my experience, those are sometimes the most important days to show up for yourself.) Sometimes you won't show up, and then you'll have the chance to be gentle and remind yourself that you always get to try again.

The next most important thing you'll need to remember is that **there are no rules here**. There's no right and wrong. Throughout the book I'll offer suggestions for how you might approach a technique, or a prompt, or a way to tune in to yourself. These are just suggestions to get you started! What I hope you'll discover as you practice the techniques offered here and become more adept at communicating with your inner self is that no one knows what's right for you except YOU. You are in charge here! You make the rules. If something that I suggest doesn't work for you, then don't do it. If you know a better way for yourself, then do it that way!

This might feel uncomfortable if you're someone who likes to follow step-by-step instructions and know exactly how something is going to turn out. To get the most out of this process, you'll need to embrace the unknown and trust the unfolding of it all. There is no direct path laid out here; my words will simply guide you forward as you create your own spiraling path inside yourself and then back out again.

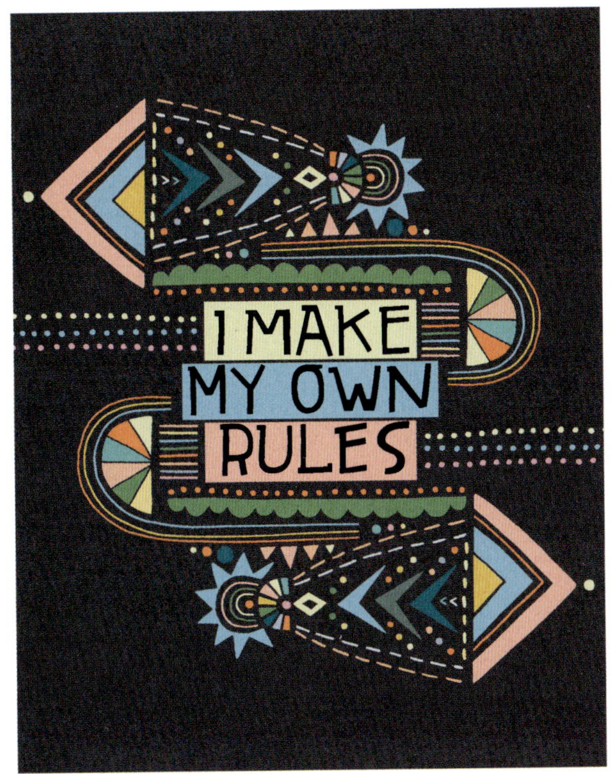

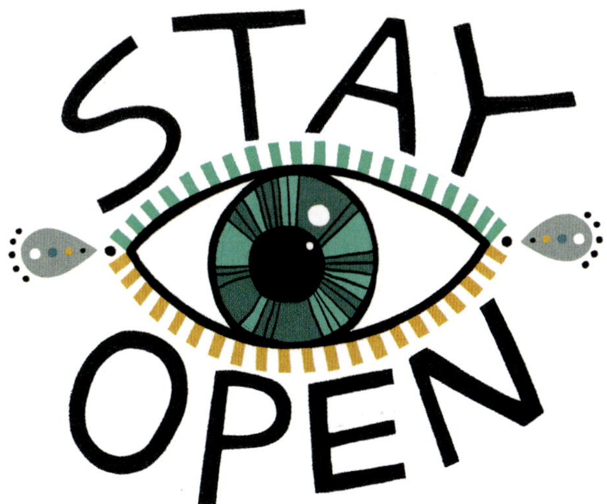

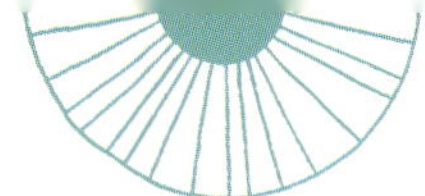

ARTMAKING FOR HEALING AND PROCESSING FEELINGS

RYAN'S DEATH WAS a catalyst for me to begin navigating the complex world of my emotions. I discovered that emotions are like waves. They start small and rise, they swell, then they peak and recede. Harvard brain scientist Jill Bolte Taylor says that emotions actually only take ninety seconds to fully pass when you allow and accept them. Ninety seconds! Like many of us, though, I've spent much of my life resisting uncomfortable emotions. I mean, who wants to feel pain or sadness or fear? I certainly didn't. Many of us pick up this notion that if we're feeling "negative" things it means we're doing something wrong. That we're not good enough. Or that it's just too much and we won't be able to handle it.

I'll never forget the day this changed for me. It was in the early days after Ryan's death, and I was alone in my car driving home. I'd spent days surrounded by family, and it was one of my first quiet moments alone. And I broke down. I began sobbing so hard that I had to pull over and park so I could just cry. There was no resisting it this time. The wave was so powerful, it felt like I would be in it forever. But then . . . I wasn't. I cried, and then it passed. (I think it might've taken longer than ninety seconds, though!) I felt emptied out and yet filled up at the same time, and then I drove home. It was the first time I'd simply let a wave make its way through my energy field without resisting it, and it was a revelation. I began to practice letting the waves come. And when they did, the pain grew and swelled, and it felt terrible and difficult, and then it receded and passed and I felt refreshed and better. Every single time.

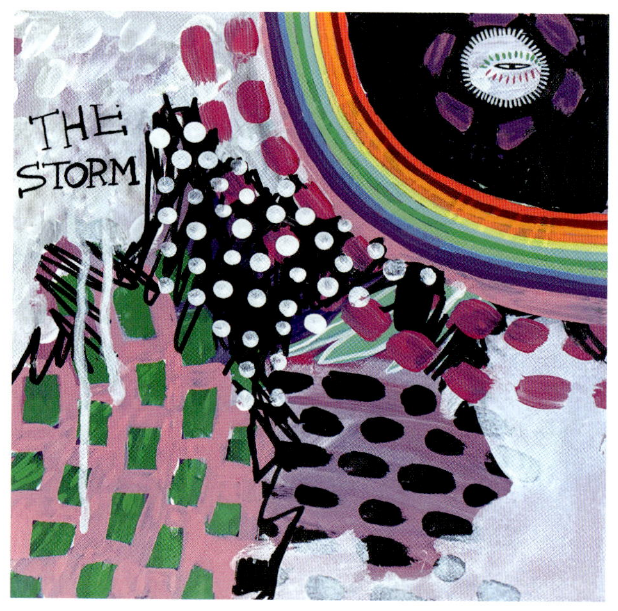

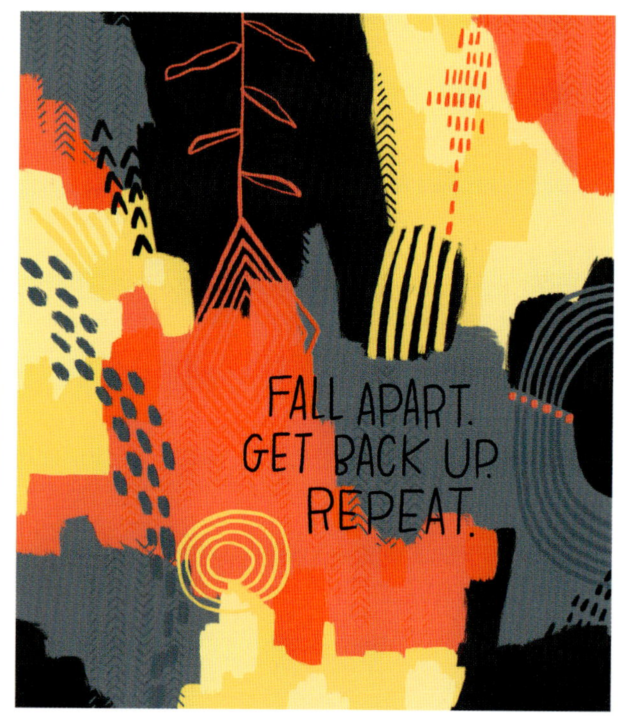

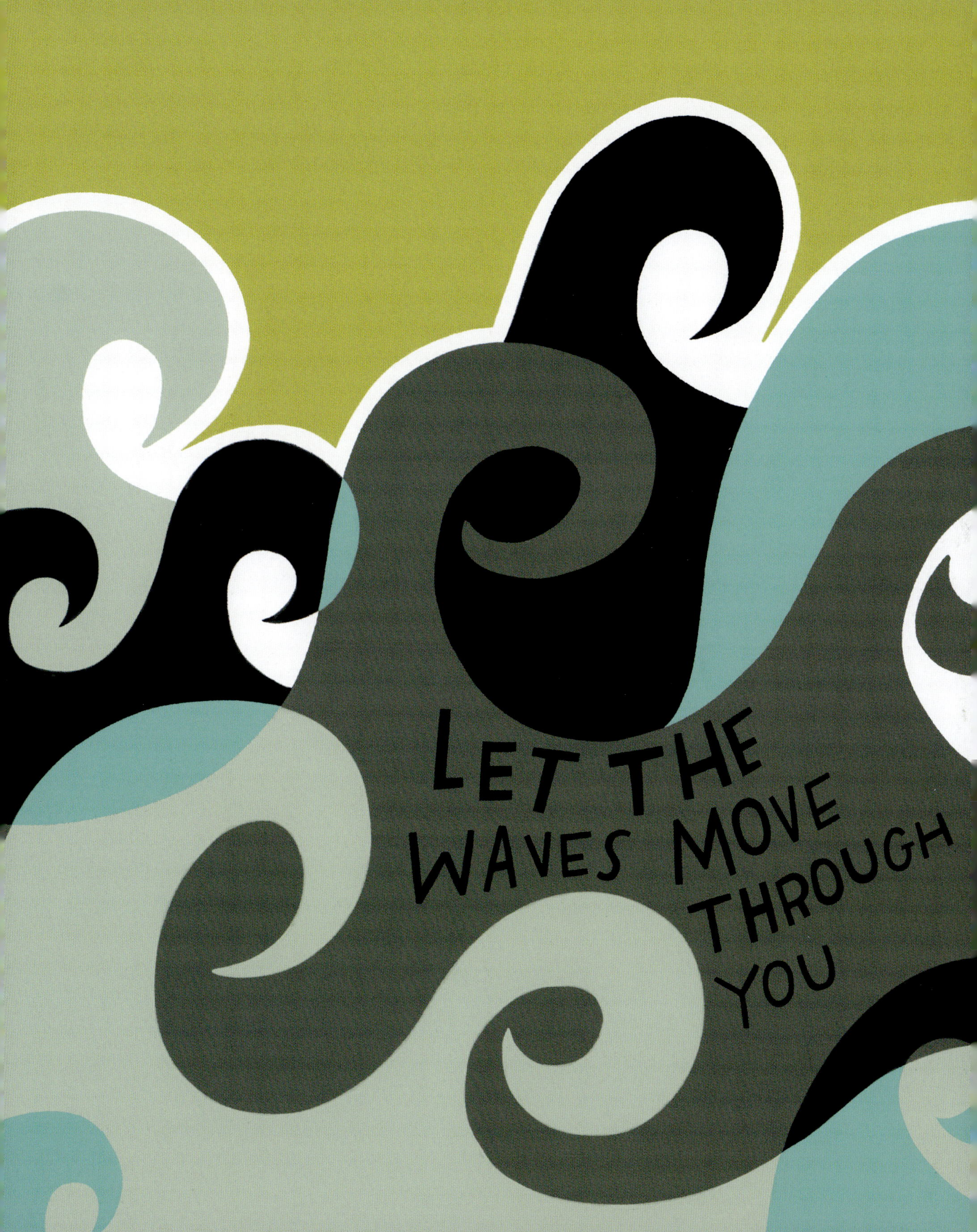

LET THE WAVES MOVE THROUGH YOU

Six months after Ryan died and not long after my baby girl was born, I started a 100-day project called "100 Messages to Myself." Early mother-hood is an easy place to get lost. So is grief. Facing the strange reality of navigating both those places at the same time, I realized I needed a way to stay tuned in to myself and to continue practicing identifying, acknowledging, and feeling my feelings as my life morphed and shifted around me. Having successfully completed a couple of 100-day creative projects before, I intuitively settled on the "100 Messages to Myself" theme as a way to show up for myself in a small way each day. What I didn't know at the time, though, was how impactful and healing the project would be for me.

Each evening after my baby and toddler were asleep, I sat on the couch with my iPad or a sketch-book. I got quiet, I turned my ears inward, and I waited for a message from my innermost self—the voice that wants nothing but the best for me. Life was difficult in those early days after Ryan's death and Georgia's birth. Through listening, hearing a message meant just for me, and then drawing I was able to calm myself. To acknowledge where I was. To comfort myself. To figure out how I was actually feeling. To heal. I never had a plan. Each day was its own experience. I just had to show up and my inner self took over from there.

Making art centered around my own words to myself was a lifeline. It still is. Sitting down to make art became a way to have a conversation with myself and to process the beautiful mess of my life. Because that's what it was—a big messy swirl of all sorts of emotions that were hard to sort out. This was my way to untangle myself each day.

What do I need to hear today?
What do I need to know?
What will make me feel better right now?

As I asked these kinds of questions while sitting in the quiet, I discovered the answers were already inside of me. All I had to do was ask and then listen. Seeing the messages from my intuition reflected back to me on the page is a deeply healing and affirming experience. I can still look at a piece I made in those early days and remember what I was feeling, why I needed those specific words, and how it helped me heal. The power of this artmaking practice in my life is undeniable. I hope it will be powerful in yours, too!

Sometimes your messages will be profound and deeply personal. Sometimes they'll be more generic. Sometimes they might surprise or embarrass you. They might make you cry. Or laugh. Trust that whatever comes is meant for you in that moment. Honor it. Ask it what it has to teach you as you make art around the message.

No one has to see what you create. The art you create from and for yourself is only for YOU. Don't hold yourself back wondering what other people might think about what you're hearing, saying, or making. None of that matters. Turn off the judgment! Make it personal. The more real, raw, and vulnerable you allow yourself to be, the deeper your potential for healing and growth.

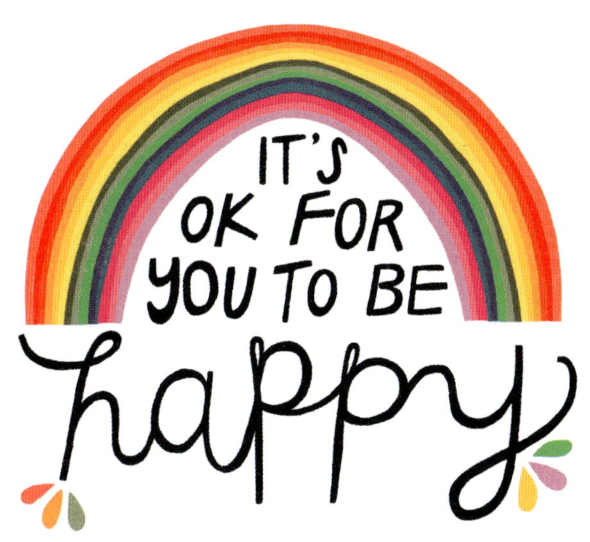
IT'S
OK FOR
YOU TO BE
happy

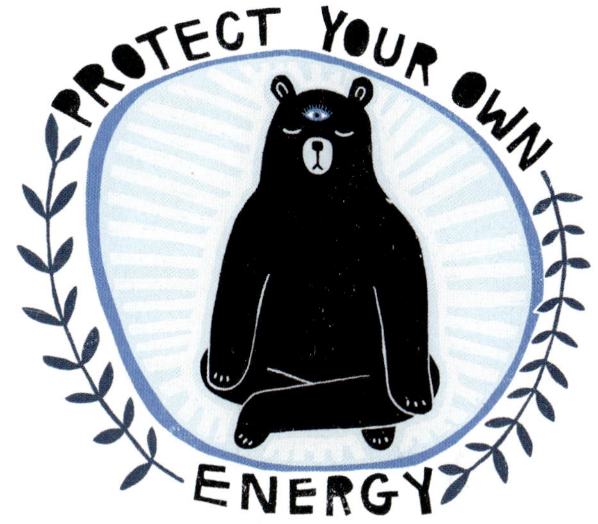
PROTECT YOUR OWN
ENERGY

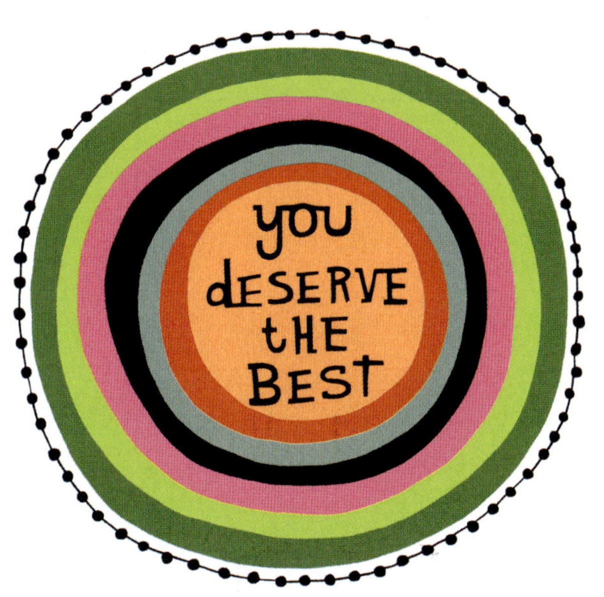
you
DESERVE
THE
BEST

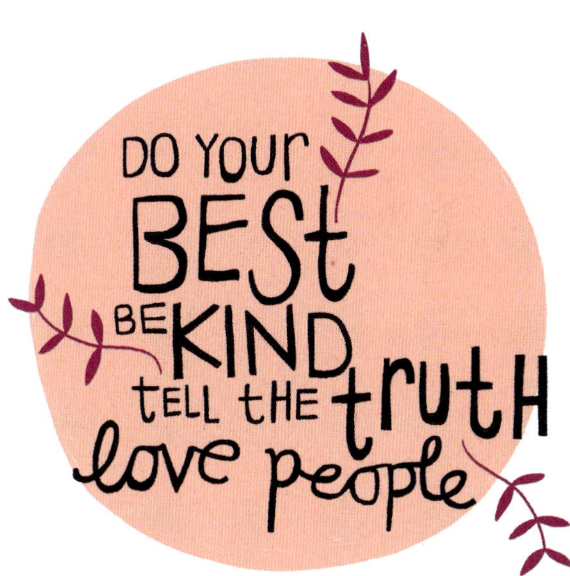
DO YOUR
BEST
BE KIND
TELL THE TRUTH
love people

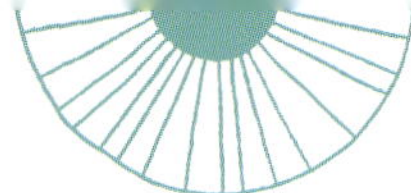

GETTING SET UP

WHERE YOU SETTLE in to get quiet and create is up to you. Depending on what materials I'm using, my go-to spots for intuition-based artmaking are on my couch with my iPad, at my painting table in my studio, or on the floor of my studio with a sketchbook and markers.

As I mentioned before, there are no rules here, and that applies to the materials you choose to use to create your images as well. In the pages to come, you'll find suggestions and examples for art supplies like paint, markers, colored pencils, collage, and digital drawing. You can choose to focus on something specific, or every day you can try something new. The parameters are up to you. (Try this: Start practicing now and ask your inner voice what artmaking tools you should use!)

So while there are no rules, I do have a few suggestions that will help you get a smooth and successful start:

- Keep it simple and choose supplies that are already familiar instead of something you've never used before. Using familiar tools will allow your mind to focus inward more easily because it won't have to concentrate as much on what your hands are doing as it would if you were learning to use a new medium.

- Make your artmaking area cozy and inviting, somewhere you're excited to spend time! Your space doesn't have to be large or extravagant . . . a corner of a dining room table, your bedroom floor, or an area in the basement can all be transformed into magical places where your intuitive creativity can come out to play. (I've created art in all these places over the course of my creative life so far!)

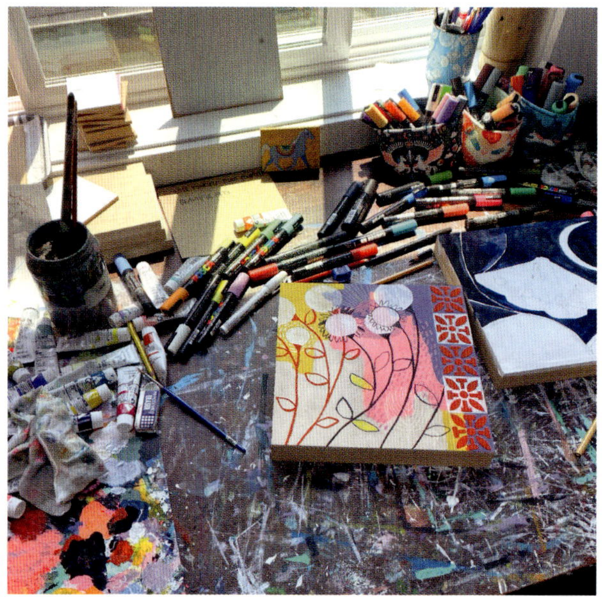

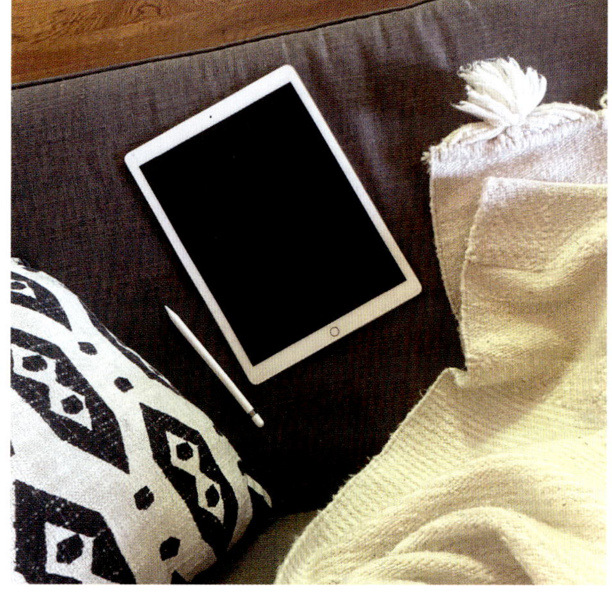

- Decide which supplies you're going to use and gather them up. Get the supplies laid out and ready in a way that appeals to you so when you sit down, you're all ready to go. If you have to run around and gather things up, it will slow the process.

- If you can, try to create a routine and sit down to create around the same time every day. Set an intention for how often you'd like to play and practice. I'd suggest at least a few times a week to really get into a good rhythm.

- Create a ritual for yourself to get into your intuitive space. Perhaps you could light a candle, recite a little intention/prayer/mantra for yourself, close your eyes and take some deep breaths, bring a cup of your favorite tea with you . . . anything that will help you settle in and mark the beginning of your artmaking time for self-care.

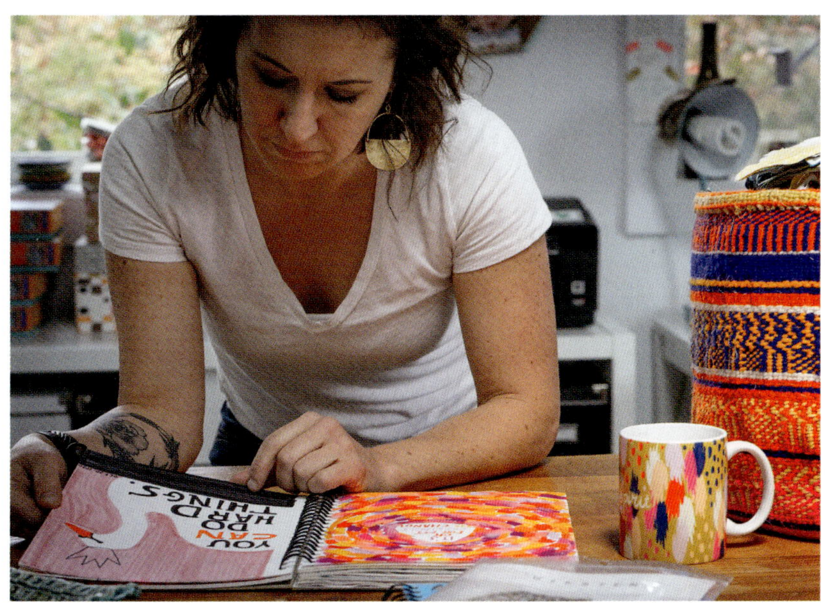

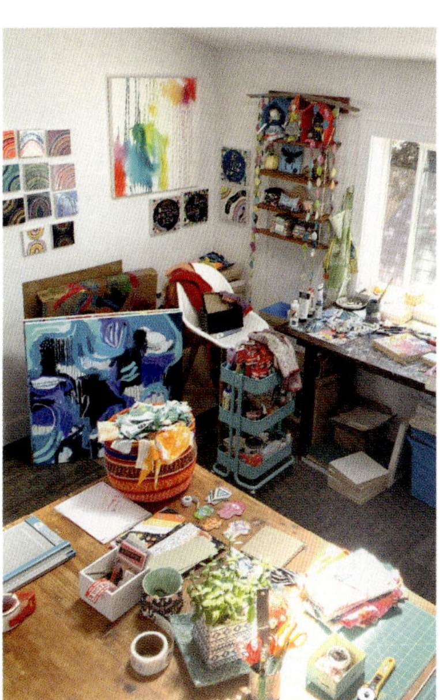

MY INVITATION TO YOU

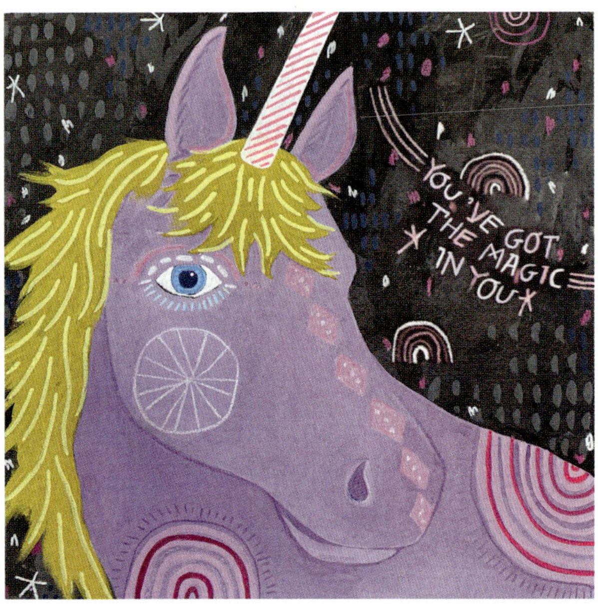

THIS BOOK IS an invitation into yourself.

Every day that you choose to sit down quietly with yourself to listen in and show up without a plan will strengthen your ability to hear what your inner voice has to say to help guide you down the unique path of your own life.

This book is an invitation to make a commitment to yourself. To dive in, to get curious, to be raw and vulnerable, to face what's painful and hard, to savor what's joyful, and to acknowledge and accept the reality of your life as it happens each day.

As you practice, your relationship with your intuition and with yourself will deepen, soften, and expand.

It won't always be easy. But it will always be worth it.

Whatever you do, just keep showing up.

Keep going.

Let yourself be a beginner.

Take a tiny step. Then another.

Allow your path to veer.

Make a mistake.

Keep going.

Have a good cry.

High-five yourself.

Give yourself permission to not have all the answers.

Allow heartbreak. Allow joy.

Revel in your success.

Feel the fear and do it anyway.

Forgive yourself.

Keep going.

Take the day off. Take the month off.

Then keep going.

Think back to where you started and see how far you've come.

Let it all go.

Reframe it. Shift your perspective.

Love yourself. No matter what.

Make art. Be true.

I believe in you.

You have magic inside you.

Keep going.

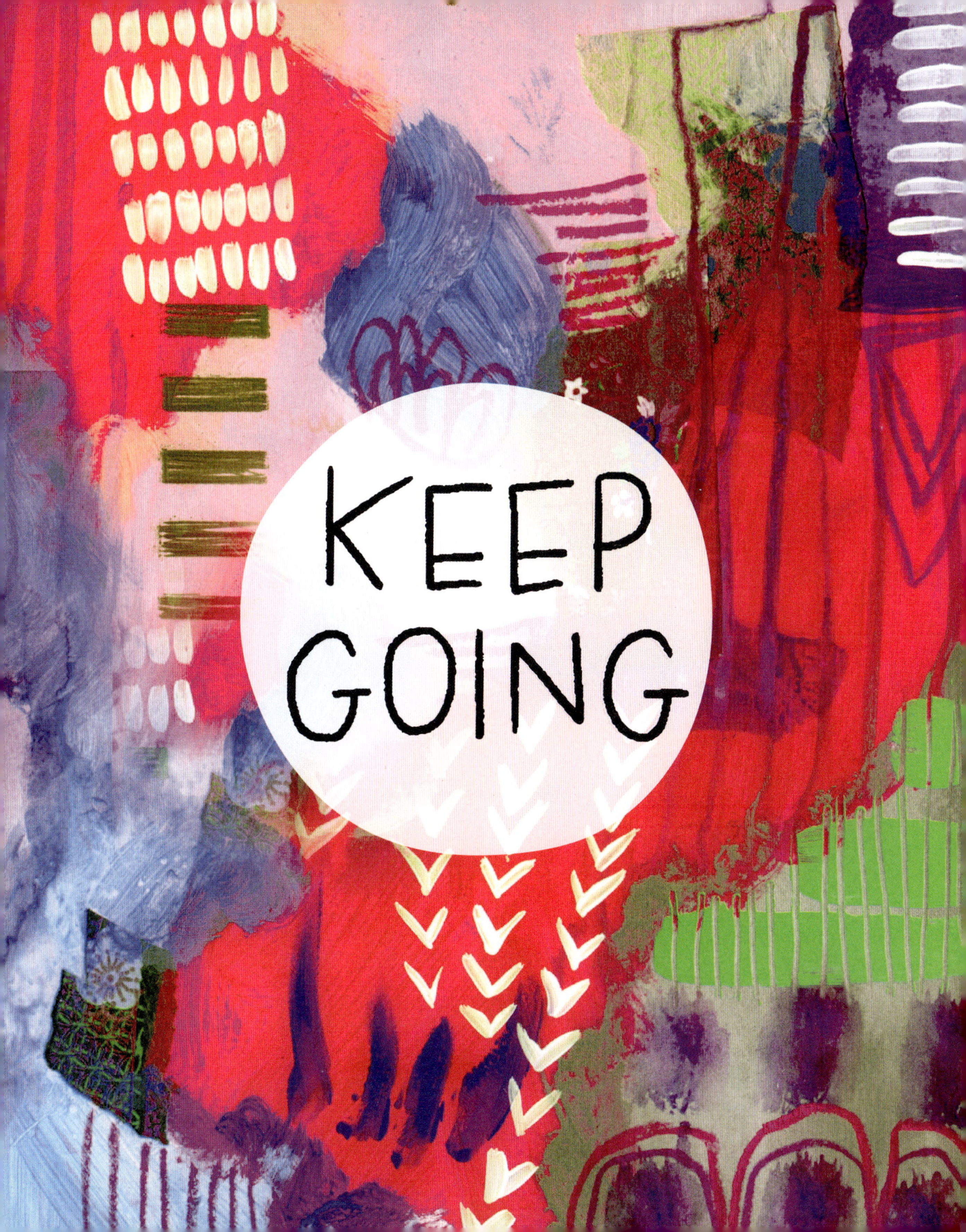

KEEP
GOING

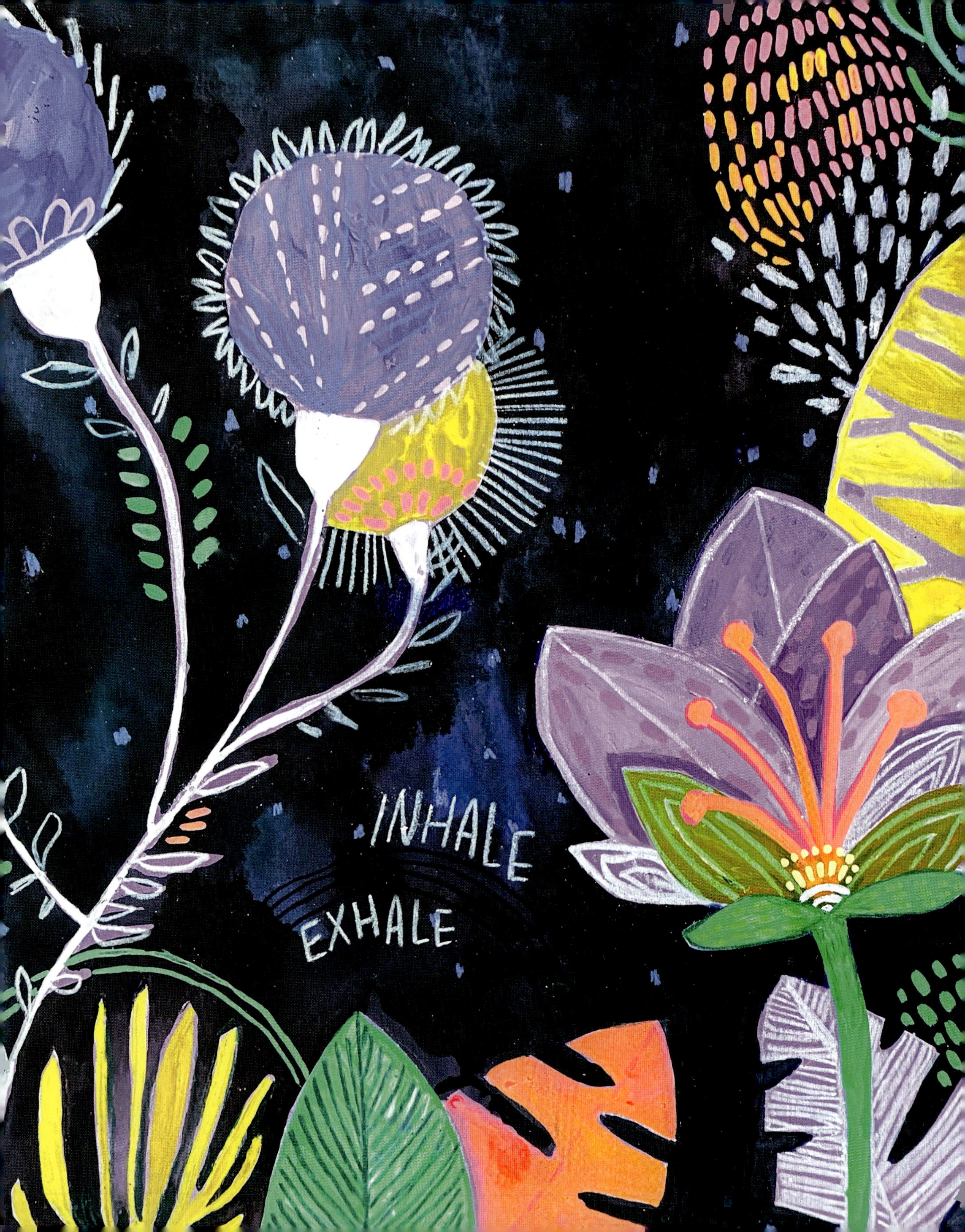

INHALE
EXHALE

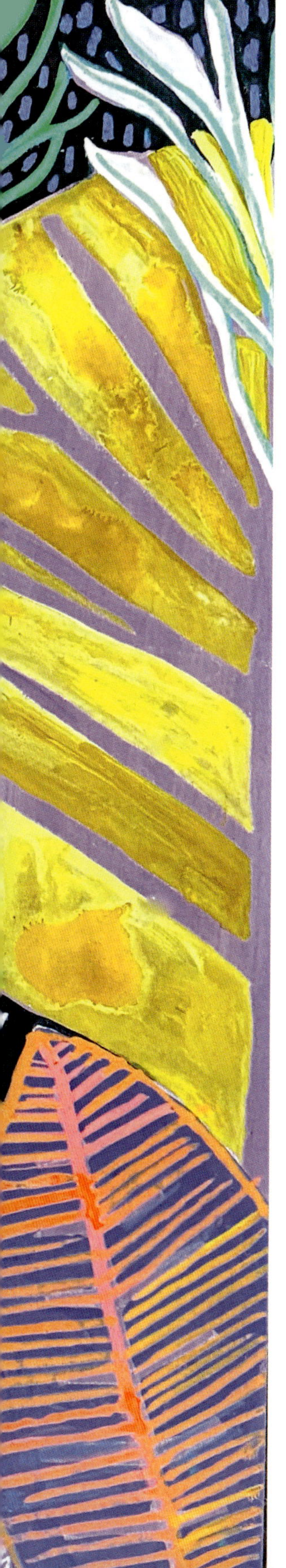

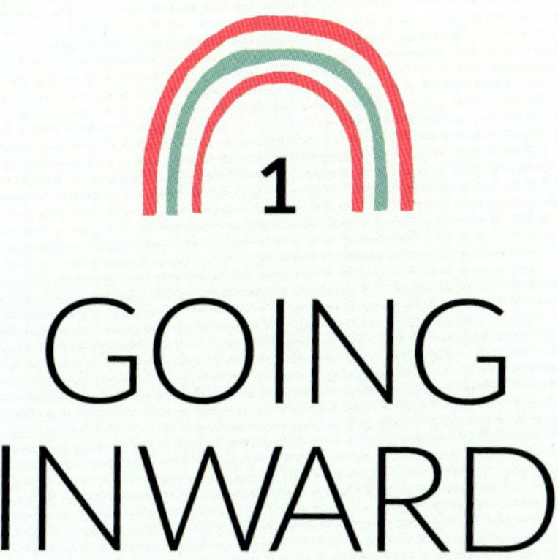

1

GOING INWARD

AT THE HEART of this process is a deep connection to yourself. Making art that's centered around messages from your wise inner self is less about the finished piece and more about your inner experience. As I said before—considering yourself "an artist" is not required here!

In this chapter, you'll learn some techniques for tuning in to your inner voice and hearing what it has to tell you. You'll begin to discover your own unique and personal processes for getting quiet and making space for meaningful messages to emerge. You'll get more familiar with the ways your innermost self communicates with you, and you'll strengthen that relationship each time you sit down to create. You'll find that your practice becomes a sacred place where you can return any time you're feeling lost, frazzled, confused, or afraid . . . and you'll learn that answers, comfort, guidance, and clarity are available to you whenever you need them.

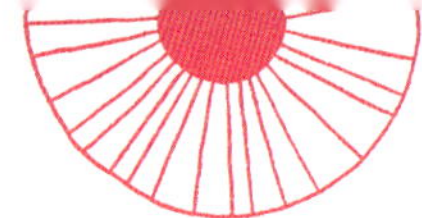

YOUR JOURNEY BEGINS

SO HOW DO you go about the business of communicating with your inner self and listening to your intuition anyway?

It's not always easy to hear your own inner voice. In fact, from the time we're small kids many of us learn to ignore what our inner voice/gut has to say (I'm raising my hand here!), and even worse—sometimes we tune it out completely. Sometimes we pick up false beliefs that other people's voices and opinions are more important or more correct than our own, and we stop trusting and listening to ourselves. Sound familiar? We all fall into this trap in one way or another.

The good news, though, is that your inner voice is always there and it'll never leave you, no matter what. Every single person on the planet has one. No exceptions. Your inner voice is the part of you that's connected to the great mystery of it all. YOU are a part of the great mystery! Call it whatever feels right to you—the universe, God, the wild unknown, Great Spirit, the great beyond . . . there are so many names for the unnameable mystery of it all. Whatever you call it, you're a part of it, invisibly connected to it at all times, and you have access to it in each and every moment.

So even if you've tuned it out for years and might not even understand the idea of listening to your gut because it's buried underneath the murky

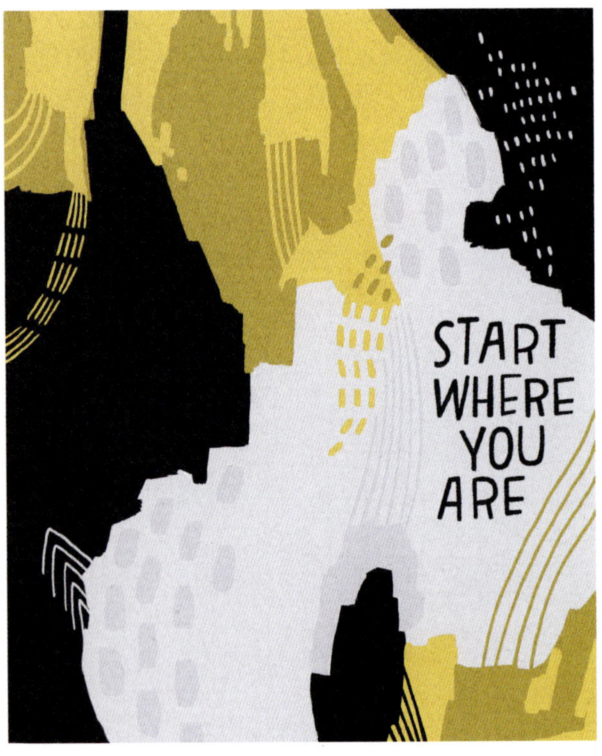

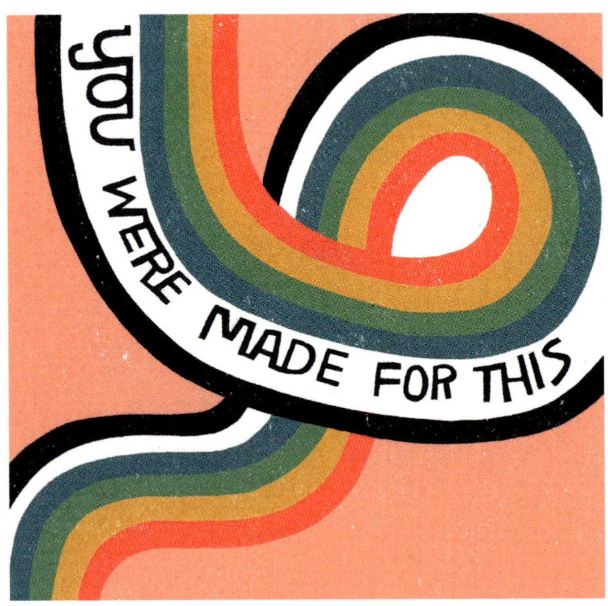

swirl of chattering thoughts in your mind, your wise inner self is there patiently waiting to be rediscovered. Your wise inner self is NOT the chatter. It's deeper. Quieter. Calmer. Whenever you're ready, it's there to gently begin showing you the answers and all the guidance for your own life that you could ever want or hope for.

Everything you need is already within you!
Isn't that cool?!

Think back on your life. Chances are, there have been times you've heard and listened to your inner voice without even necessarily realizing it. Maybe it's a decision you made that didn't have a logical explanation but it just "felt right." Maybe it was a sense or a knowing that you had about someone or something. Maybe it was an image that popped into your head to comfort you when you were afraid. All these kinds of experiences are your inner voice working its magic, helping you navigate your days, whether you're aware of it or not.

So wherever you are on the listening-to-your-inner-voice spectrum—from completely ignoring it to faithfully navigating your entire life by it—let's start to unwind all that so you can start getting cozy with your powerful inner self. Wherever you're starting from, it's perfect. It's never too late, and you're exactly where you're supposed to be at this moment in time.

Here we go!

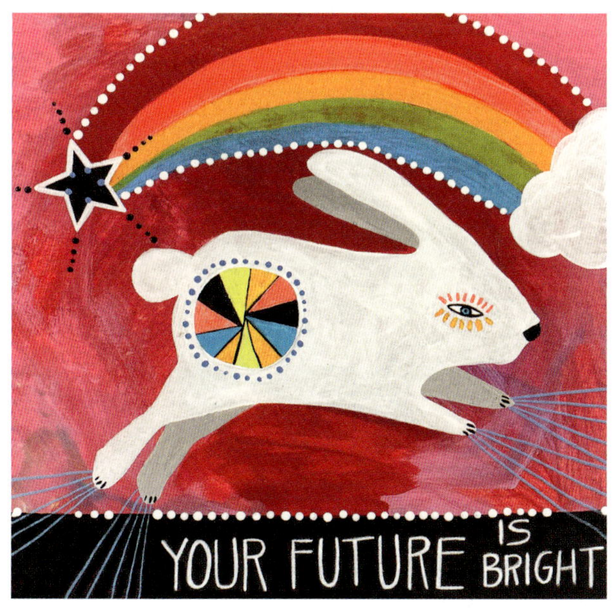

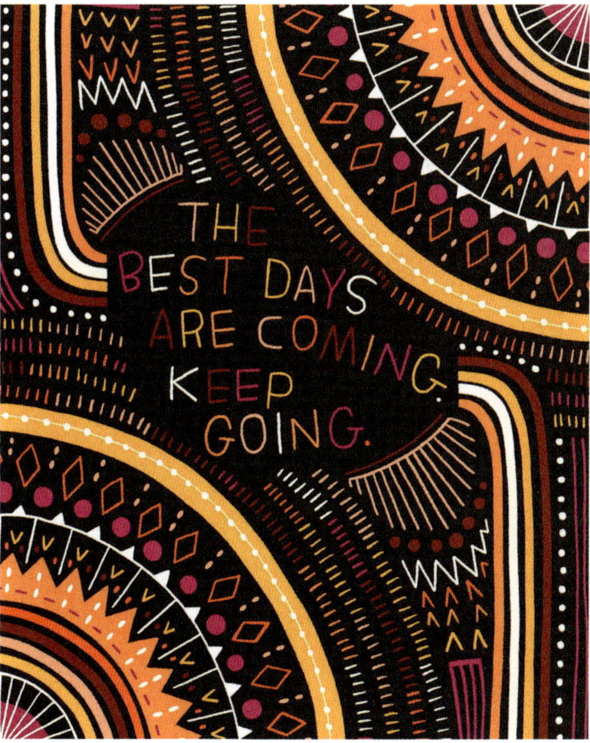

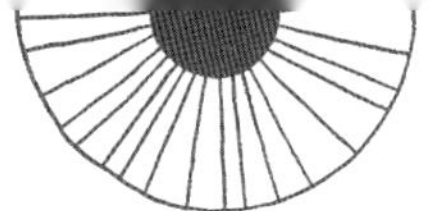

MAKING YOUR PROCESS SACRED / TAKING YOUR PROCESS SERIOUSLY

AS WITH ANYTHING, the more intention and energy you put into this practice, the more you'll get out of it. This process is not meant to be difficult, but that's not to say it's easy. Some days you won't want to show up, but the more you do, the bigger the reward will be: Calm. Satisfaction. Pride. Connection. Presence. Comfort. Self-care.

Once you've got the hang of it, it'll be easier to tune in and listen. You'll be able to discern what is your true inner voice and what's just the rest of the chatter in your mind. But especially in the beginning, it's important to make a commitment to yourself. I committed to 100 days. You certainly don't have to commit to the same thing, but take some time to think about what might make sense for you. How often can you realistically carve out some time to sit down, get quiet, and make art just for you? What time of day might work best? How can you eliminate distractions and set yourself up for success? How can you make it something you look forward to and not just another thing that you feel like you have to do?

This process is not meant to feel like a chore. It's meant to feel like a gift you're giving to yourself.

Creating space for yourself is sacred business. Author Stephen Covey wrote, "Be patient with yourself. Self-growth is tender; it's holy ground. There's no greater investment."

Invest in yourself and your well-being. Take yourself seriously. Show up for yourself. Keep your word to yourself. Treat your creative process with care. Treat it with kindness. Treat it with respect. Nurture it by showing up, and then by continuing to show up, even when parts of your mind are saying you don't want to. Sometimes showing up in those particular moments is the most potent and important of all.

Create beautiful new habits that nourish you. Maybe you can replace evening TV watching with quiet, intuitive artmaking instead. Or perhaps you can wake up earlier than normal and create in the quiet dark of the morning. Perhaps your lunch hour is spent sitting quietly tuning in for messages instead of scrolling on your phone. Only you'll know what you have the capacity for, and the changes you make don't have to be big or dramatic. Subtle small shifts are great, too!

When my firstborn was three months old, I began
a daily project. I began to notice how easy it was
to let my creative practice fall away because I
was consumed by new motherhood, and that if
I wanted to keep creating, I would have to be
very intentional about it. Artmaking is vital to my
well-being, and I take that seriously. I also decided
it was important to me that my son know me as
someone who has my own interests, passions,
dreams, and career *in addition* to being a mother.
And so I decided to commit to a project, creating
an animal a day for a year. I gave myself space to
skip some days, because I somehow intuitively
knew that there would be days I just didn't have
it in me to make anything at all, and that I had
to let that be okay. I also didn't make any rules
about how the animal was created. Some days it
might be a five-minute sketch in a sketchbook.
Some days it might be a more finished piece, like a
painting, if my son napped well or if time allowed
in other ways.

To this day, it's one of my favorite and most
precious projects. I noticed that small steps and
small efforts can create something big over time.
After a year of creating animals, I had more than
160 paintings to show for it. A large, personally
meaningful series was born out of my taking my
commitment to my creative practice seriously, and
making time to show up for it nearly every day
was a huge gift to myself.

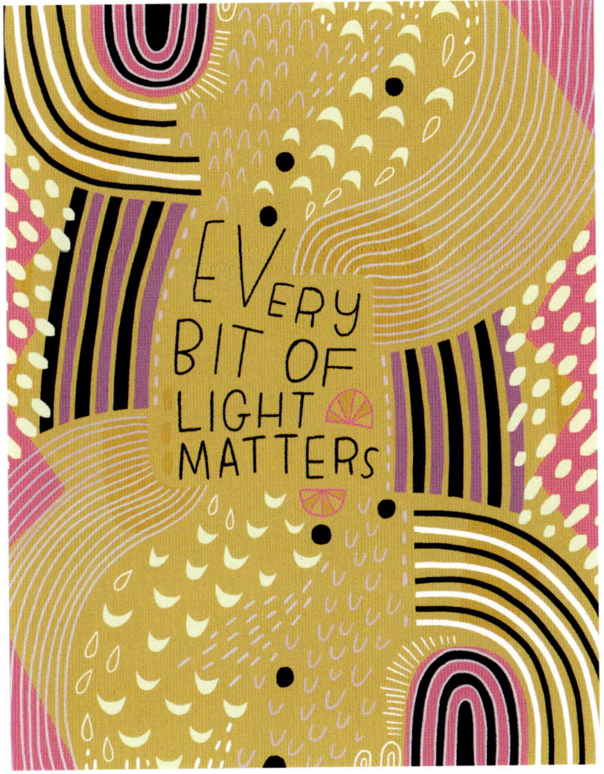

So, wherever and however you choose to create,
believe that it matters. What you're doing for
yourself matters! Every bit of light that each of us
adds to the world in the form of learning to love
ourselves more matters. (That includes you!) It
adds beauty and goodness to our world, which our
world needs in a big way.

See? This is sacred, important business here!

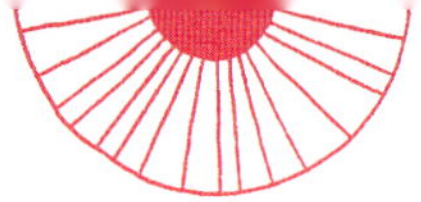

SINKING DOWN
AND SETTLING IN

WE MODERN HUMANS are often pulled in many directions, and our energy can be scattered and disorganized. We live so much of the time outside of our own bodies, energy focused outward rather than inward. For example, at any given time I'm thinking about where my kids are, where they need to be, projects I'm working on, emails I haven't answered, chores needing to be done, appointments I need to make, texts I need to respond to, new ideas that I don't want to forget . . . you get the idea. We all have some version of this depending on what our lives look like. It's easy to get caught up in the to-do of it all and rarely (if ever) take the time to check in with ourselves!

When I began intentionally creating this kind of artwork on the couch in the evenings after my babies were asleep, I used this time as a way to check in with myself—to sink down and settle in. It felt like a sigh. A relief. A big, long, deep breath. A pause. I'm not used to pausing. Pausing feels like a luxury that I don't have time for. But ironically, when I make pausing a priority, everything flows more easily—in artmaking and in life in general. It's all connected. It's all intertwined.

When you sink down and settle in, you're forgetting about the to-do list. You're forgetting about time and obligations for a little while. (Don't worry—they're not going anywhere!) You're pulling all those strands of outward-reaching energy back into your body and into the present moment.

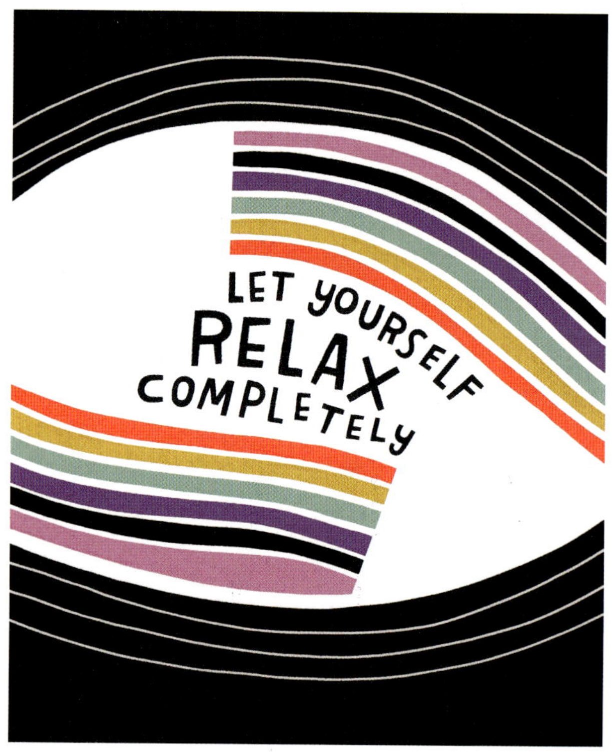

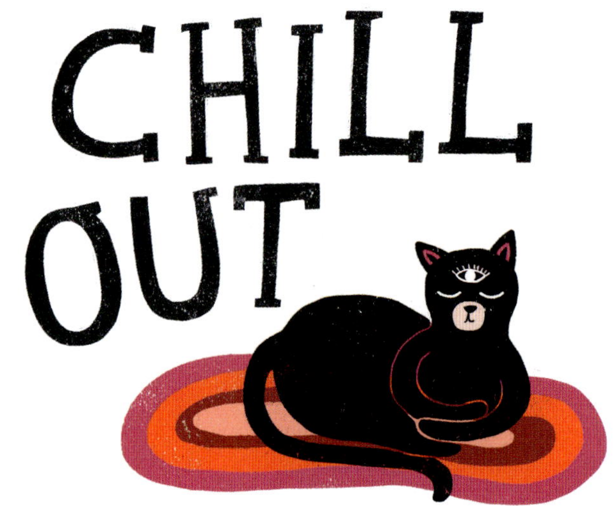

Close your eyes and breathe deeply. Inhale and exhale, as many times as you want to. What feels good? What do you need right now? How can you offer it to yourself?

Practice getting back inside your body. All the worries, all the fears, all the judgments and voices and people and roles you play can all melt away, just for a little while . . . Anytime a thought pops in, simply imagine pulling that outward energy back into yourself.

Stay there until you feel settled. Relaxed. Open. Soft. Calm. Light and loose.

When you're there, you're ready to listen and receive. And so the magic begins.

Now, as with everything in this book, this is simply a suggestion. You might already have some kind of practice you use for sinking down into your quiet inner self, like a certain way of meditating, dancing, walking, hiking, chanting, yoga, cooking, driving . . . There are as many different ways to tune in to yourself as there are people on the planet. Everyone is different. So if that's the case for you and you want to ignore everything I'm saying here and do it your own way, then do it! Only you know what's best for you.

The point is that you'll need a way to get into your body and let go of the chatter and your scattered energy. As you practice, you'll find it easier and easier to drop into that state whenever you need to, whatever you happen to be doing. It won't take as long and you'll be able to spiral in and out of yourself to get what you need, when you need it. You'll be able to drop down and check in with yourself anytime you please. It's a very useful skill to have, I promise!

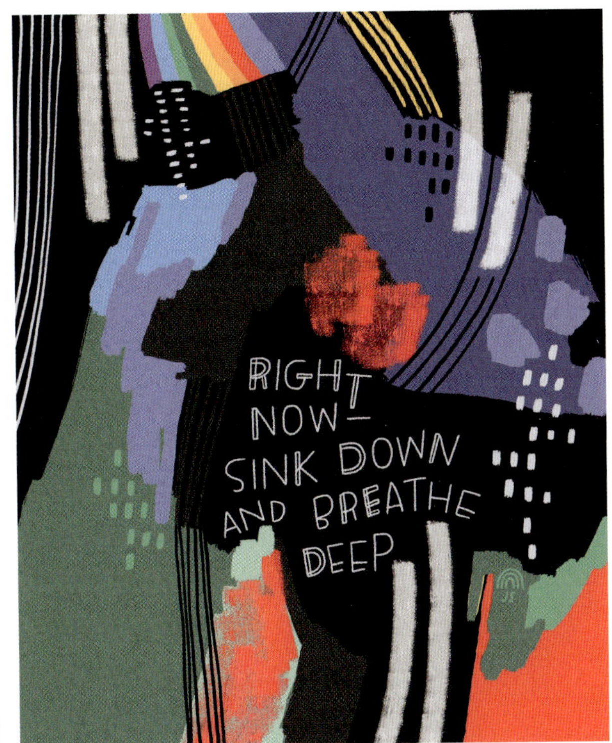

Pausing feels like a luxury that I don't have time for. But ironically, when I make pausing a priority, everything flows more easily—in artmaking and in life in general.

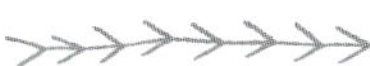

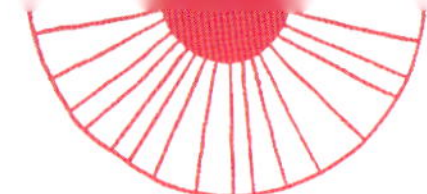

GETTING INTO ACCEPTANCE

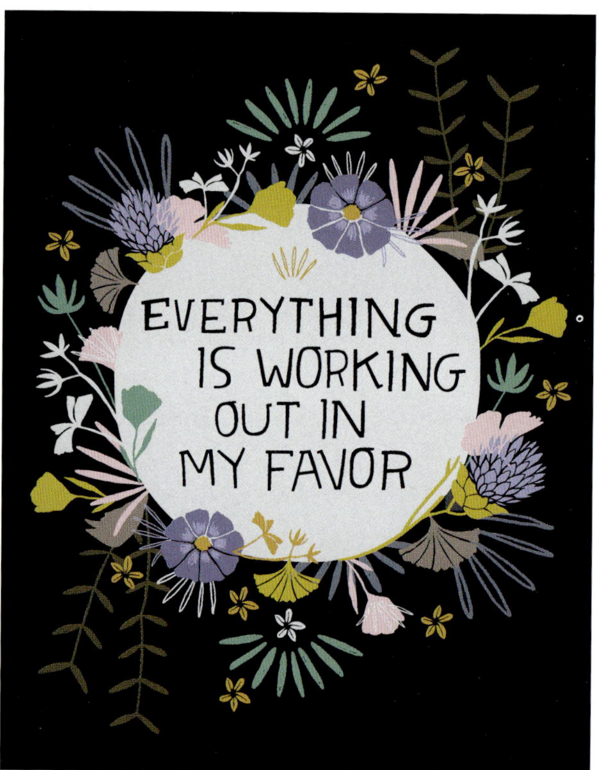

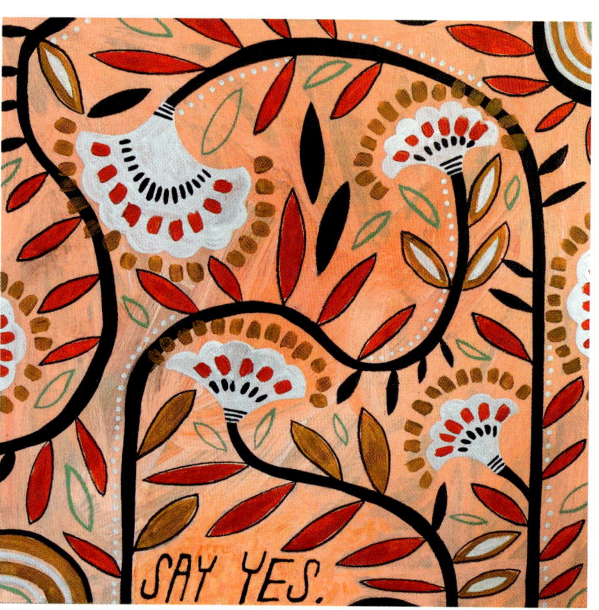

YOU CAN LOOK at your life and the world through so many different lenses. Some are disempowering, but others lift you up and help you see the silver linings in everything you walk through.

Radical acceptance is accepting what comes, whatever and however it shows up, and is based on the idea that suffering doesn't come directly from pain but from our attachment to pain and the stories we create about it. According to Skyland Trail, radical acceptance is "when you stop fighting reality, stop responding with impulsive or destructive behaviors when things aren't going the way you want them to, and let go of bitterness that may be keeping you trapped in a cycle of suffering." This idea may seem foreign (and maybe even completely false sometimes!), but you know who can help you get into this radical acceptance? Yep, you guessed it: your inner voice.

How much time do most of us spend fighting reality, wishing things were different, thinking things should be different, wondering why life isn't going according to the way we selfishly think it should?

SO. MUCH. TIME.

While I was out for a thinking walk one day (which you'll read more about in a minute), listening for a message for myself, I heard these words: **Everything is working out in my favor.** Since then, this has been my favorite lens to look at my life through. If everything is working out in my favor, then every experience must be useful to me in some way. It must be leading me forward on my journey somehow. This helps me accept the challenging things that I encounter along my path. It helps me get curious. It reminds me to accept what's in front of me rather than resist it. Because the fact is, in the moment, things can't be any other way than the way they are. There's no way to change it. And that's where the radical acceptance comes in. It's a willingness to say yes to life, however it shows up.

So, what's right in front of you, right now?

That's your life right there.

Whether it should or shouldn't be how it is, according to you, really doesn't matter now, does it? Because the fact of the matter is that what's real in your life is what's real in your life. Simple as that.

And getting on with the business of accepting it exactly as it is, as challenging as that prospect might be, is the name of the game. That's what I'm learning, anyway.

The resistance to what is, is what causes the suffering. The surrender and the curiosity about what is, is what causes expansion. Joy. Magic. Miracles.

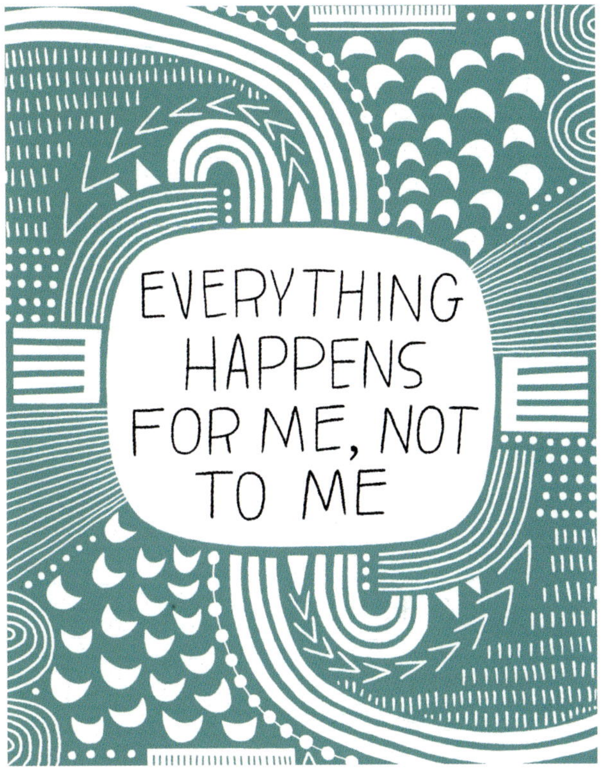

Every moment is a new chance for a new awakening into the reality of the present moment.

In every moment, acceptance is available.

Setting an intention to accept your day/your situation/your life as you settle in to listen for messages for yourself will allow your intuitive inner voice to share new perspectives and insights about you and your life. Ask your inner voice to show you how to accept and to show you the way. I promise you'll receive answers.

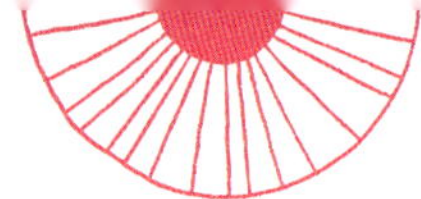

TUNING IN

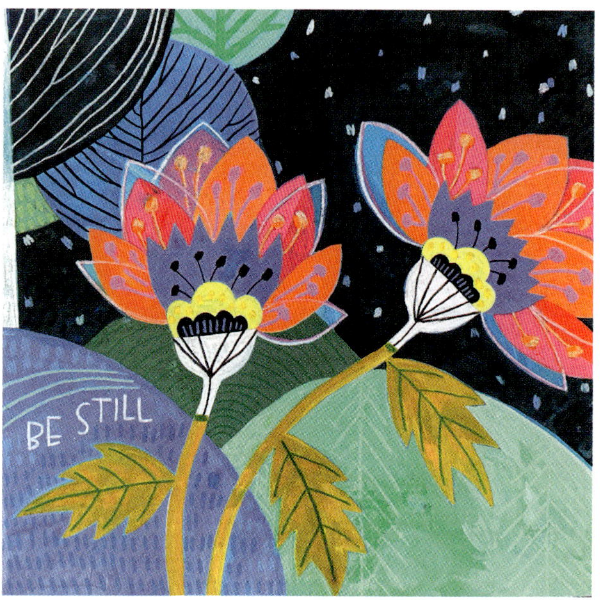

IF YOU'RE UNFAMILIAR with hearing your inner voice, it might take a bit of time to figure out how it best speaks to you. How you tune in and hear your inner voice is a personal process; there are as many ways to tune in as there are people on the planet! So while I have some suggestions here, please know that this is by no means an exhaustive list. There is no "right way" to hear your inner voice. These are simply suggestions that you're welcome to use and adapt as you need to make them work for you. You might even discover or already have your own process that's not mentioned here at all. That's awesome, too!

Here are a few of my tried-and-true suggestions to get you started.

Thinking Walks

My most beloved and reliable way to get in touch with my inner voice is to go on what I call a "thinking walk." A thinking walk can happen anywhere. I simply set out for a walk in my neighborhood with the intention to hear a meaningful message for myself for that day. As I walk, my mind wanders. I don't pay much attention to my thoughts and instead lightly listen for something deeper. I've learned to discern my fear voice and all my mental chatter from my real and true voice that only wants the best for me. The messages I receive on these walks feel like a deep knowing. Like clarity. Like something that simply showed up in my mind without me having to think about it. There's a sense that I get when the message is just right, like a piece of a puzzle that clicks into place. Sometimes I bring my phone or a small notepad with me so I can write down the message(s) I receive so I don't forget by the time I get home (that's happened before)!

Meditating

Meditating is one of those things that can feel intimidating and like you have to get it "right," but really it's just about getting quiet and calm and turning inward.

Try this visualization to get you started: Close your eyes. Take a few deep breaths. Set an intention to receive a message from yourself. Empty your mind. Imagine that all your energy is like tentacles, reaching outward into the world, scattering and pulling you in different directions. Next, imagine pulling those tentacles back into your body, all your energy contained within yourself. Let go of your day and your worries and your thoughts and simply be right here, right now. Each time you find yourself carried away by thoughts, imagine pulling the tentacles of that energy back into yourself. Refocus your intention. As you breathe, keep a curious and open awareness for any voices, words, or images that you might see, feel, or hear.

Creating without a Plan

Diving in, creating without a plan, seeing what happens, and keeping your hands and/or body busy is a great way to occupy the thinking part of your mind so the quieter, deeper part has space to come through and speak to you. Let your mind settle and wander as you listen inwardly with the intention of receiving a message. Create simple, familiar, or random shapes or make repetitive marks on paper, canvas, or any other surface. Keep your hands moving and don't pay much attention to the final outcome. Focus on the inner process!

You could try the following:

- Doodling (pen, pencil, marker, or even on a digital screen like an iPad)
- Smearing paint and making marks on a canvas
- Drawing with your eyes closed
- Drawing with your nondominant hand
- Collaging colorful bits of paper or random words
- Painting with your kids to loosen up your mind

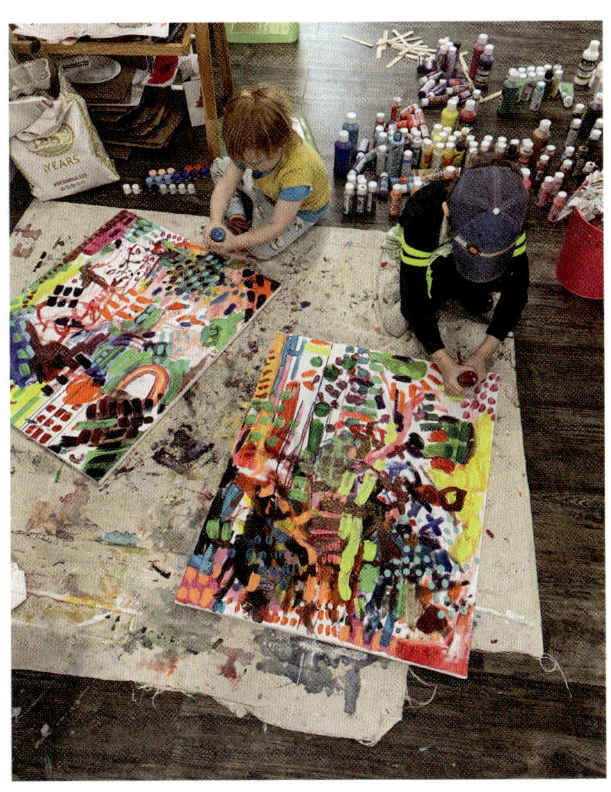

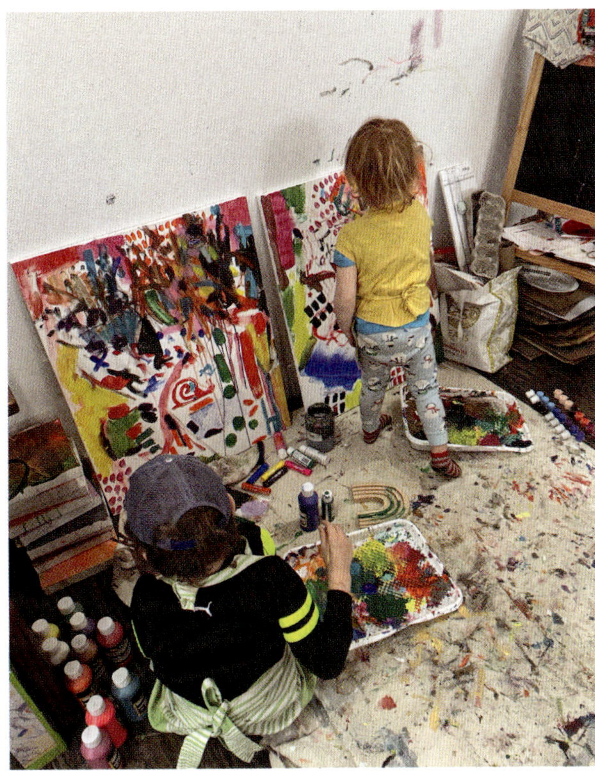

Taking a Shower or Bath

The shower is one of my favorite places for receiving inner guidance! I often find myself surprised when messages and clarity drop into my awareness in the shower, because I'm not usually expecting it! But something about my hands and body being busy allows my inner voice to communicate with me more effectively. Sometimes I intentionally tune in while I'm in the shower. Relaxing in a bath might work better for you; both are well worth a try!

Getting Outside into Nature

This method is related to the thinking walks but is more focused on the actual setting. Sometimes simply being in the beauty of nature and reveling in the rejuvenating surroundings—a river, the ocean, a forest—can cause your mind to relax more than usual, giving your inner self more room to guide you.

Going for a Drive

Your inner voice can sometimes talk to you more easily while driving because a part of your mind is occupied, allowing your deeper self more space to come through. Set an intention to receive inner guidance as you get in the car and see what happens. It often works like a charm!

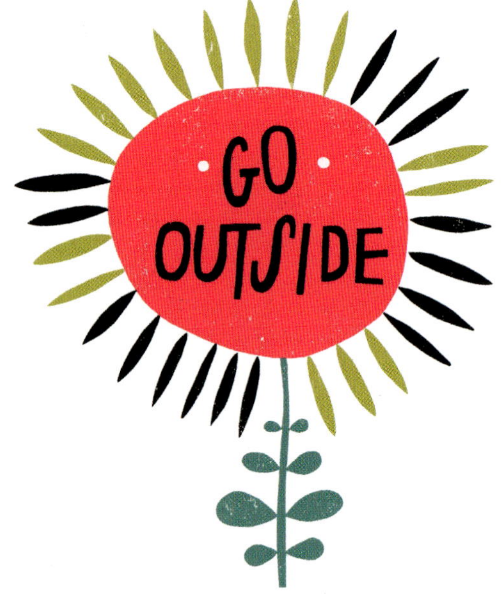

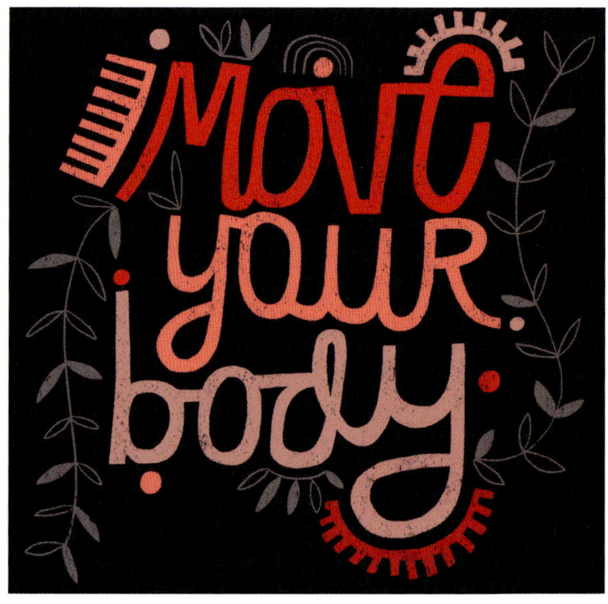

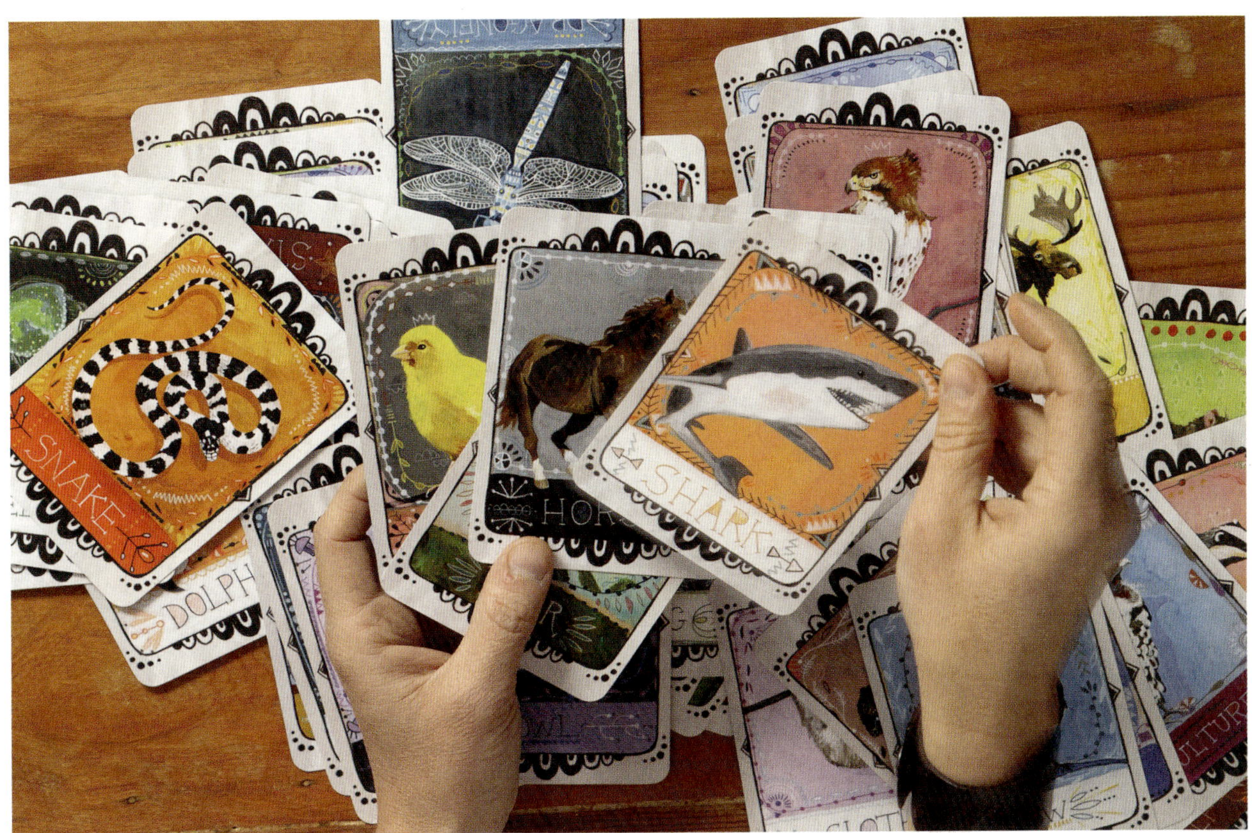

Moving Your Body

Dance, walk, run, jump, ride your bike . . . anything to get your body moving! Doing something active might be just the ticket to quieting your thinking mind and sinking into hearing the voice of your intuition.

Using Oracle or Tarot Cards to Assist You

I love oracle and tarot cards. I even created and published two oracle decks of my own! When using these kinds of tools, I like to ask open-ended questions, such as "What am I supposed to know today?" or "What guidance is most useful for me to follow right now?" Then I can interpret what the card(s) are communicating to me by using my intuition and reading about the card's meaning to decipher the message that's meant for me. I'm often surprised by how much clarity and insight into my life this method can offer!

NAVIGATING IN THE DEPTHS

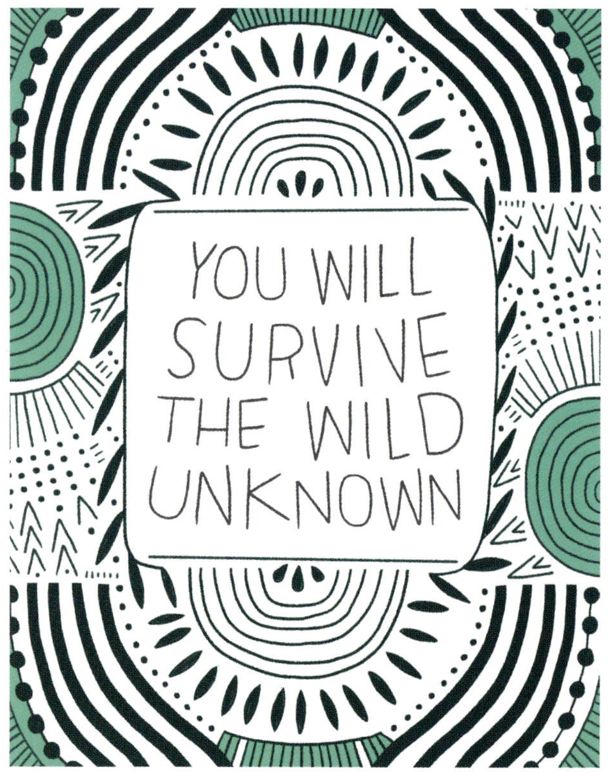

NOW THIS MIGHT all sound well and good, but once you get down to the business of actually trying to get quiet, oftentimes what happens is that your mind starts chattering away. Does this sound familiar? All sorts of unhelpful thoughts and ideas begin to creep in! I have a feeling you're probably nodding your head in agreement here, right?

Humans are complex and tricky beasts. I don't have a grasp on why our minds work the way they do, and I probably never will, but I am getting more familiar with the different parts of my mind, my patterns, and the wild variety of ways my mind tries to trick me. Learning to decipher your internal patterns and mind tricks will be incredibly useful as you go along in this process!

So what tricky business might you encounter as you're beginning to sink down and settle into your inner depths? And what can you do to smoothly make your way through so you and your inner voice can connect and make some magic?

You'll most likely hear a lot of different voices and thoughts running through your mind as you try to make contact with your true inner voice, but what all these voices come down to and have in common is one thing: FEAR.

Your fear voice has good intentions. It wants to keep you safe by reminding you of all the ways you could potentially get hurt, or fail, or embarrass yourself, or not be good enough. It'll remind you of all the times those things have already happened.

The problem is that fear wants to hold you back so you never, ever change. And that can keep you stuck and sad, you know?

Fear can show up in your mind and your life in a lot of unhelpful ways: resistance, procrastination, resentment, rebellion, self-sabotage, self-judgment, self-hatred, despondency, hopelessness, shame . . . to name a few.

I think you probably get the idea that we don't really want fear to be steering the ship here.

This may sound like bad news, but it's actually good news, because as soon as you realize that you've encountered something in the fear category, you immediately know it's not true. Like I mentioned in the last section, your inner voice always wants the best for you. This voice will create inner peace instead of anxiety. If it sounds like garbage: it's fear. If it's making you feel bad: fear again! Sometimes it'll be sneaky and trick you into thinking it has your best interests at heart, but if you really step back and examine it, fear is trying to keep you small or to stay in what's familiar in some way every single time. Even if what's familiar isn't even all that great!

So rather than buying into fear's nonsense, you're invited here in this book to learn to simply say "no thank you" to all these fearful thoughts and carry on your way. Fear isn't going anywhere, unfortunately. You can acknowledge that it's there trying to help you (it does love attention, after all!), but let it know that it's not the one in charge. *You* are in charge. Your inner voice is the only one you're to listen to when you're down in your depths.

The more you practice, the more you'll discover the unique ways that fear tries to trick you. It's different for everyone. You'll start to learn the ways you sabotage yourself by listening to fear instead of letting your inner voice guide you. We all do it! But the cool thing is that you can build this practice like a muscle. For example, when you start going to the gym, it usually sucks. It's nearly impossible to remember the reward that comes with it—feeling great afterward!—and the resistance is high. As you keep your commitment to yourself and continue to go to the gym, it's easier to simply ignore the resistance because you know it's going to feel great when you're done working out. Ignoring fear will be the same—once you've done it enough times and know what's on the other side, listening to your fear won't be all that alluring anymore.

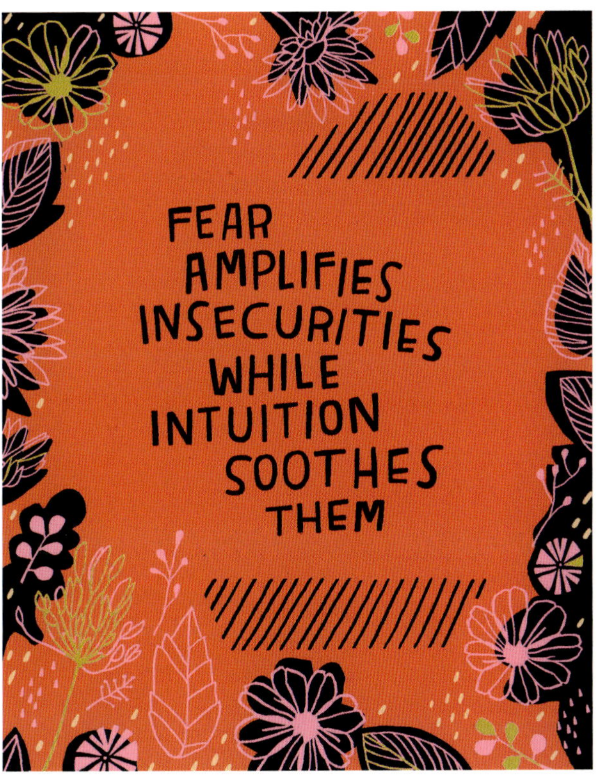

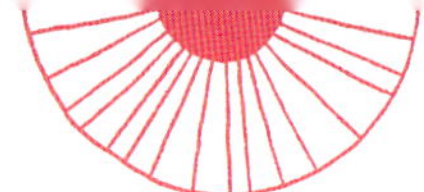

HEARING YOUR INNER VOICE

SO NOW THAT you know your fear voice is separate from your true inner voice, you might be wondering, "Well, what does my inner voice sound like anyway? What exactly am I listening for?"

Your inner voice can communicate with you and send you messages and signals in a lot of different ways. For example, you might:

- Hear a voice in your mind that sounds like your own voice
- Hear a voice in your mind that sounds different than your own
- Feel words and sensations
- See words in your mind
- See images in your mind

- See visual signs in your outer world
- Feel a full-body knowing
- Feel a gut sense/hunch (which may or may not make sense in the moment)
- Receive something in a dream
- Have an idea come into your mind

Your innermost self might even communicate with you in some other way that's not on this list! It might feel tricky at first, and you might hear all sorts of chatter and judgments about what you should or shouldn't be doing as you tune in and listen. That's okay! Just keep going. Your unique relationship with your intuition will grow and deepen and become stronger as you practice intentionally listening to it. There's no right way or wrong way; there's only *your* way. And you'll create and discover your way as you keep moving forward. Remember, all you need is to be willing, curious, and open!

However you start to receive the messages meant for you, keeping in mind a few important things about your inner voice will make it easier to decipher what's true and to ignore the unhelpful thoughts that will also inevitably surface. These unhelpful thoughts may seem fine at first but are, in fact, just other voices and thoughts, likely based in fear, trying to trick you into believing they're helpful.

You can run your thoughts through these filters as you get started, to begin deciphering what's true for you and what's not:

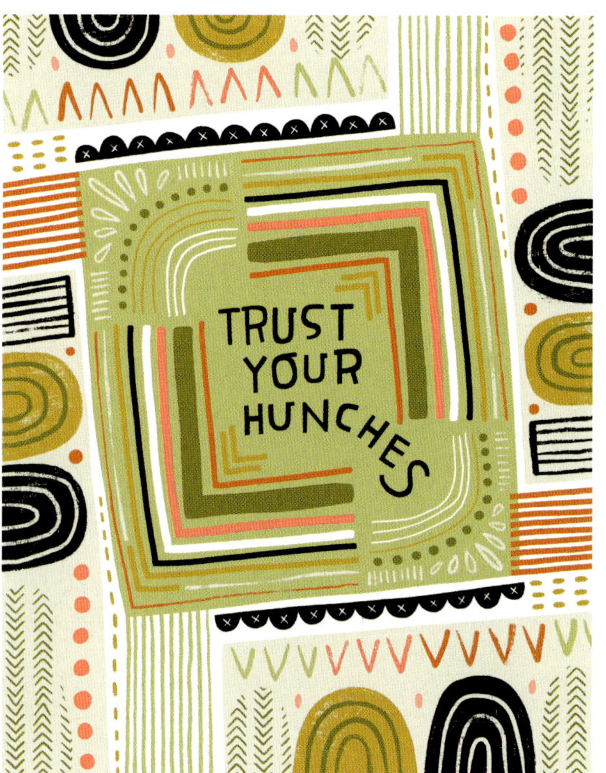

Your Inner Voice *Always*

- Wants the best for you and will lead you toward self-growth and self-love
- Only speaks to you kindly, compassionately, and encouragingly (and perhaps firmly sometimes!)
- Feels like a confident, calm knowing in your body, not only in your mind
- Wants to help you create inner peace
- Tries to get your attention, so trust your hunches
- Speaks kindly about others

Your Inner Voice *Does Not*

- Speak negatively to you
- Judge, shame, criticize, or intimidate you
- Want to keep you small
- Create internal chaos or anxiety
- Speak negatively about others
- Justify bad behavior or decisions
- Always give you the answer you *want* (this is why we so often ignore it!), but it always gives you the answer that's right for you and is what you need

Remember, everyone has a fear voice. It's just part of being a human. But these fearful thoughts are often rooted in old things that aren't even true in your life anymore! Your fear voice projects your past onto your current life and onto your future to make sure you never stray too far from where you are (because in ancient times, straying too far from where you are might mean getting eaten by a tiger! Or being separated from your clan! Or something else terrible!).

Your unique relationship with your intuition will grow and deepen and become stronger as you practice intentionally listening to it. There's no right way or wrong way; there's only your way.

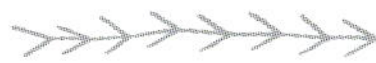

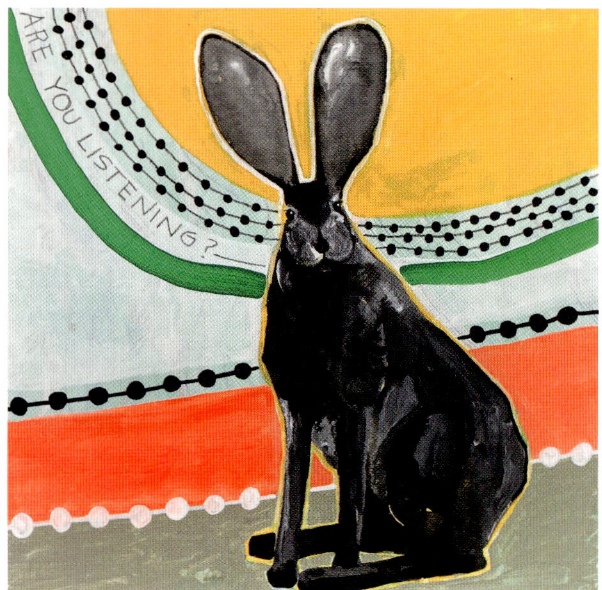

Now, I'm not talking about legitimate fear when you're actually in danger. That's different, and other parts of you will kick in to try to keep you safe in situations like that. I'm talking about the voice that wants to keep you small. The one that shames you. The one that reminds you of all the times you've failed, disappointed yourself, embarrassed yourself . . . The voice that makes you feel bad about yourself, compares you to other people, tells you that your dreams aren't possible so why bother even trying. That voice can seem pretty darn real . . . but it isn't.

The thoughts your fear voice thinks are *never* true.

Your fear voice shows up in all sorts of ways, but some examples include a scarcity mind-set (believing you'll never have enough), comparing yourself to others (believing you're not good enough), procrastination, worry and anxiety, not keeping your word to yourself or to others, not following through, judgment, laziness . . . and the list goes on and on. I'm sure you can add a few of your own here!

Your fear voice believes it's keeping you safe by reminding you of all these scary things that don't feel good. It makes you think that if you stray too far from what's familiar, even worse things will happen. But what actually happens is that your fear voice keeps you stuck. You don't grow, you don't change, you don't move forward, and you miss out on your life. It keeps you fearful instead of free. See how sneaky that is? It tells you you'll be free and safe if you listen to it, but in fact it just keeps you feeling small and afraid.

A simple way to think about it and a good filter to run your thoughts/messages through is:

Does this thought lift me up, or does it keep me down?

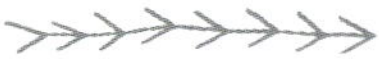

If it lifts you up and wants the best for you: it's your true inner voice.

If it keeps you down or small: don't believe it!

Be honest with yourself when running your thoughts through this filter. It can be tricky sometimes, because your true messages might feel uncomfortable. You might not want them to be true, so you might ignore them for a while. Sometimes you'll continue to believe that what your fear voice tells you is true, either consciously or unconsciously. This is all okay! It's totally normal and part of this practice.

The more you practice, the easier it will become. You'll discover that your true inner voice always leads you in the right direction. The more you harness its power and follow its guidance, the more solid you'll feel within yourself. Nothing that anyone says or thinks about you and your life will matter as much as what you know in your gut is right for you. Your self-confidence will grow.

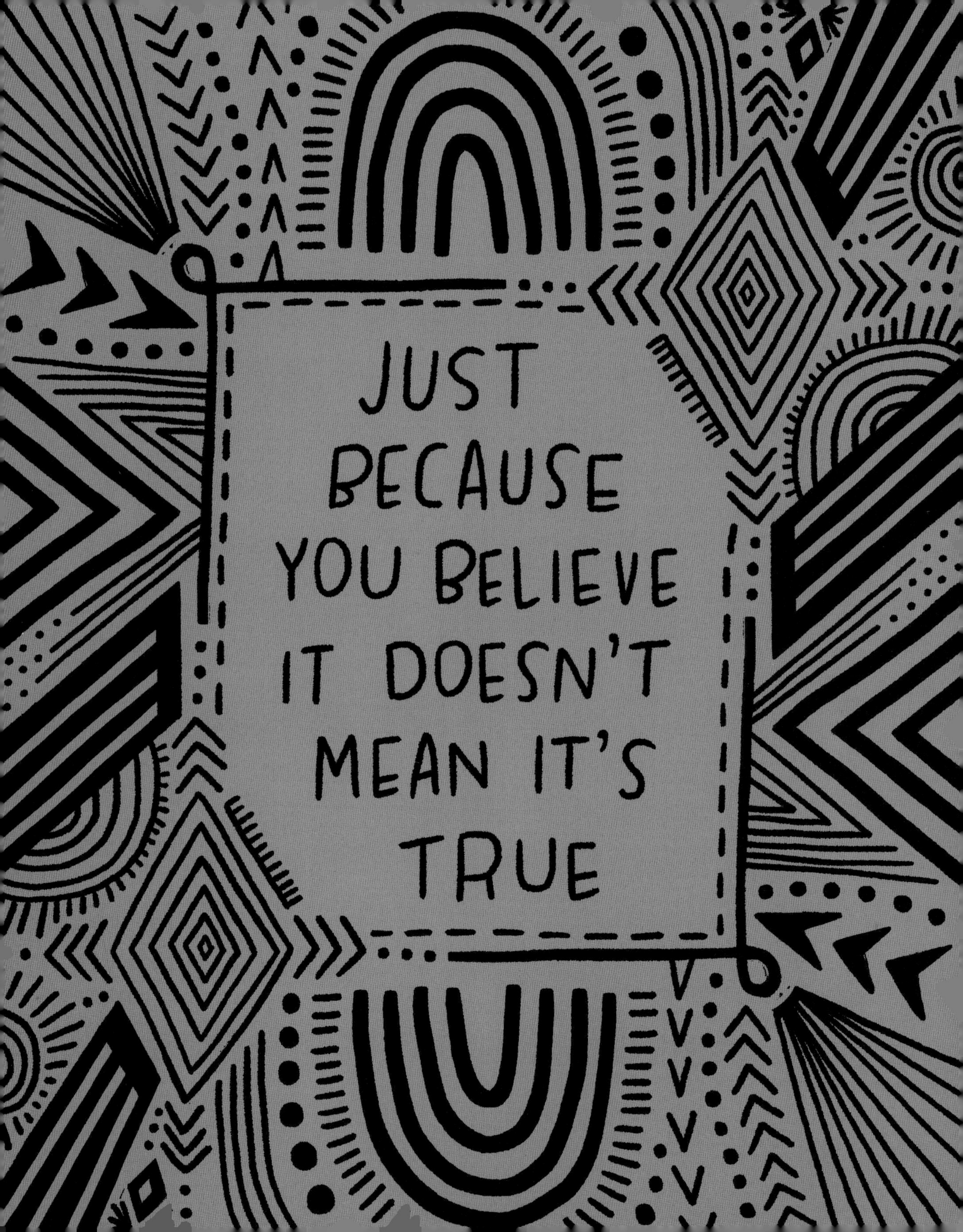

JUST
BECAUSE
YOU BELIEVE
IT DOESN'T
MEAN IT'S
TRUE

Your respect for yourself will skyrocket. You'll trust yourself above all else, because you know that your inner voice will never lead you down an unkind path. People who live life guided by their intuition and their inner voice are guided by light, not darkness. You will move closer and closer to being internally unshakable.

How I Hear My Own Inner Voice

In the introduction I shared about the voice that spoke to me in my mind the morning that Ryan died. This was a more dramatic example of hearing a powerful voice inside myself than I usually experience—it was spontaneous, and it caught my attention immediately—but this is typically how I receive messages from my intuition when I'm intentionally listening for them as well. I tend to hear the actual words within my mind, and they are accompanied by a sense of calm knowing in my body. I've practiced so much now that it's not difficult for me to discern what is a true helpful message and what's some other voice inside me. Sometimes, though, my inner voice communicates through images. It's much less frequent, but I love this type of connection!

In 2007, Ryan and I moved from my hometown of Boulder, Colorado, to Atlanta, Georgia. Ryan had been wait-listed for a graduate program that would lead to medical school and was accepted into the program at the last minute. He left early to find us an apartment and to start school, and I stayed back to finish packing up our house and left a week later, driving across the country on my own in my old, somewhat unreliable 4Runner. The trip was lovely (I've always loved long drives on my own), but I was nervous about my car the entire time. I was afraid the engine was going to give out, and my fear got particularly bad on the last day as I drove through the mountains of Tennessee. No other cars were around, and my

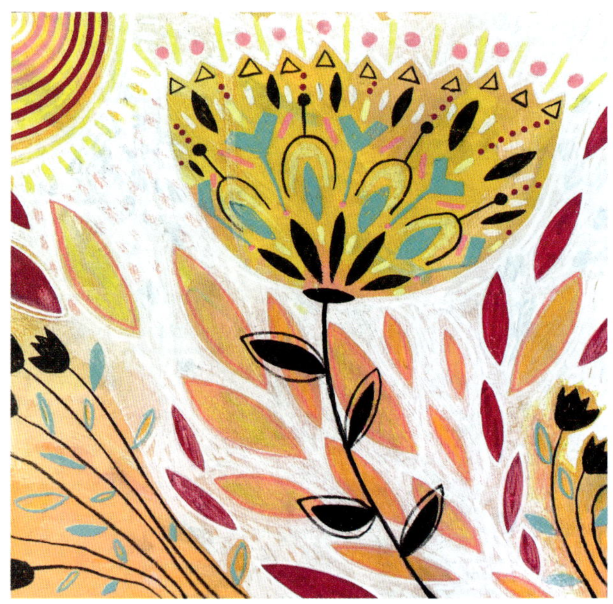

anxiety slowly grew with each mile that I drove. And then all of a sudden, out of nowhere, I saw a silver cord appear in my mind. The cord flowed out from the front of my car, attaching it to Atlanta, and I intuitively knew that the cord was pulling me safely along and that everything would be okay. I was instantly calm. It was the strangest and most comforting sensation, trusting that cord. Each time I started to feel nervous, I remembered the cord and instantly felt better. And guess what? I made it to Atlanta without any car problems!

My inner self unexpectedly and spontaneously communicated with me that day, just like it did the morning that Ryan died. The messages were delivered in different ways—one as a voice in my mind, the other as a powerful image—but they were both an instant comfort and created a deep knowing within that I would be okay.

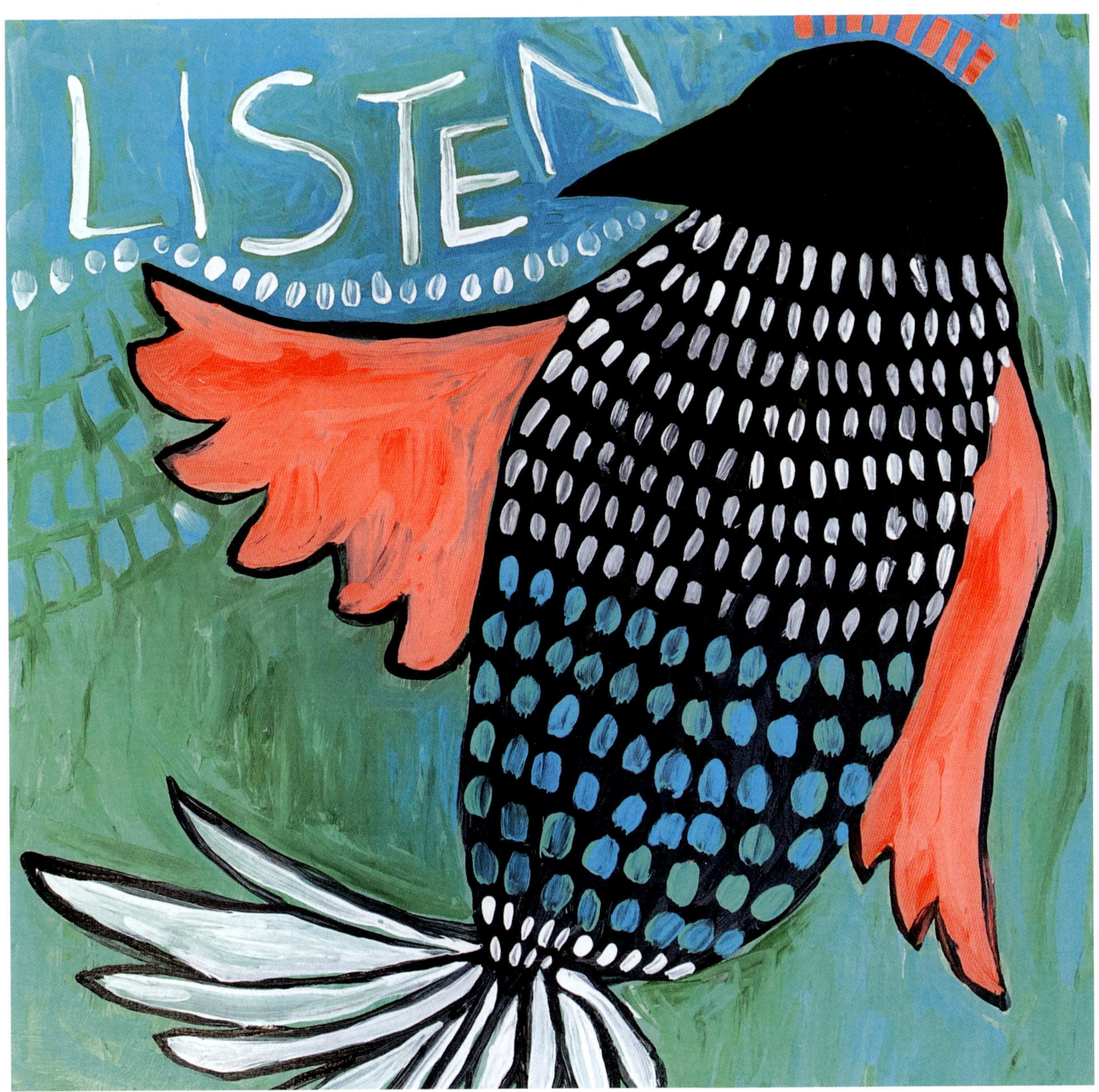

These types of loud, clear, spontaneous communications happen for me from time to time and are always powerful and mysterious; most often, though, my inner voice feels more like a quiet internal conversation that I can tune in to. It's my internal navigation system that's always on and always leads me where I'm meant to go when I remember it's there for me to use.

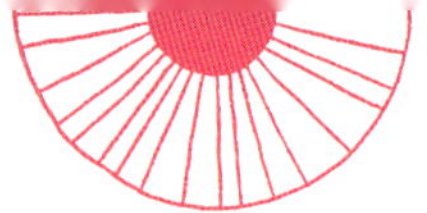

EARS OUTWARD, HEART FORWARD, MIND INWARD

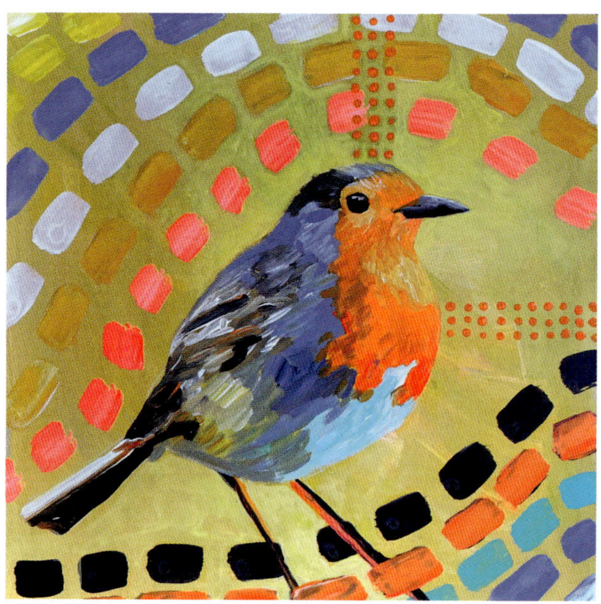

BEFORE THE PANDEMIC started, I used to go to a yoga class once a week. I loved the teacher because she had such a grounding and calming presence. She always shared a bit about what was going on in her life at the beginning of class and how she saw it through the lens of yoga, and while I sat on my mat with my eyes closed, open and receptive to her words and the space and the energy around me, insights about myself would often flow into my awareness. A phrase would often catch my attention and relate to my own life in such an uncanny way that it felt like a message just for me, like my inner self was perked up listening for exactly the bits to pull out of what she was saying that I needed to hear the most.

Some of my favorite phrases that transformed something within me in the moment were gathered there on my yoga mat and are reflected in some of the artwork in this book. Phrases like:

- Be calm like a warrior.
- Let go and empty out to lift higher.
- Learn to sit with it.

I learned a valuable listening skill in that class that I've carried with me into the rest of my outward life. Wherever I go, I listen—inwardly and outwardly at the same time. My ears are focused outward, and when something catches my attention I can simultaneously process what I hear through my inner filter: my heart, mind, and intuition.

I can inwardly ask myself questions like:

- Is this useful for me?
- What can I learn here?
- How can this help me know myself better?

Sometimes an overheard snippet of a conversation might catch my attention and almost eerily relate exactly to something I'm going through in my own life. A conversation with a friend or family member might later turn into a piece of art based on an aha moment that I had or something they said while we talked. I always pay attention to people's energy, and sometimes the way someone simply *is* can spark a powerful realization or message within me. Sometimes it's a word on a billboard, or someone's T-shirt, or a feeling that washes through me when I see something beautiful, or painful, or ugly.

Everything is information, ripe with potential to help you transform your inner world. When you begin to walk through life this way, you'll be looking for signs and clues and insights everywhere you go. And without a doubt, you'll find them! There are gifts and riches for your inner self everywhere you go, if you're willing to be open to seeing them. It's an active way of engaging with the world and might not be familiar; it's easy to be on autopilot and simply go through the motions of life without actually paying attention. Have you ever been in the car driving somewhere and then arrived at your destination with absolutely no recollection of how you got there or what happened along the way? That's what I'm talking about! Many of us (me included) go through so much of our lives this way, not really paying attention.

But once you start paying attention, the magic begins. Your inner voice is dancing with life, in conversation with the universe, all the time, and you can either tune in to that or not. It's up to you. There's so much to discover about yourself when you focus outward and inward at the same time, and the power in the messages you receive may surprise you.

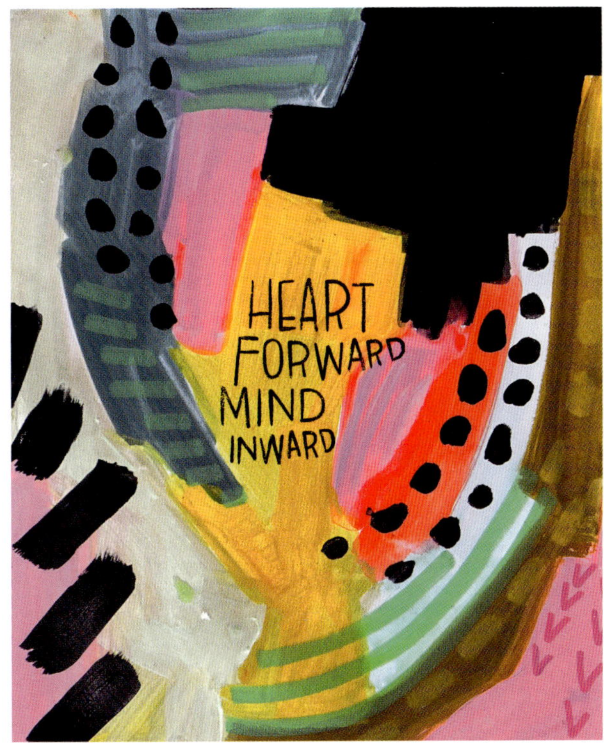

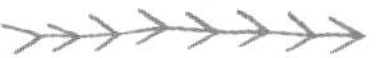

Everything is information, ripe with potential to help you transform your inner world.

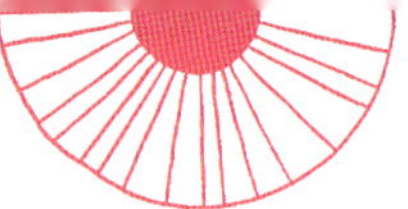

YOUR MESSAGES

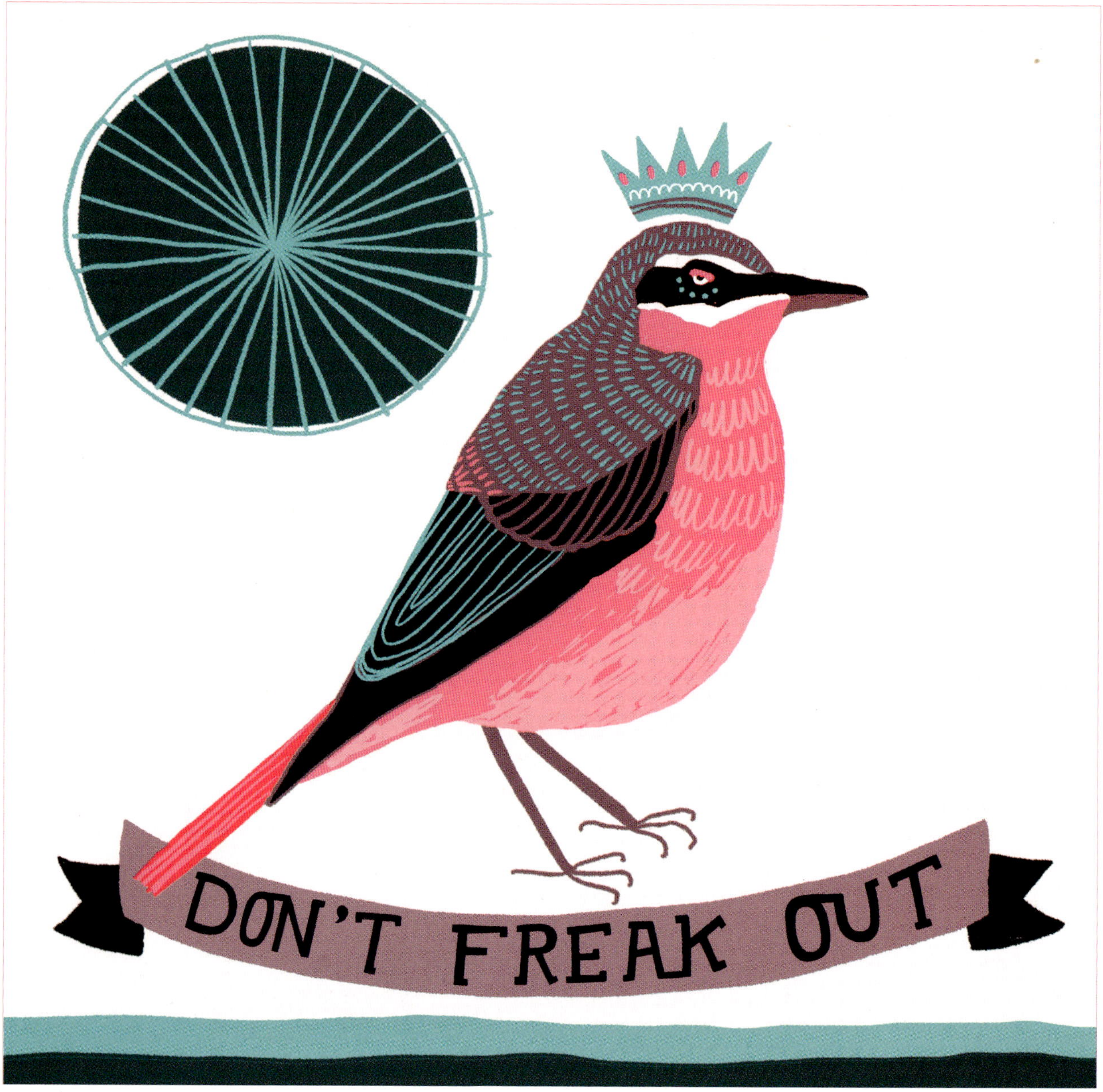

AS YOU MIGHT be starting to realize, your inner voice will communicate with you differently on different days. While that might seem a little strange and it would definitely be easier to know exactly the types of things you're going to hear, it's definitely more exciting to be surprised every day! A friend said to me once, "Every day is strange . . . and that makes sense because every

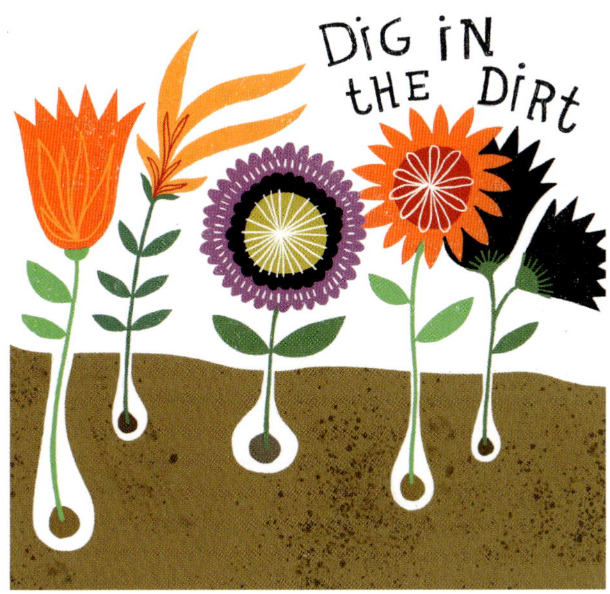

day I've lived was new to me that day." Every day is brand new. Every day is different. Life is complex and beautiful and terrible and hard and joyful, sometimes all at once. It makes sense that our inner voices would need different ways to communicate with us! There are so many variables at play within our inner human worlds.

Some days your messages will be more universal and generic, and other days they'll be laser-beam specific to whatever you're currently experiencing. Some days you may get one word, some days you may get a sentence, some days you may get an image with no words at all. It really depends! What every message will have in common, though, is that it's tailor-made for you and exactly what you need to give to yourself in that moment for comfort and support.

When I look at the images on these pages, I can remember exactly what was happening in my life when I heard the messages and created the images. I made the "Don't Freak Out" bird image during a tough phase when my baby girl wasn't sleeping and life was HARD. I'd just about had

it because I was so exhausted, and I was trying to keep my cool. This one helped me defuse the situation for myself a little bit on that particular day. Similarly, the "Quit Whining" painting was one I made when I was complaining internally a LOT and feeling sorry for myself. This was a bit of a tough love message for myself and it was surprising! It helped me get out of my head, buck up, and change my attitude a bit. It also helped me take it all a little bit less seriously (which is something I often need!). The "Dig in the Dirt" image was a suggestion from my inner voice for a specific thing I could do to bring me back into balance with myself.

The most important thing to remember is that the messages you receive will be in service of your highest good. Your wise inner self wants only the best for you and knows exactly what you need to feel inwardly comforted, supported, and loved.

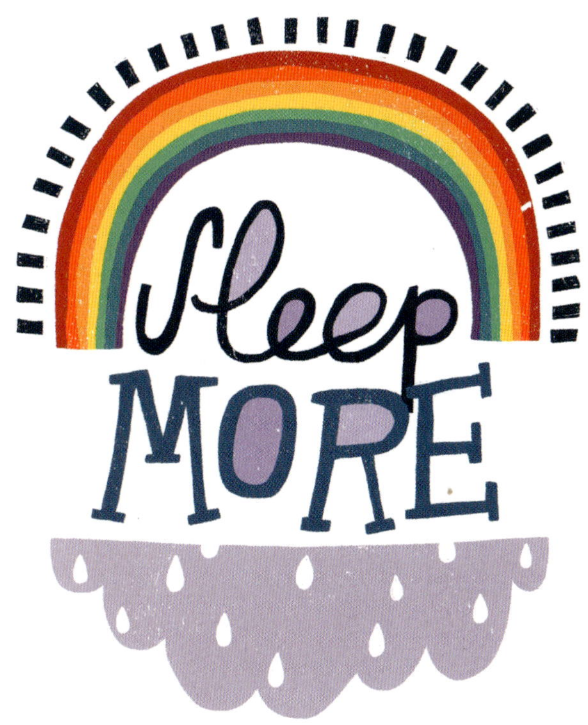

It's also important to try to keep an open mind. If your messages usually come through in one way—for example, seeing words in your mind—this doesn't mean your inner voice won't potentially surprise you along the way to get your attention in some other way. I'll give you an example from my own life.

I grew up playing the piano, and I taught myself to play the guitar when I was fifteen. I've always loved to sing and I started writing songs, which turned out to be a powerful way for me to express myself and process my feelings as a teenager, college student, and young adult. As time went on and I began working as a visual artist, my life got busier and songwriting fell away. My guitar sat mostly untouched for many years.

In late 2020 I was going through a rough patch, and for some reason I had a hunch to pick up my guitar. I didn't know why, because I'd tried picking up my guitar a few times over the course of the years it sat mostly unused, and I always put it down again almost immediately. I was embarrassed about how bad I was and how much my fingers hurt, and I was ashamed that I let something that was once so important to me fall away completely. But I followed the hunch and picked it up that day. My old guitar that I bought at age fifteen didn't feel quite right in my hands, and another hunch told me to buy a new, inexpensive guitar. This guitar changed *everything*. It felt great in my hands, and it made me want to play it! So I began to play again. Mostly I just tried playing old songs that I wrote in my early twenties, but one night I had a wonderful, strange, and rare experience while in the shower. While I was absentmindedly washing my hair, I heard a song lyric and a melody. It just showed up in my mind. I got out of the shower, sat down on my bed

with my guitar, and in less than an hour I wrote an entire song. The song is for myself. It's written from my wise and true inner self to my more human self.

It's the only time so far that I've received a message in the form of a song in this way, but it was a magical experience that I'll never forget. My inner self knew that this song was in me, waiting to be born. My inner voice knew how to transform my panic into something beautiful and useful. I felt the nudge, I listened and followed it (even though I didn't know why at the time), and I got exactly what I needed at that time in my life. That song came from somewhere higher and deeper within me, exactly when I needed it. I still play that song for myself whenever I need comfort and support. It's profoundly healing. And the best part is that I've continued to write songs since then and am so glad to have this creative outlet as part of my life again!

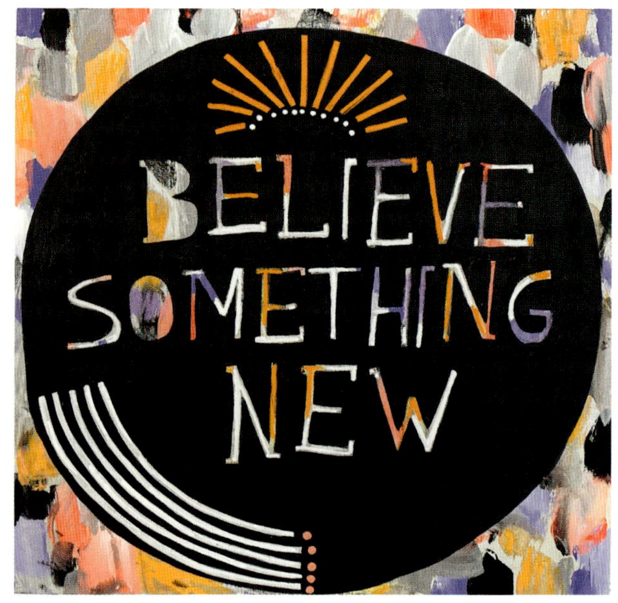

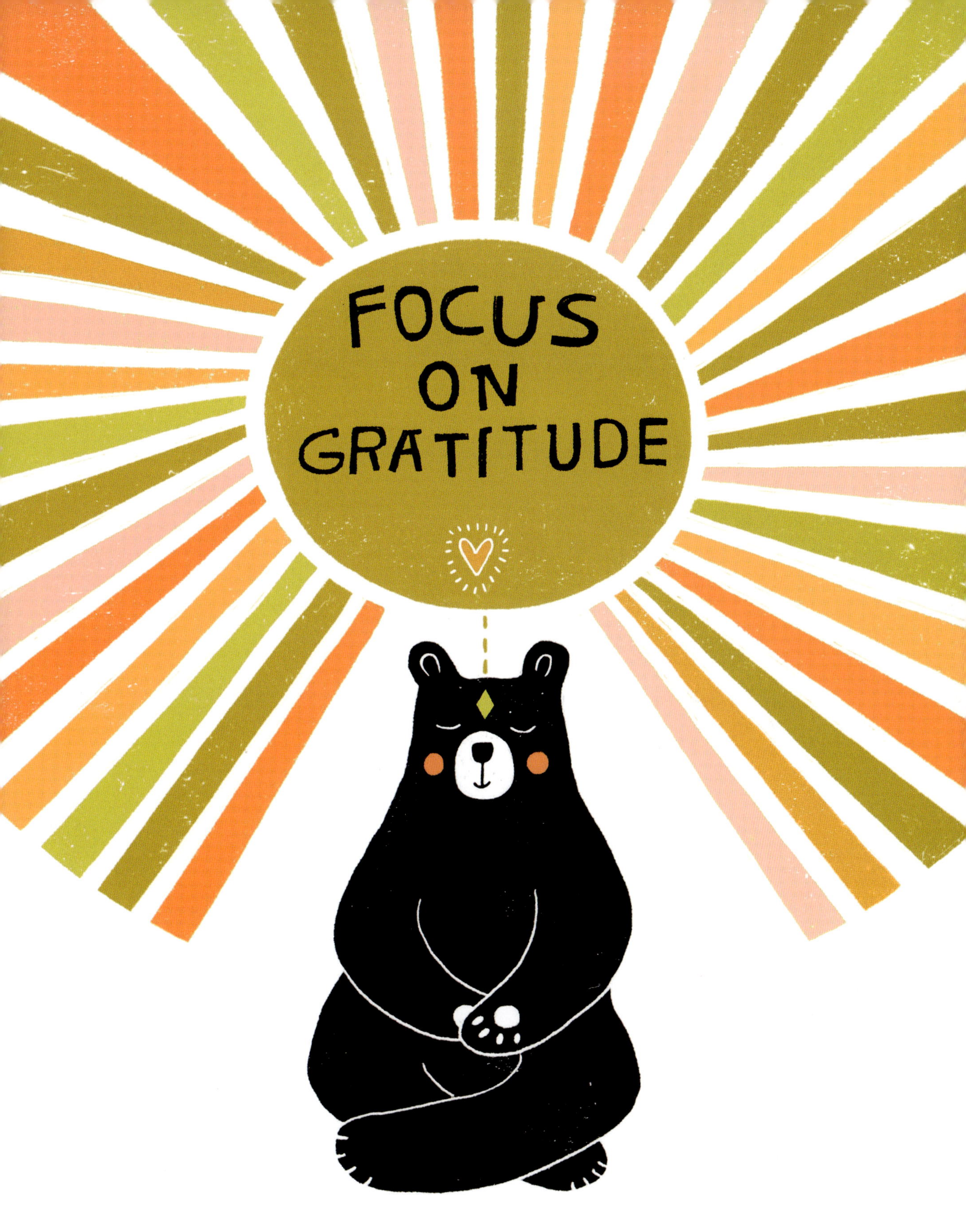

FOCUS
ON
GRATITUDE

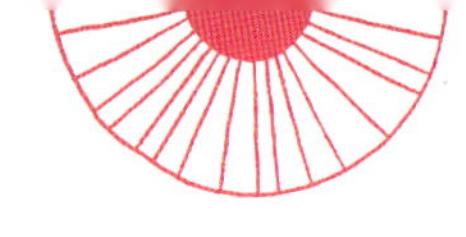

PROMPTS

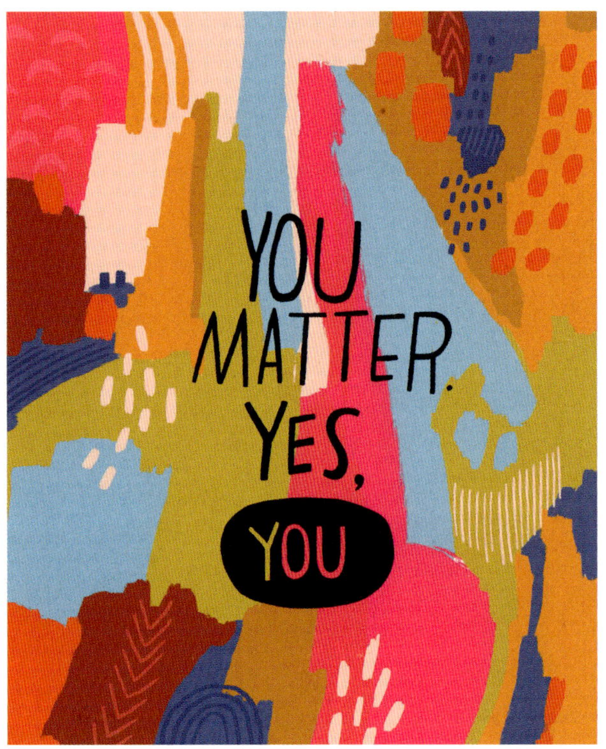

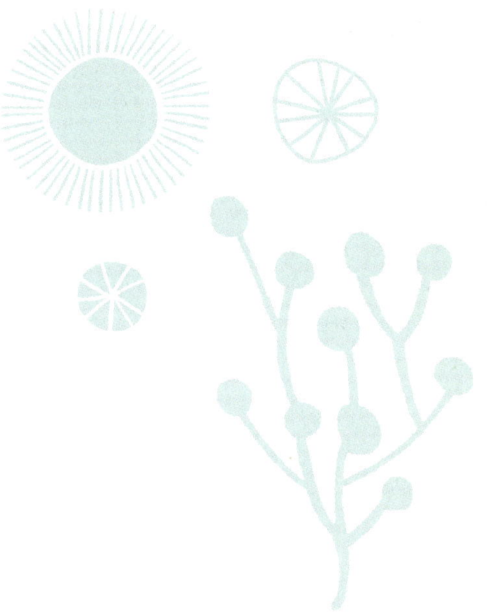

SOMETIMES A BIT of help tuning in to hear what your inner voice has to share with you can be useful, like a little kick start. Prompts are helpful as a way to ease yourself into the process of listening for messages for yourself. When you're first beginning, and especially if you're feeling a little intimidated or unsure that you'll even receive anything at all, you might find it's easier to focus if you're listening for something specific.

You'll see a lot of examples from my own work for directions you can take these prompts in, but please know that you can interpret them however you like and however it makes the most sense to you. Your brain doesn't work the same way as mine (we're all so unique!), and the messages you hear and the art you make using these prompts might vary wildly from mine. That's awesome! Try not to judge or censor yourself.

Some of the prompts are simpler and more direct, while others are perhaps a bit more esoteric or might not make sense on certain days or in certain situations. You don't have to use these in order—they're here for you to pick and choose and to use as often or as seldom as you'd like. Skip over any that you don't like, change them however you'd like, or do the same prompt over and over. Remember, there are no rules! YOU get to decide for you. Give yourself permission to trust yourself.

I've provided some different kinds of examples for each prompt to help inspire you, but please just use these as a springboard for your own creativity!

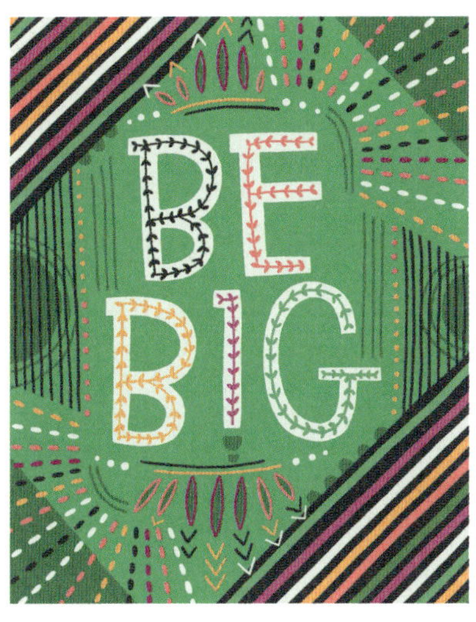

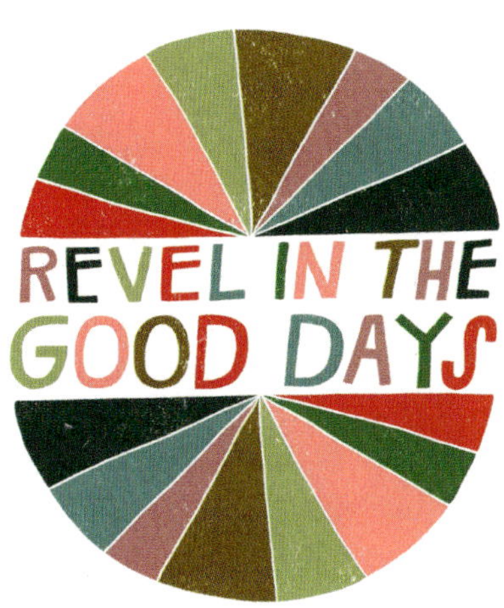

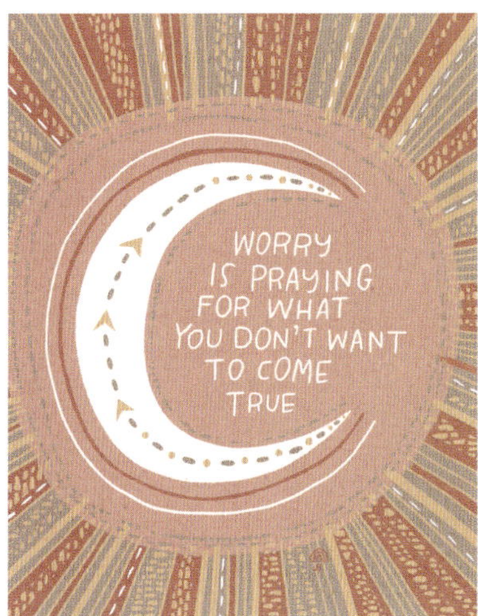

Identify a Feeling

What's a feeling that's alive inside you right now? Listen for a message from that feeling!

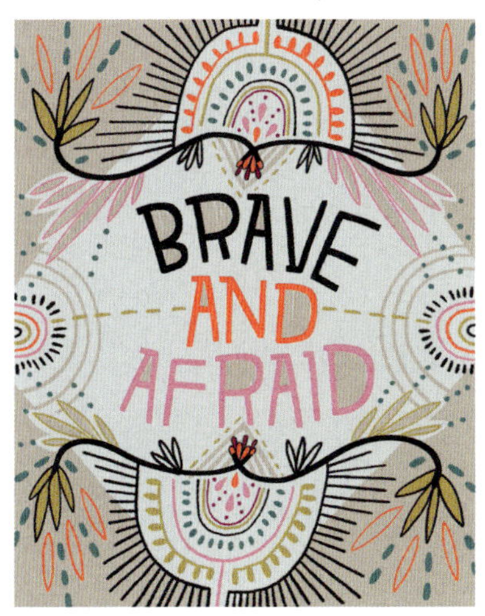

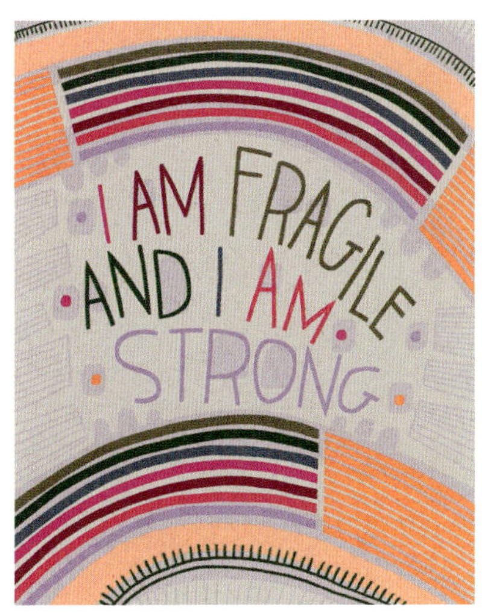

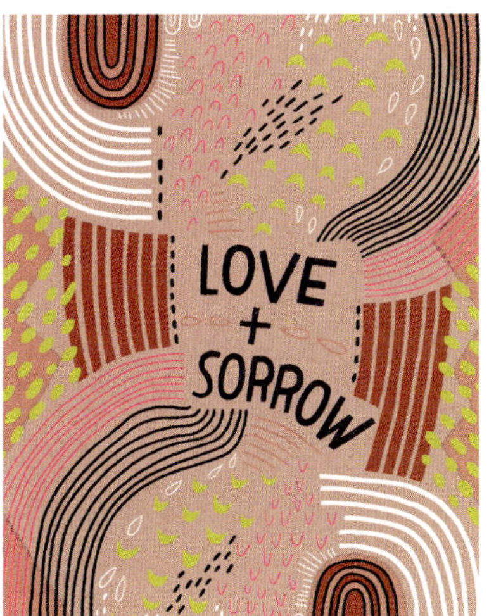

Identify Simultaneous Conflicting Feelings

Sometimes opposing feelings can exist within you. Can you find some?

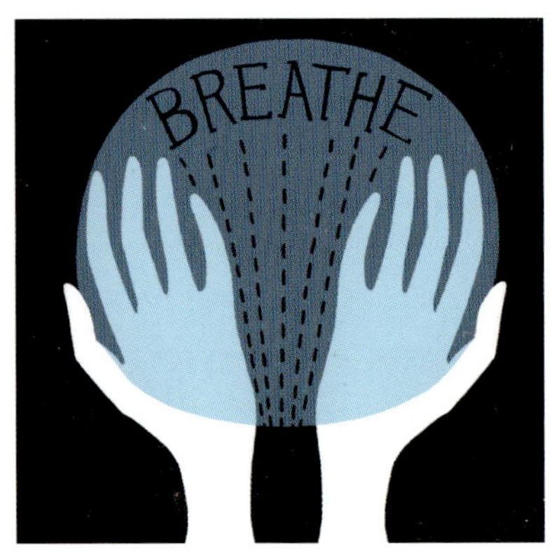

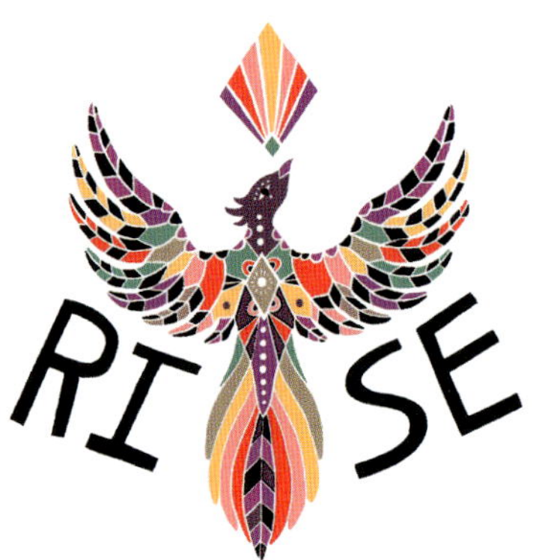

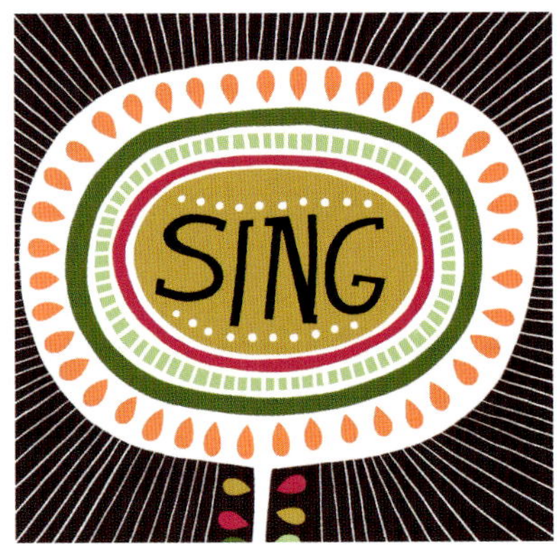

A Message in One Word

What one word would be helpful to you right now?

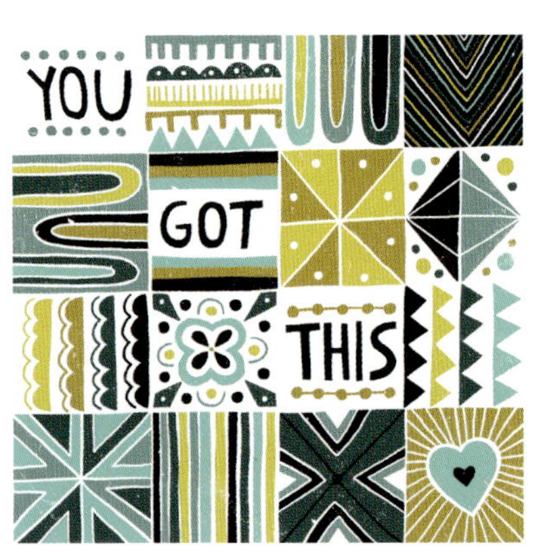

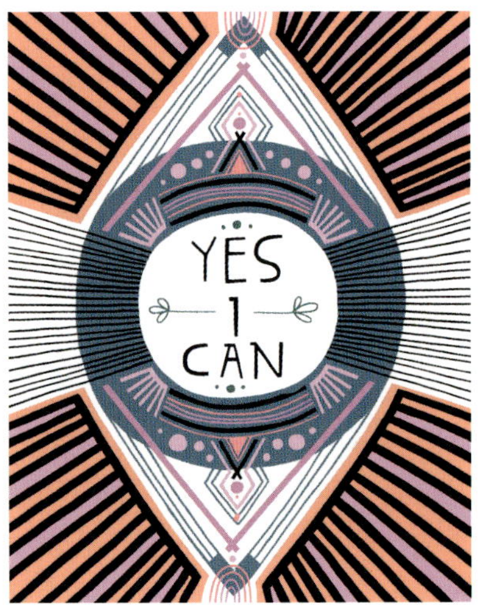

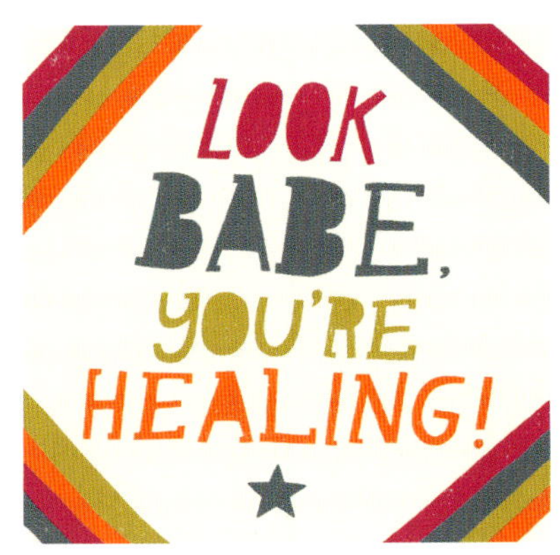

Cheer Yourself On

What is your wise inner self saying to make you feel amazing right now?

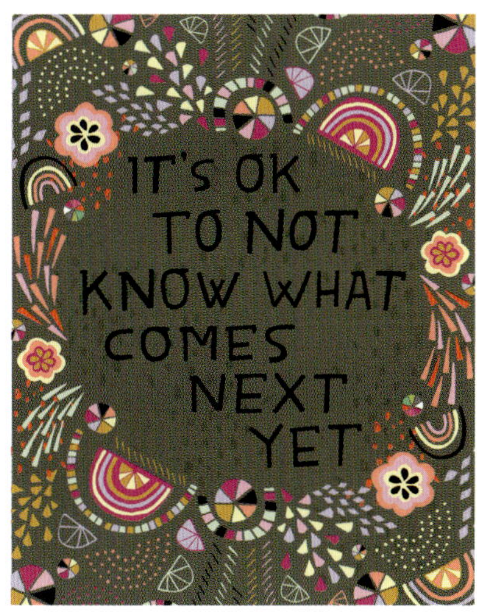

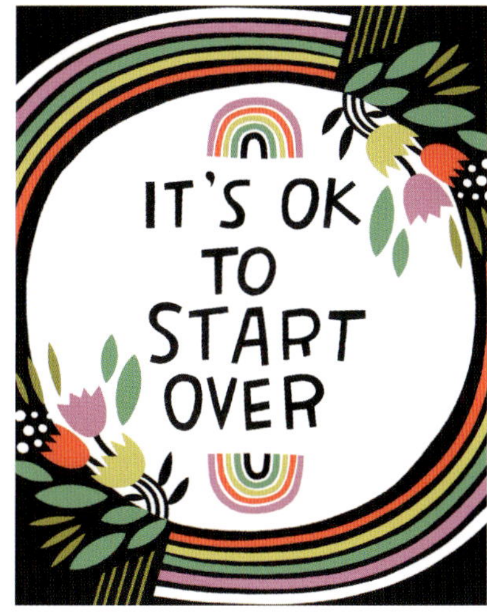

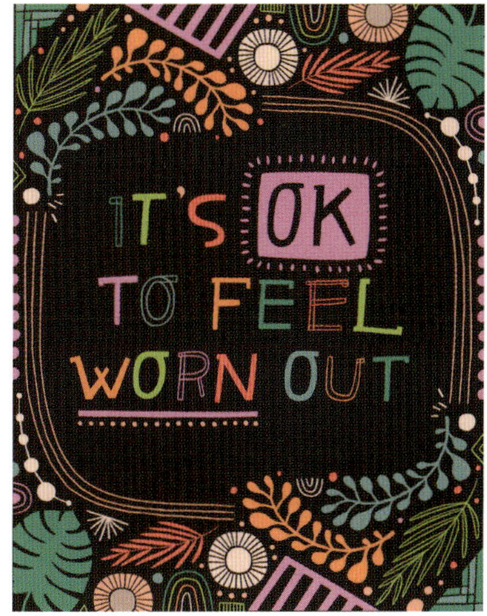

Complete This Sentence: It's Okay To . . .

What's the first thing that pops into your mind to fill in this blank?
What can you give yourself permission for?

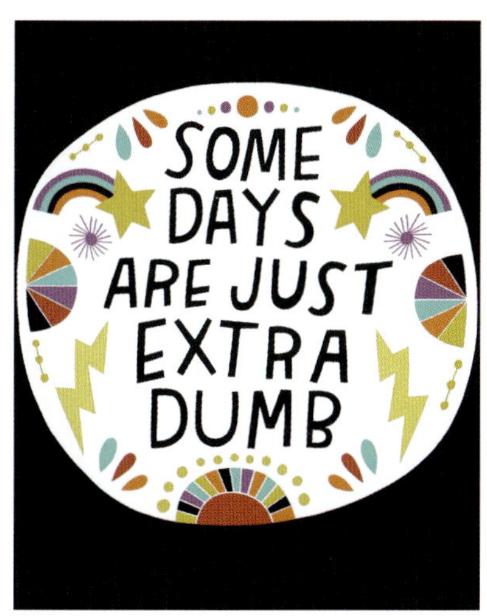

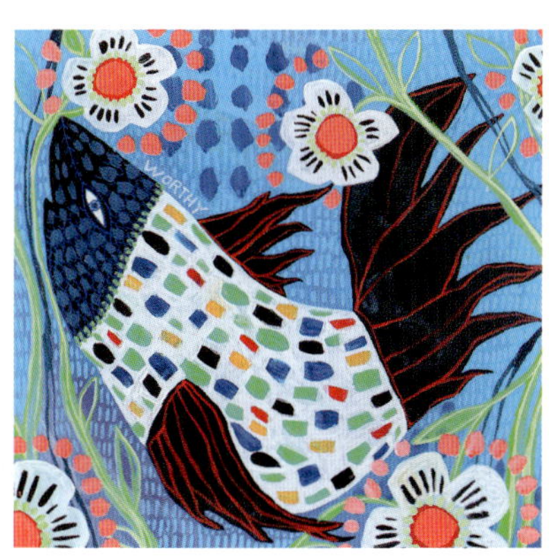

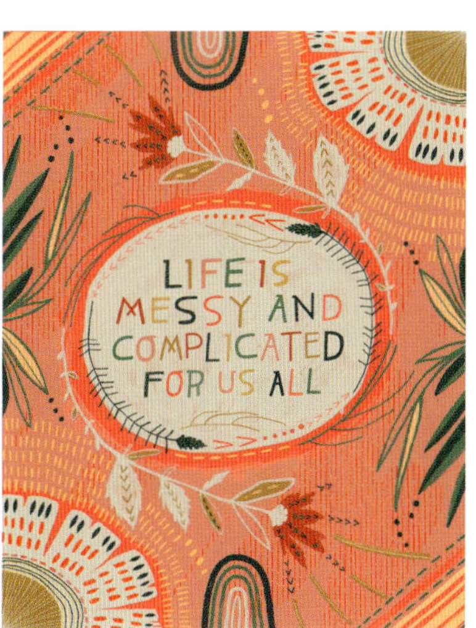

Respond to Your Day

What wisdom does your inner voice have for you to help
you integrate any experiences you had today?

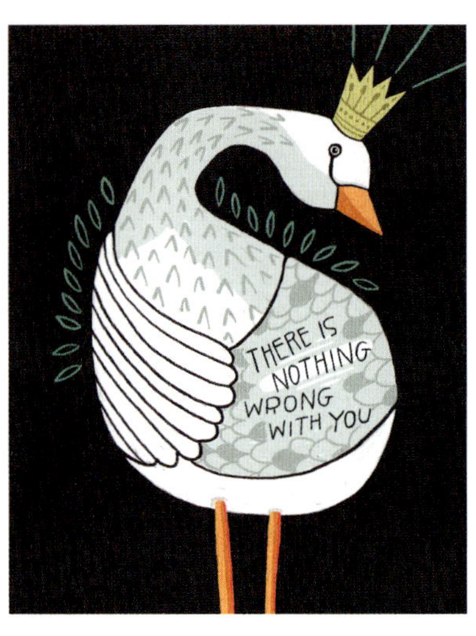

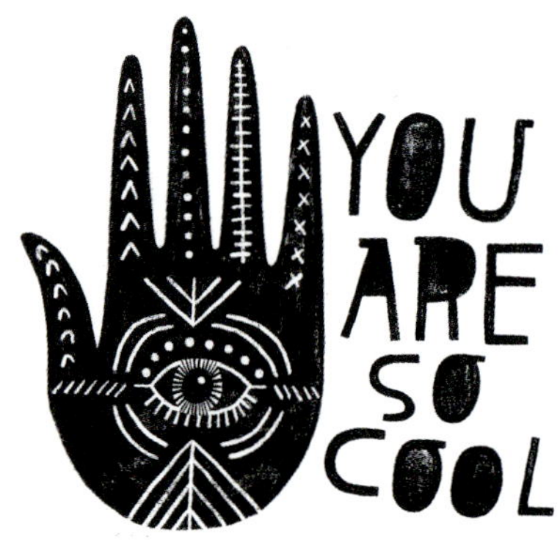

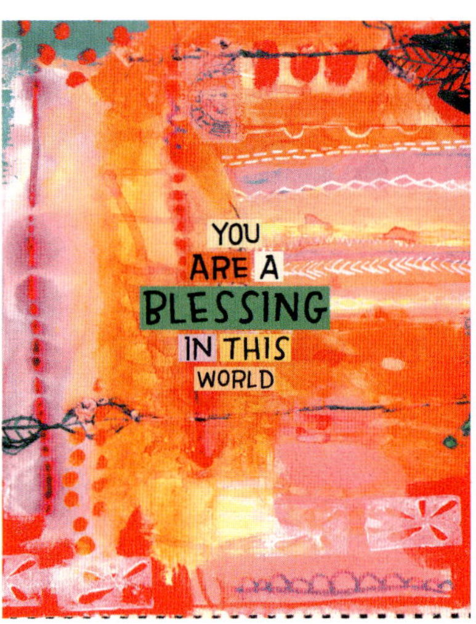

What Would a Best Friend Tell You?

Your best friend wants only the best for you!
What supportive words would that person say to you right now?

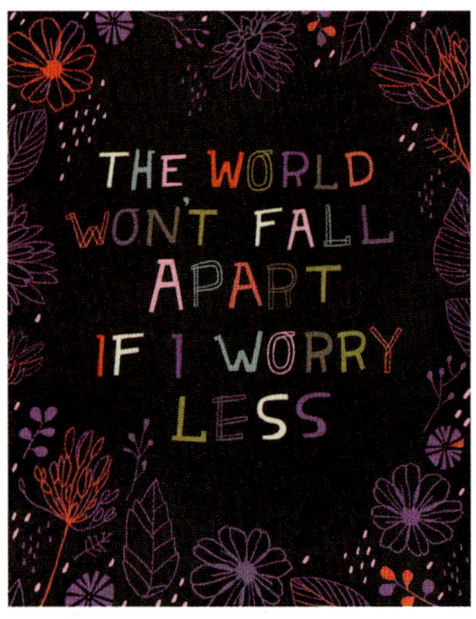

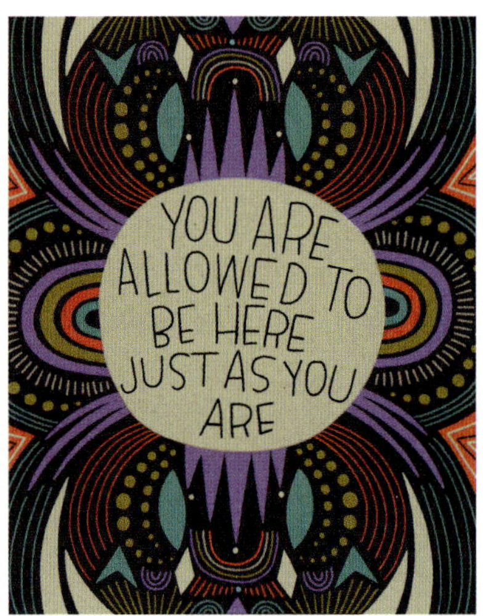

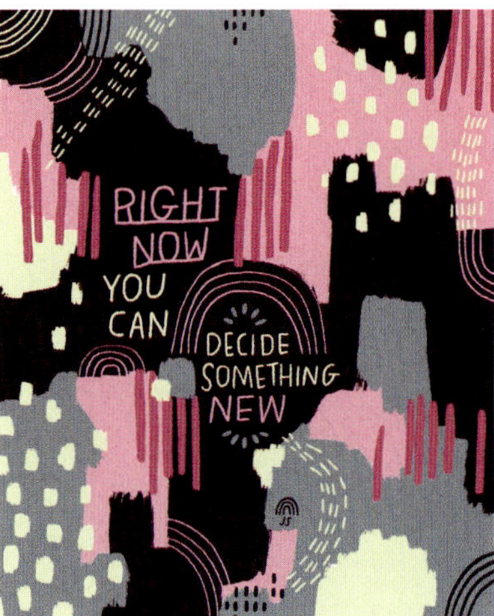

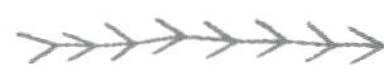

Give Yourself Permission

How are you holding yourself back? What can you give yourself permission for?

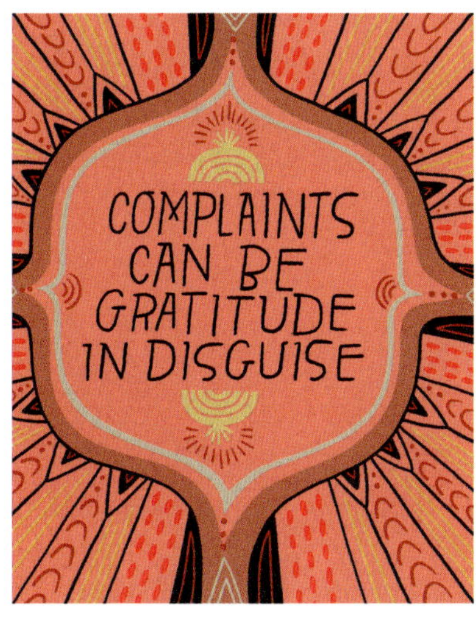

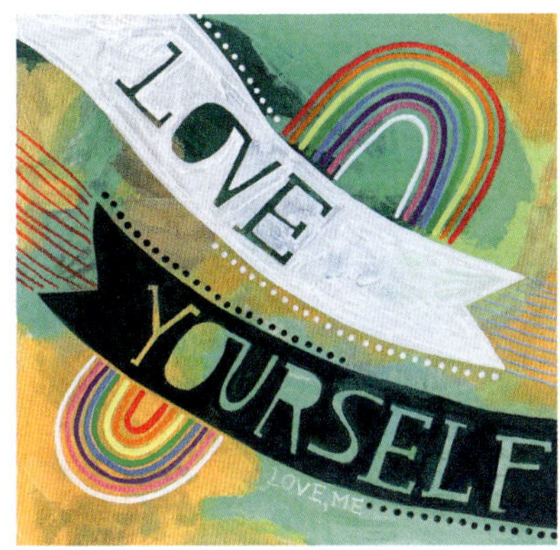

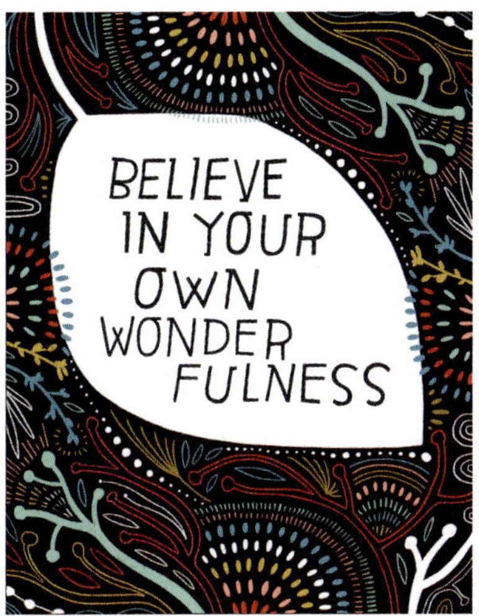

Address Unkind Thoughts

What feelings are at the root of your unkind thoughts, toward yourself or others?
How can you accept and acknowledge that part of yourself?

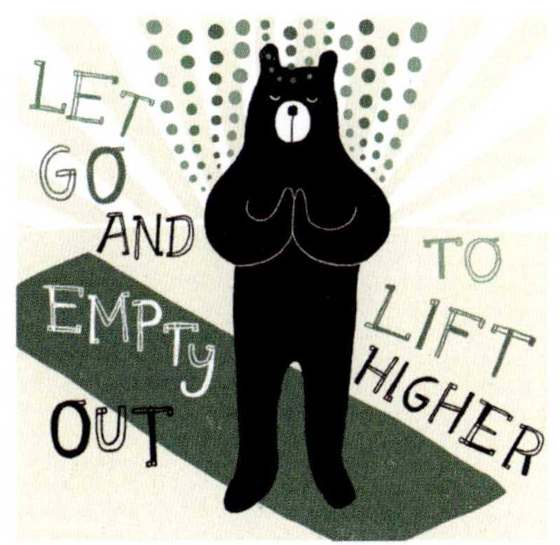

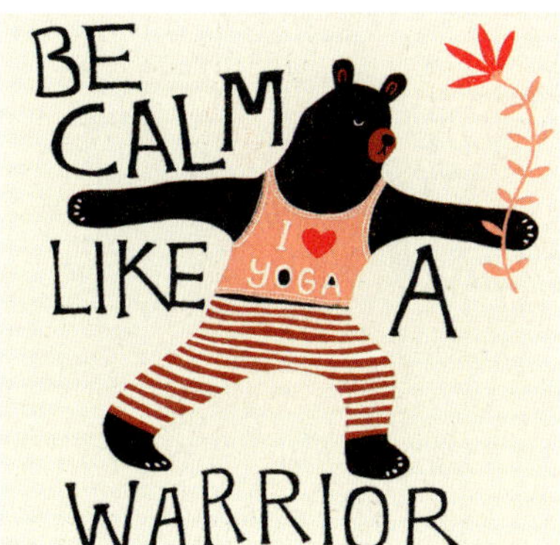

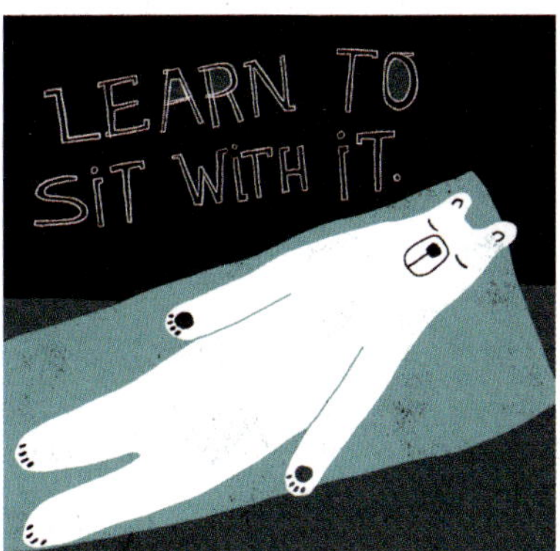

Active Listening Throughout the Day

Listen for messages as you go about your day. Stay curious in conversations,
while reading books, listening to podcasts, in yoga class, in music lyrics . . .
you never know when or how an insight or a message will come to you!

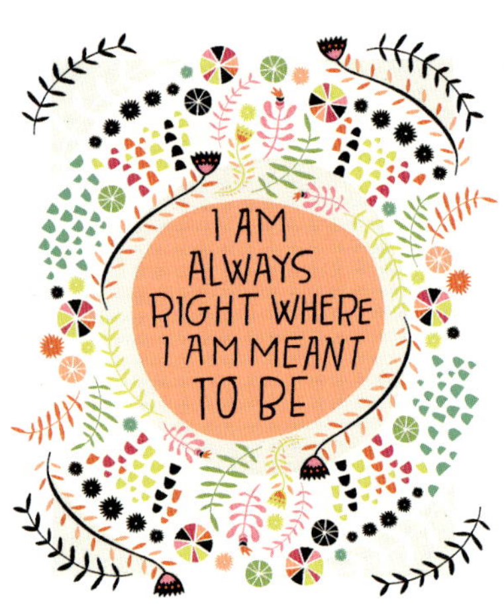

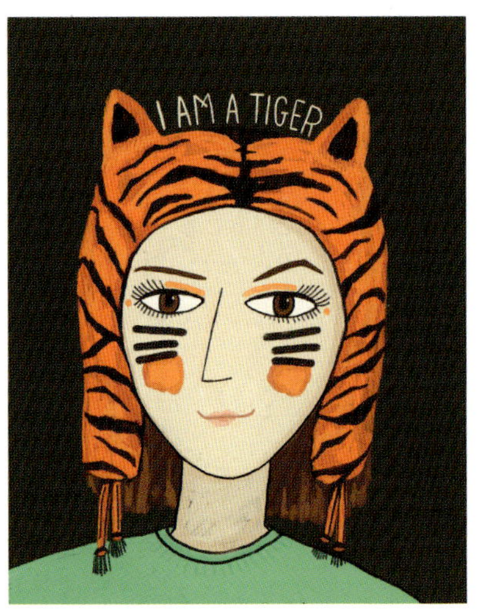

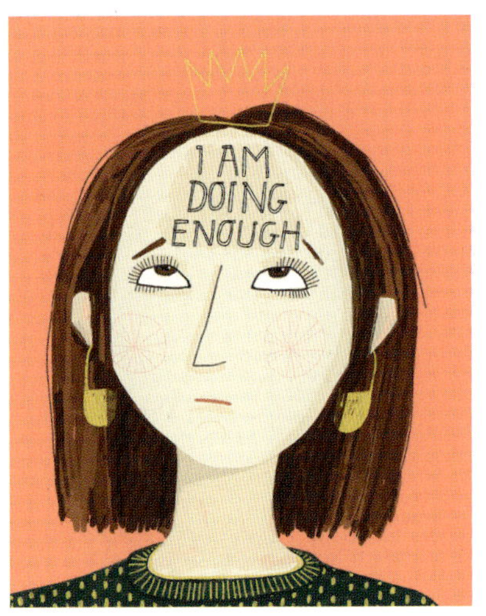

Complete This Sentence: I Am . . .

What's the first thing that pops into your mind to fill in this blank?
Don't overthink it or second-guess yourself!

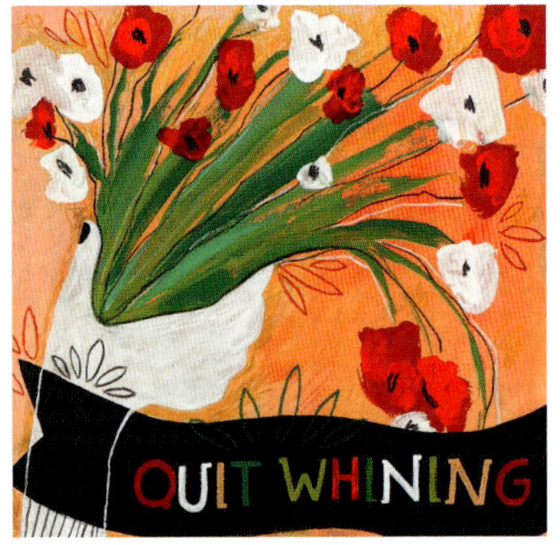

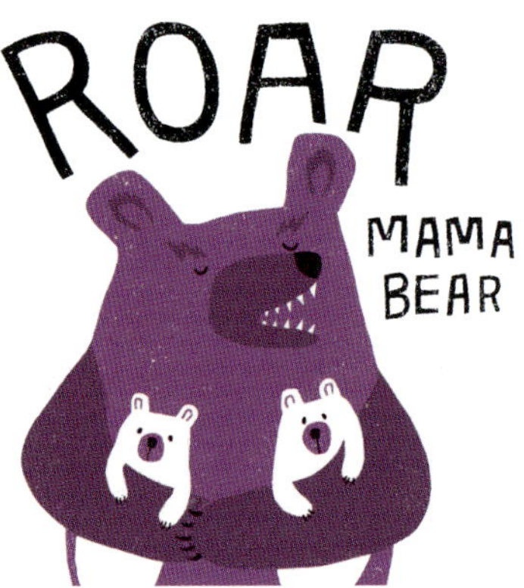

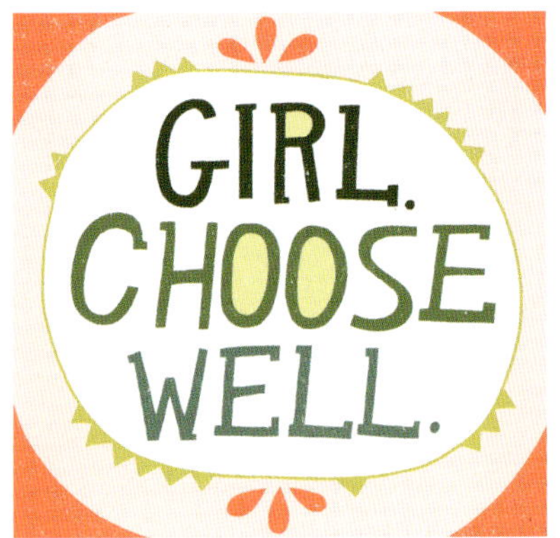

Change Your Tone of Voice

Are you normally harsh and mean to yourself? Try using kind and sweet words.
Use words you don't normally use. Give yourself a pet name. Use swear words if you never swear.

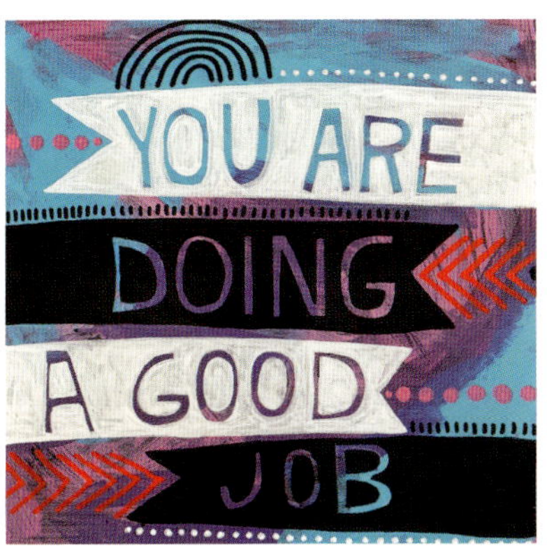

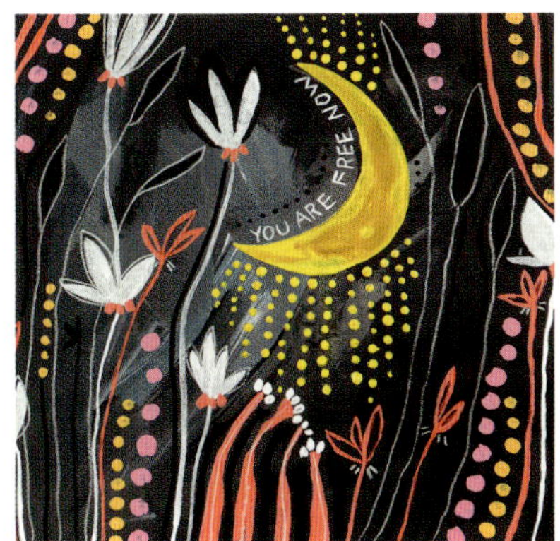

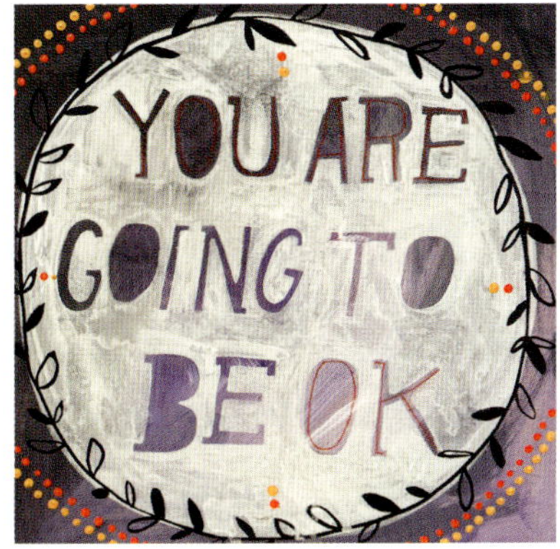

Complete This Sentence: You Are . . .

What's the first thing that comes to mind for this fill-in-the-blank?
Don't overthink it or second-guess yourself!

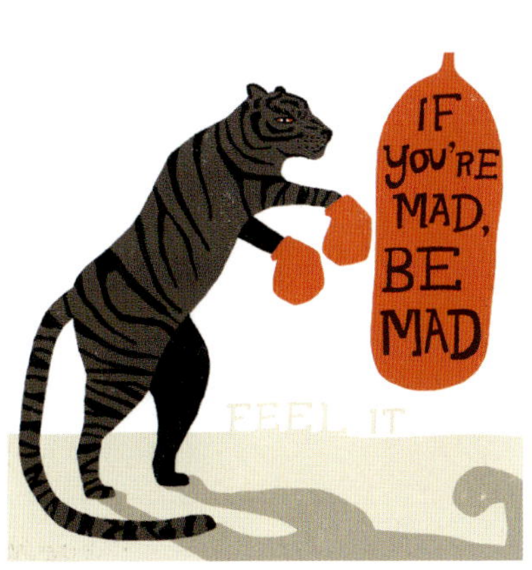

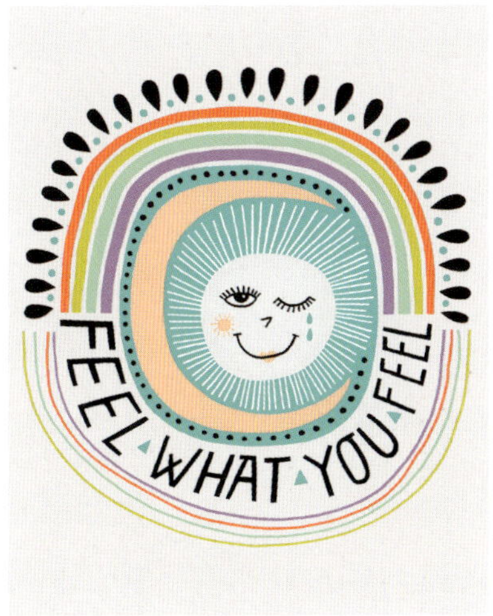

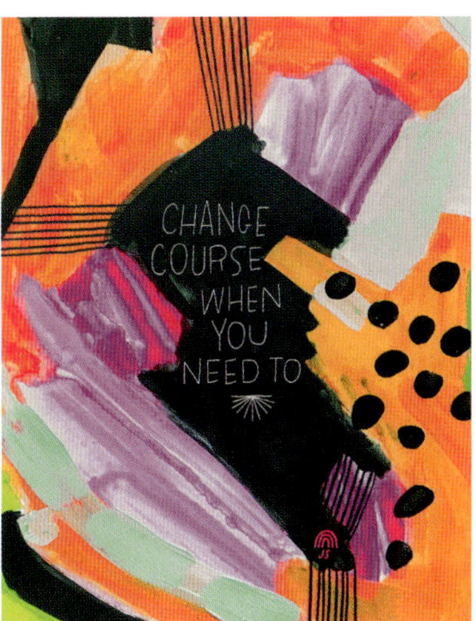

Allow Your Own Experience

Say YES to yourself. What are you resisting or wishing were different somehow?
Flip it, accept it, and say yes to it!

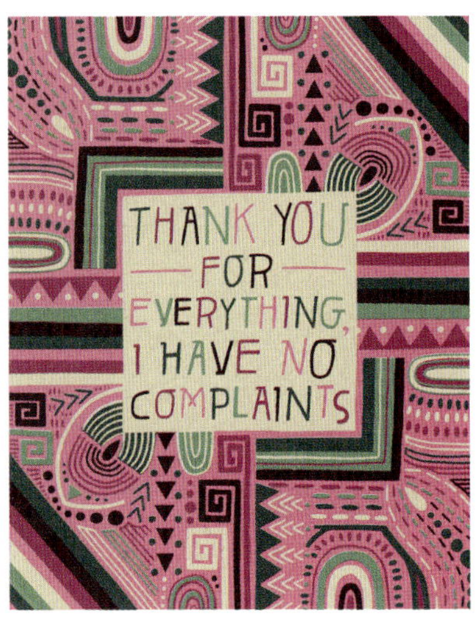

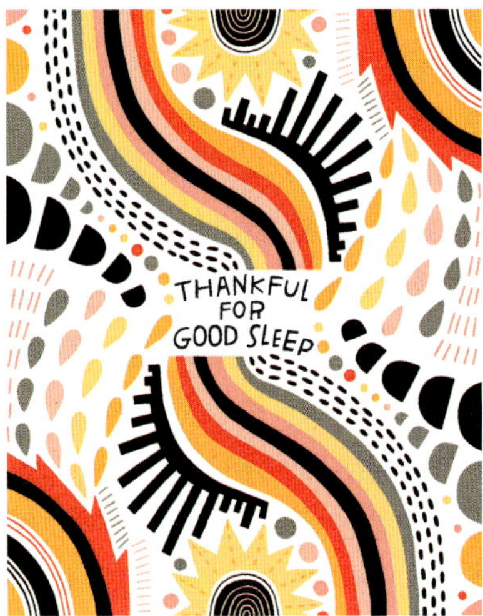

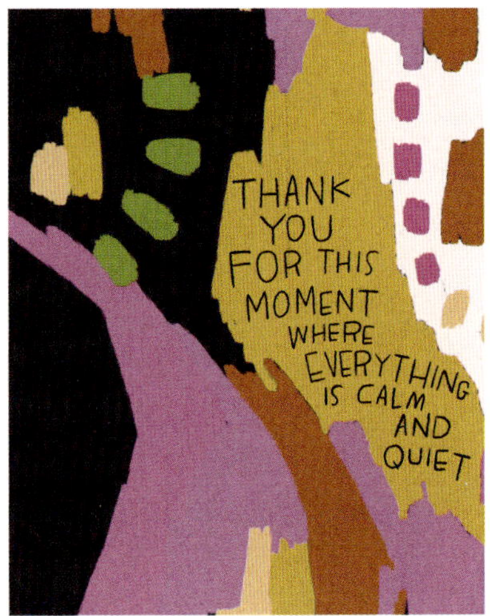

Express Gratitude

There's always, always something to be grateful for.
What are you grateful for in this moment?

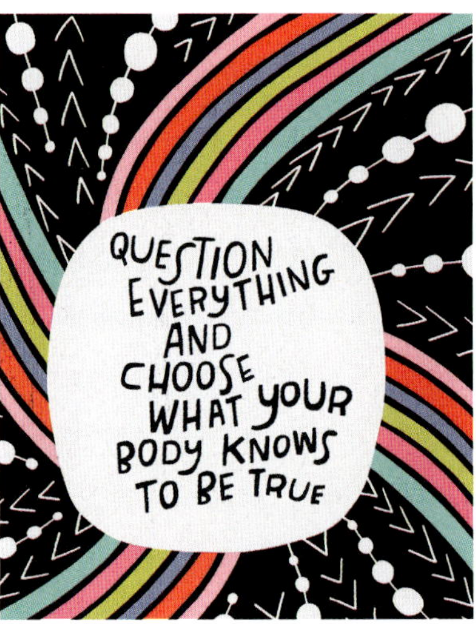

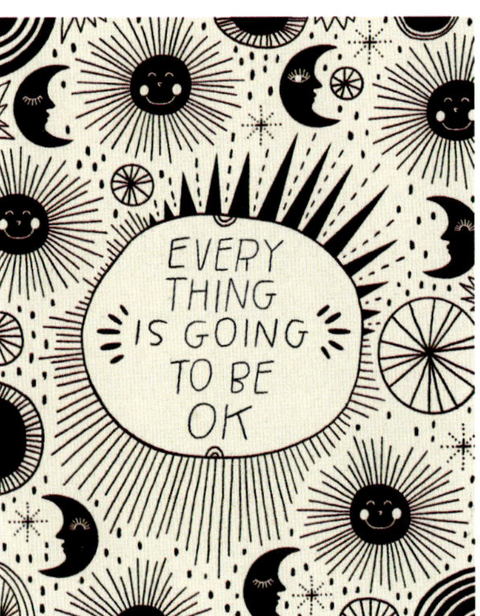

Write a Message to Your Fear Voice from Your Inner Voice

Your fear voice is trying to protect you and keep you safe as best it can.
How can you acknowledge that and also let it know it's not running the show?

*If you're feeling a little intimidated or unsure that you'll
even receive anything at all, you might find it's easier to focus if
you're listening for something specific.*

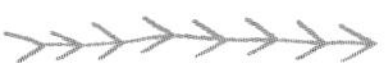

More Prompts

Here are some more prompts to help you connect
to your inner voice.

Complete These Sentences

- Permission granted to . . .
- I'm allowed to . . .
- I can accept . . .
- I get to . . .
- My superpower is . . .
- I appreciate . . .
- My pain teaches me . . .
- Today is . . .
- If I could start today over, I would . . .
- I can believe . . .
- I can stop believing . . .
- My biggest wound that still needs healing is . . .
- I can let go of . . .
- I'm ashamed of . . .
- I'm proud of . . .
- If I could change one thing right now,
  it would be . . .

Ask Yourself These Questions

- What's true for me right now?
- What do I need to be fully happy?
- What have other people told me that I believed
  but isn't true?
- What does my childhood self have to tell me
  right now?
- What do I need in this moment?
- How can I practice self-kindness today?
- What drains my energy?
- What can I do to feel better?
- Where am I out of alignment in my life?
- What does my future self want for me?

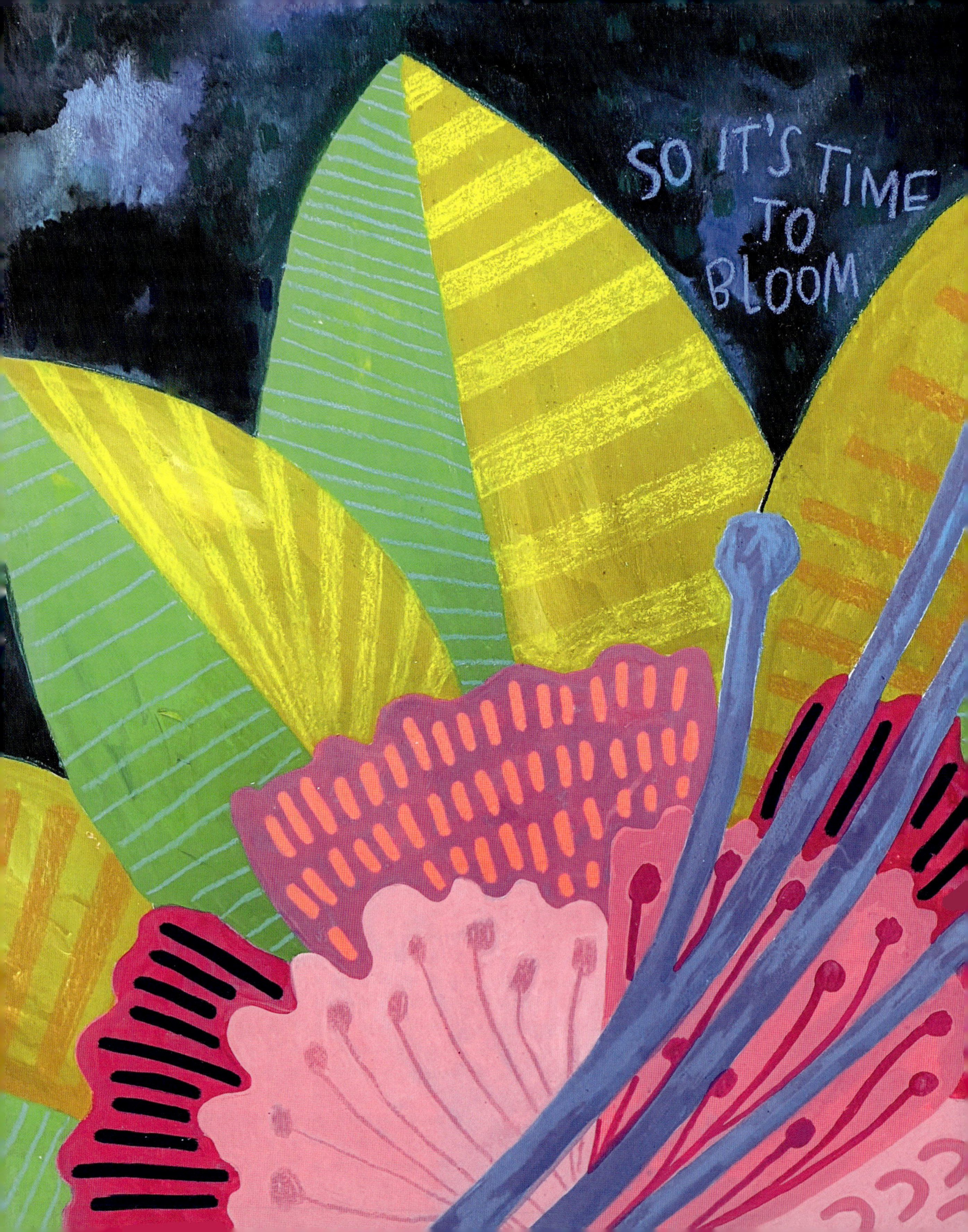

SO IT'S TIME
TO
BLOOM

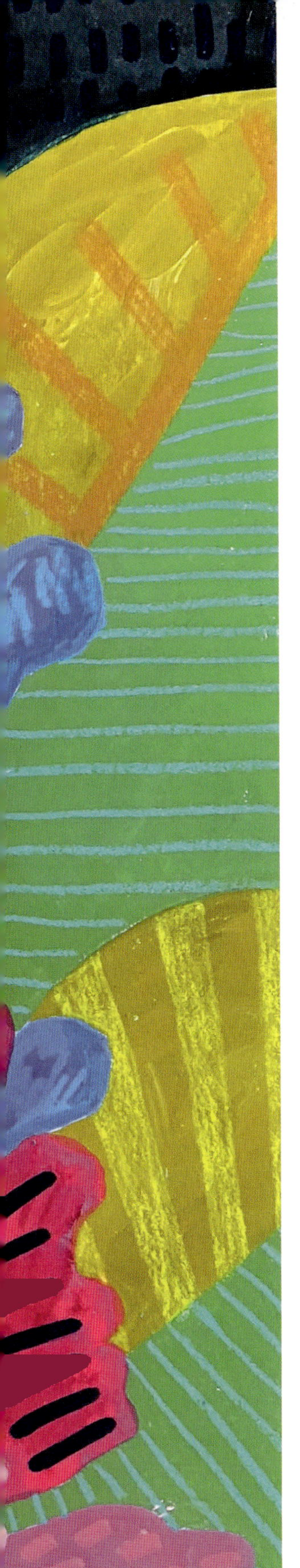

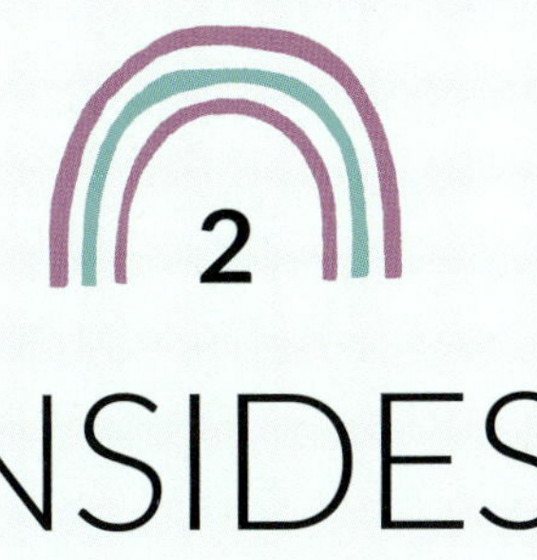

2

INSIDES OUTWARD

ONCE YOU'VE SPENT some time navigating your inner world, and you've started to get a feel for how your inner voice communicates with you, it's time for the artmaking fun to begin!

In this chapter, I'll show you a variety of techniques and tools that you can use to turn your messages into masterpieces. From a simple pen on paper to a painting on canvas, the possibilities are plentiful for how you choose to make your own personal art. You'll discover that your artwork can have lots of words or no words at all. You can use all the colors, just a few, or even just one. A simple pencil on paper will work, as will markers in a sketchbook or bits of paper torn from magazines and collaged onto the page. There are no rules here! Only you will know what feels right to visually honor and express the wisdom of your innermost self.

Let's play!

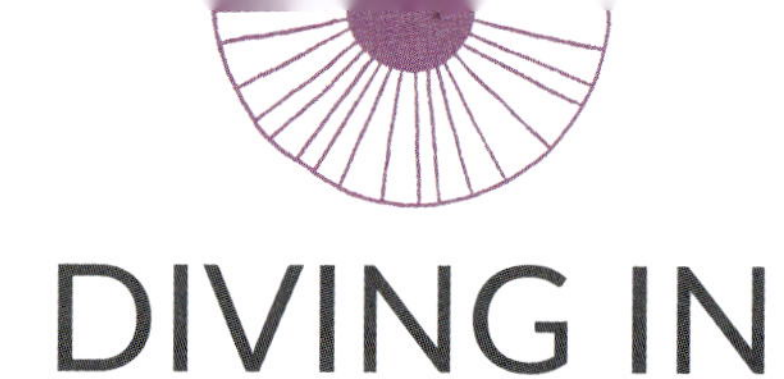

DIVING IN

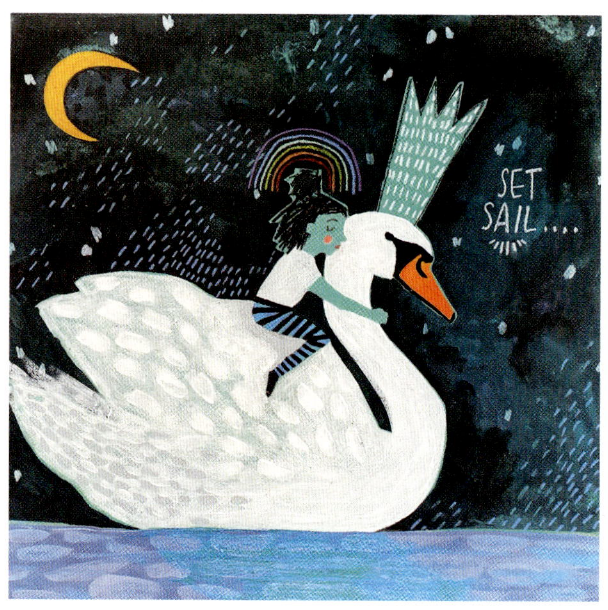

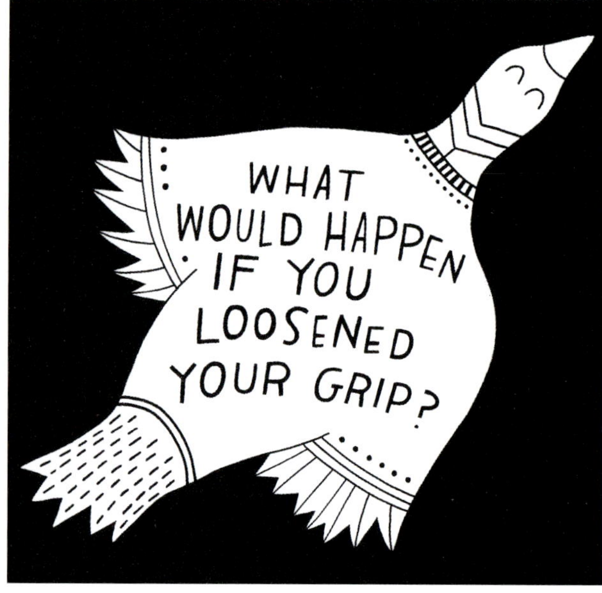

HERE WE GO, my creative friend!

It's time to loosen your grip on all the shoulds and all the judgments you have about yourself and to get curious about what's going to unfold. Whatever happens is exactly perfect, and there's no need to compare yourself to anyone for any reason. Everything you create will be useful information for you in some way. Remember that there's a lesson to gain in everything. Listen for the lessons as you go. Sometimes you'll learn a wonderful lesson or have some amazing internal revelation while making a piece of art that turns out terribly. In my view, that's a huge success!

Depending on the type of person you are, you might like to have a creative plan for yourself, or you might like to just wing it and create your artwork however it feels right each day. In my opinion, it makes the most sense to get started using techniques and materials that are familiar to you, so you're not simultaneously learning to listen to your inner voice and trying some brand-new medium for the first time! What I'm trying to say is, if you're comfortable and familiar with using markers in a sketchbook but have never used, say, watercolor, then it might be a good idea to start this intuitive artmaking adventure with the markers and sketchbook instead of the watercolor. You can always try out the watercolors later once you're more familiar with how your inner voice communicates to give you messages that you can work with.

That said, you absolutely don't have to follow this advice if it doesn't feel right for you. You might feel more creative freedom and less constraints trying out a new medium; that might free up the intuitive part of your brain in a new way. Sometimes a fresh start and a new perspective can surprise you in unexpected ways.

In my own experience, I find that getting started is often the hardest part. You can't *think* your way through this process; you can only create your way through it. Just like how you won't learn to ride a bike by reading a book about riding a bike—you have to actually get on the bike and feel your way through it—you won't learn how to hear your inner voice and make art that reflects and honors it by reading about it. You actually have to jump in and try it! You have to be willing to fall off in the beginning and practice your way to proficiency. It takes time!

My favorite painting professor in college used to tell me that I had to be willing to make the bad art in order to get to the good art. What he meant was that it's all part of the process. Nothing is wasted. You just have to be willing to start creating and to trust the mystery of the creative process.

So whatever materials you choose to work with, try to get started without overthinking it too much. Overthinking is unhelpful when it comes to creativity! Do your best not to take yourself too seriously and make sure the way you're creating is enjoyable and fun and not at all stressful.

You could even ask your inner voice, "What do you want to create with today?" and see what answer comes! The answer might be different each day. Or you might use the same medium every single day. One way is not better than another.

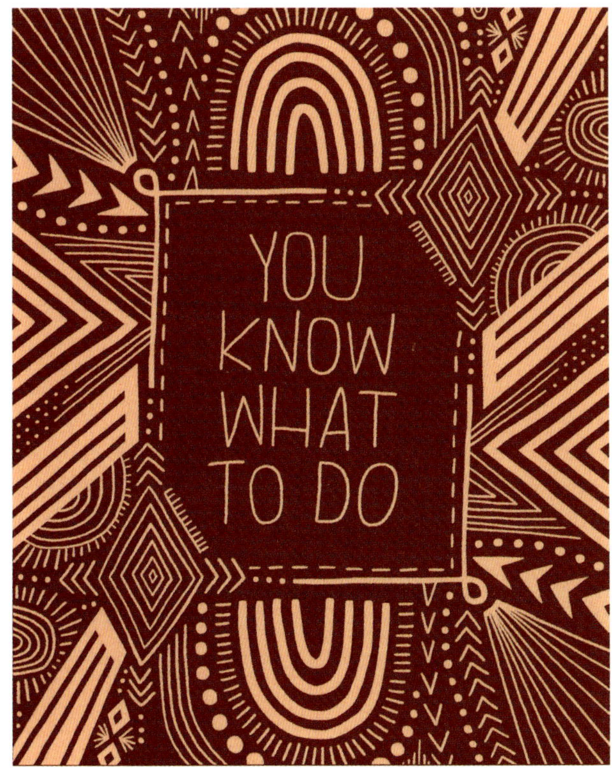

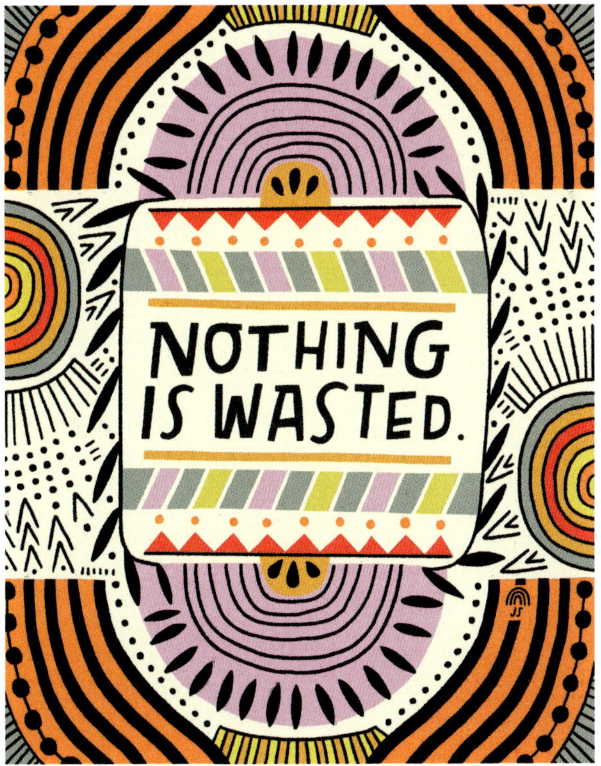

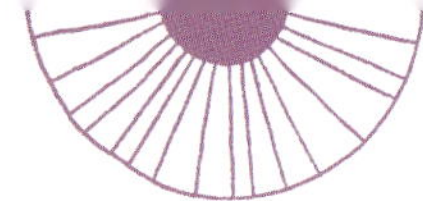

TRUST THE PROCESS

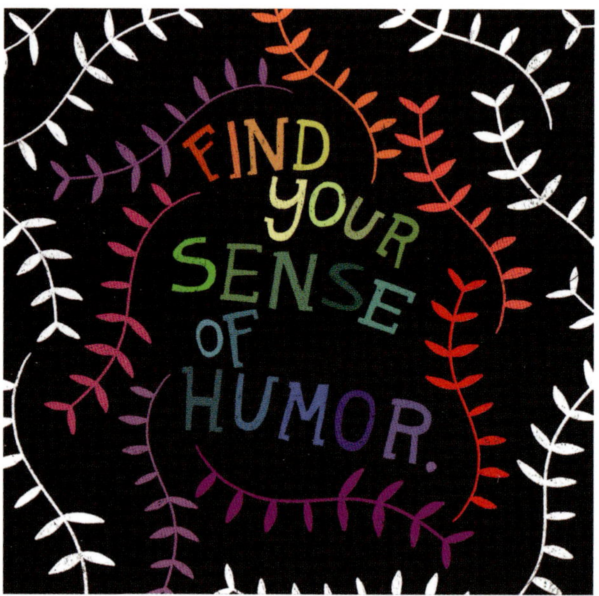

MY FAVORITE PAINTING professor (whom I mentioned in the last section) also used to tell me, "Don't get precious with your work." (He was full of wisdom!) What he meant was: leave room for accidents and surprises. Don't overthink it or overwork it. Leave room for magic.

I went through a period back then where I ruined everything I painted because I overworked it trying to make it perfect. What I discovered is that the more I loosened up in every part of the painting process, the more I loved what I was creating. It wasn't perfect, but it was human, and it was mine. I thought less and felt more. And as I did that, I started to naturally tune in and just *know* when a piece was finished rather than crossing that line and trying to erase imperfections.

The creative process requires openness and trust. Receptivity and courage. Willingness to walk into the unknown to see what you can unearth and bring forth from your magical inner world out into the light of the outer world. And that's not always a straightforward process! There'll be twists, turns, doubts, fears, surprises, and triumphs along the way. You'll make mistakes and you'll have epiphanies. You'll carve your own unique path and way of expressing yourself. The imperfections in all of that are where the true beauty is. They're marks that show where you've been and where you're going. Each line, each mark, each piece of art that you make that you don't like is leading you somewhere. Trust it. I've made so many drawings and paintings that I'm simultaneously embarrassed by and proud of. Not everything is going to be a masterpiece. You're going to make things that suck. That's just part of the deal, sweets. And when you do, you just have to keep going, remembering that you have to be willing to make the mediocre and the bad art in order to get to the good art. You have to be willing to keep showing up, even when it doesn't feel good. Because there's so much goodness on the other side of that, I promise.

So, don't get precious with your artmaking. Don't take it so seriously. Find the humor in it! It's supposed to be fun. Laugh when you make something ugly. Something so beautiful it makes you cry might be right around the corner. You just have to keep creating and see what happens, trusting the unseen path in front of you.

The words that come to you are the words that come. The art that you make is the art that you make. As you practice, do your best not to attach any stories around good or bad or artist or not-an-artist to anything that you're doing. Try not to compare your messages and artwork to mine, or to anyone else's. Just get into your own mysterious flow. The magic is in the surprises along the way.

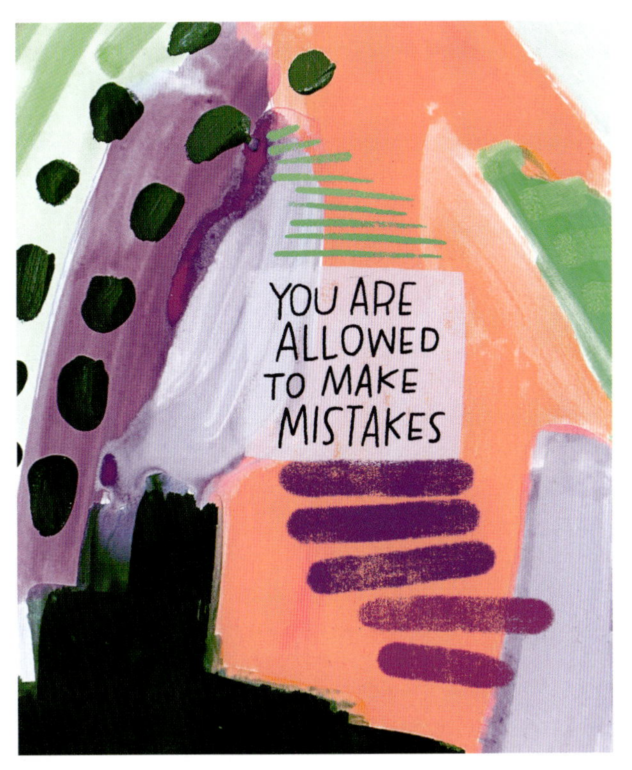

YOU ARE
ALLOWED
TO MAKE
MISTAKES

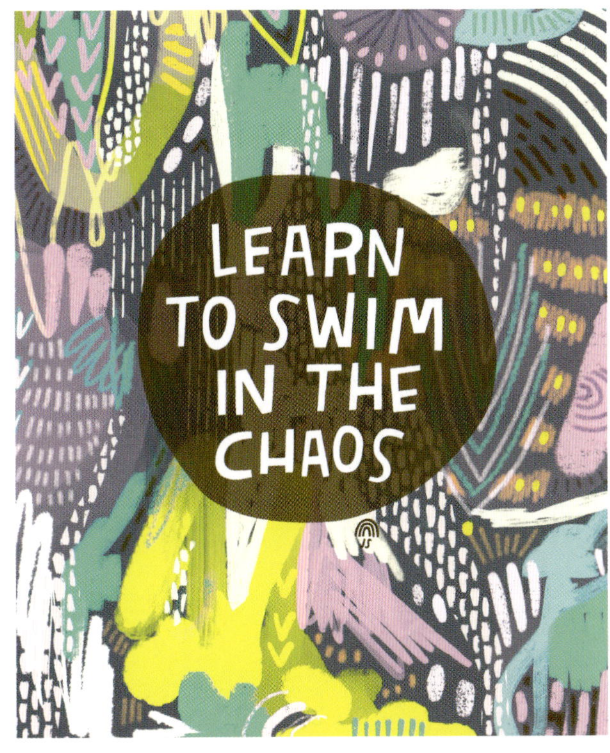

LEARN
TO SWIM
IN THE
CHAOS

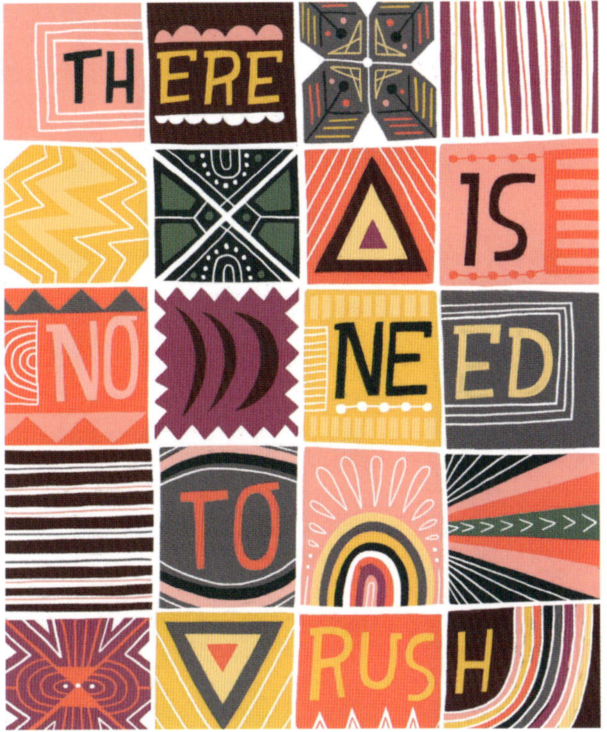

THERE IS
NO NEED
TO RUSH

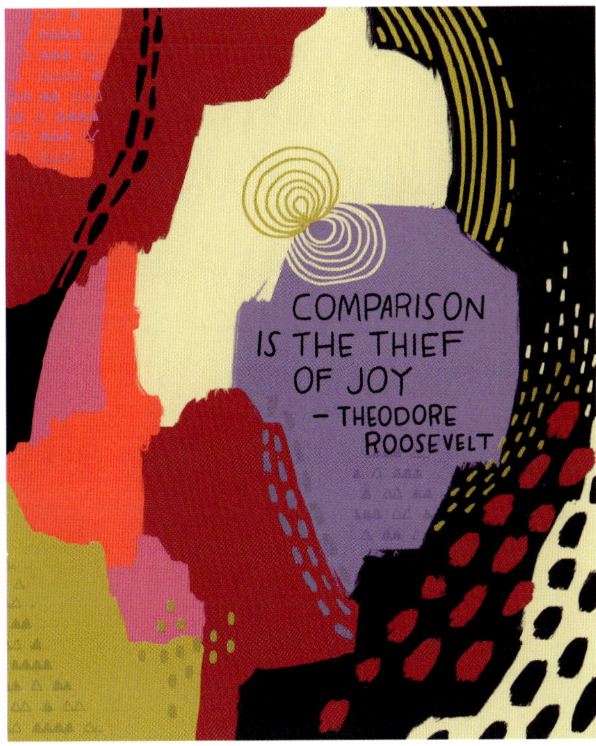

COMPARISON
IS THE THIEF
OF JOY
— THEODORE
ROOSEVELT

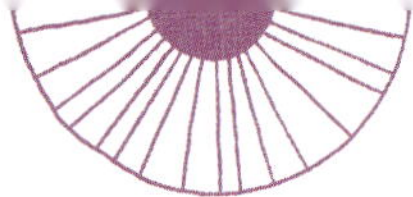

YOUR INNER CHILD

WHEN I WAS a little girl, I'd sit for hours on the floor with a pile of markers and paper, blissful and lost in my own inner world, coloring to my little heart's content. Some of my earliest and best memories are of those times. It just felt good to make stuff! Kids are so good at not overthinking things, aren't they? They just do what feels good. They don't judge themselves along the way. They allow themselves the freedom to just BE. It's natural to lose some of that as we get older, of course, but it's still there, and it's still incredibly powerful to tap into that sense of childlike wonder and freedom.

To this day, when I want to tap into my creativity in an unfiltered kind of way, I sit on the floor to create. It's like I have this deep, innate sense that being on the floor is a safe place for me to let go and just be in the moment, letting creativity flow through me without judging it along the way. My childhood self remembers this feeling well, and when I put myself in the same position it's like an inner muscle memory, something I can immediately tap into for a different creative state.

Think back to when you were a child. What did you love to do the most? How did you do it? What came naturally? What did you lose yourself in? What were you thinking about or feeling? These are all clues for how you can tap into your inner voice and let it come out to play and deepen your artmaking experience!

While making intuition-based art is most definitely a "serious" thing to do in some ways, it's also not meant to be taken too seriously. If you're anything like me, you've gotten very good at taking things too seriously over the span of your life so far, and that can really block the unleashing of some radical creativity and healing within yourself! So

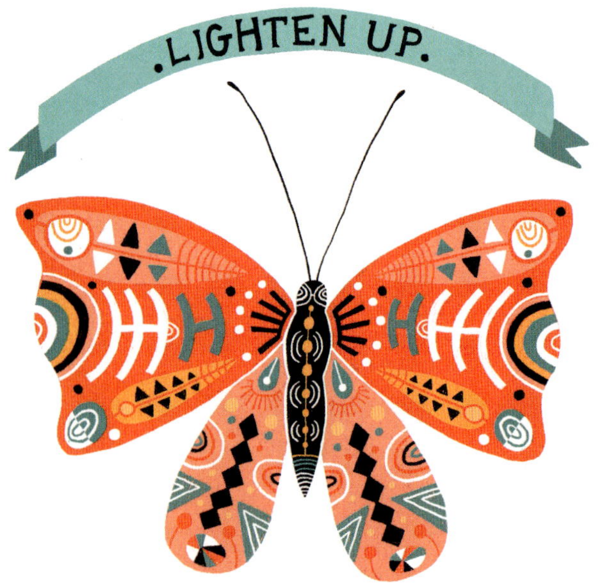

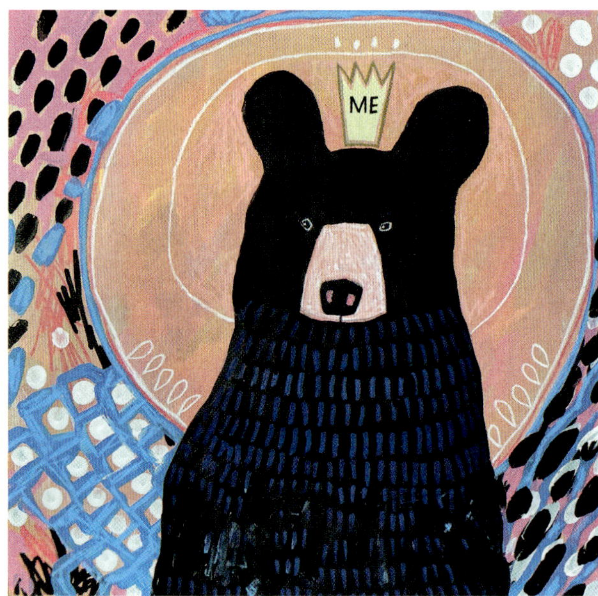

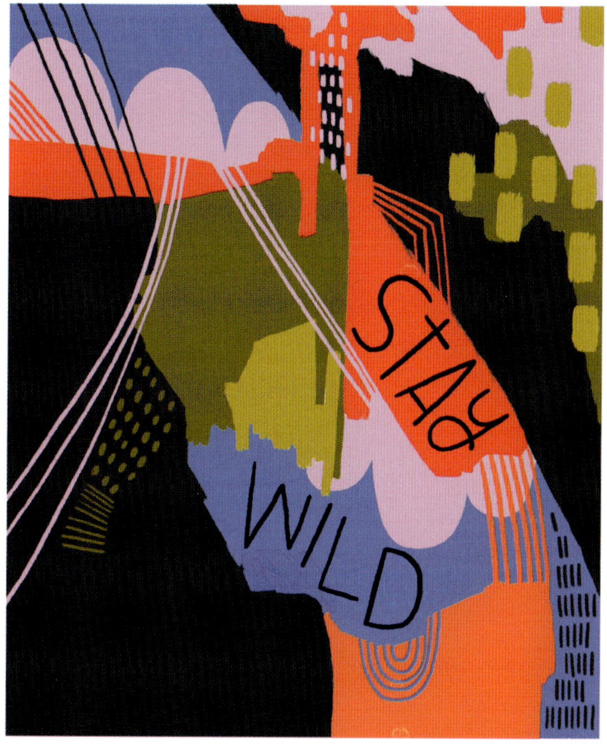

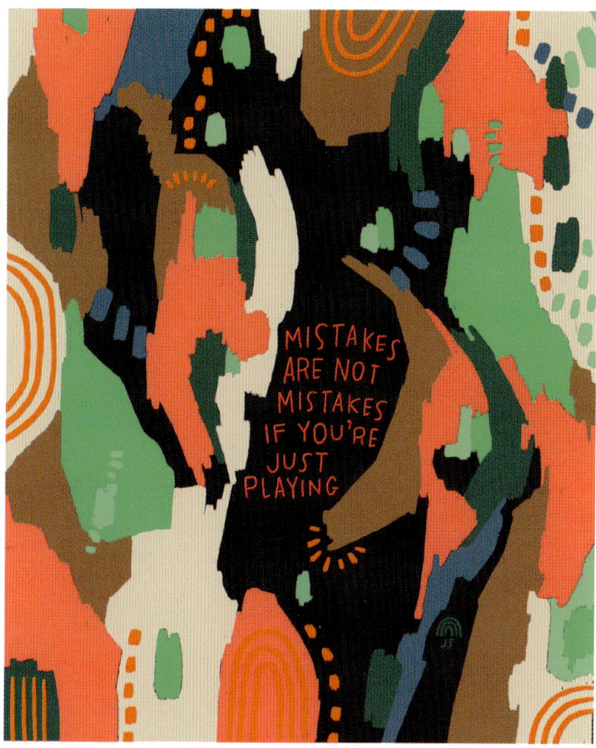

the idea is to respect your process and take it seriously, of course, but also to be loose and light and playful along the way.

Your childhood self is still alive within you. Every past version of yourself still lives in your energy field and in your memory somewhere. It can be incredibly healing, profound, and FUN to ask your inner child to come help you create. Try imagining yourself as your childhood self and listening through your childhood ears. Does that change the way you hear any messages from your inner voice? Are the messages similar? Different? These are all fun questions to ask and play around with as you create, seeing how you might best be able to tap into the most authentic version of yourself.

I also want to acknowledge that not every part of childhood is blissful and wonderful. You may have lived through painful experiences, abuse, trauma, sadness, danger, and any number of other difficult circumstances. My dad was an alcoholic, and my childhood was certainly not all roses. This is another way to invite your inner child to join you to create different types of healing. What does that childhood version of yourself, who's still alive inside you, need to hear from your inner voice now? How can you comfort that past version of yourself?

Try allowing the younger versions of yourself to come out into the light to share whatever wisdom they have. You might be surprised at the power and accuracy of it!

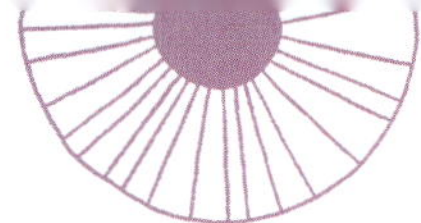

TECHNIQUES AND SUPPLIES TO TRY

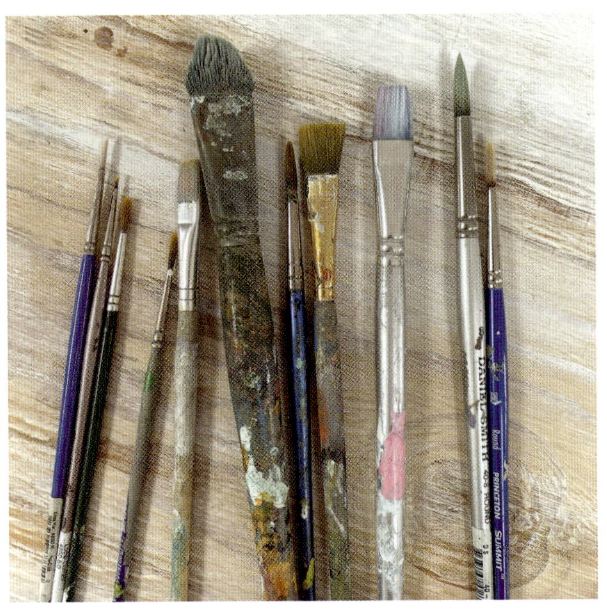

THE MATERIALS AND techniques you decide to use is a personal choice, and one is not better than another. If you're having trouble deciding what to use or where to focus, or if you're feeling at all overwhelmed or confused, the next few pages might help. It would be impossible to list all the artmaking options available to you, so I've narrowed it down to some of my favorites. Everything on the following pages will work nicely in the intuitive artmaking processes described in this book. I'll show you a lot of options for tools, materials, and supplies that you can use, but there are others not listed here that you may love (Ink! Charcoal! Chalk pastel! Encaustic!). If that's the case, please do what's best for you and use whatever your heart desires to make your own unique art. Ultimately, every single bit of this is up to you!

Paints

A lot of different types of paint exist, and some have more of a learning curve than others. In my own paintings I tend to use acrylics and acryla gouache. Later in this section I'll demonstrate my own artmaking process using these specific types of paint and my favorite brushes and tools, but these are by no means the only options. Here are a few others.

Types

- Acrylic
- Gouache
- Acryla gouache (a mix of acrylic and gouache)
- Watercolor
- Craft paint
- Tempera
- Oil
- Paint pens

When I start a painting, I tend to cover up the raw surface as quicky as I can to eliminate that "blank, scary white page staring at you" effect that can feel so intimidating. I find that once I put down a mark—any mark!—I feel like I've started, and my mind can relax. Once I've made the first mark, I try not to think too much and simply follow my intuition in filling up the entire space with color. This first layer serves simply as a starting point. You can always paint over it later (watercolor being the exception).

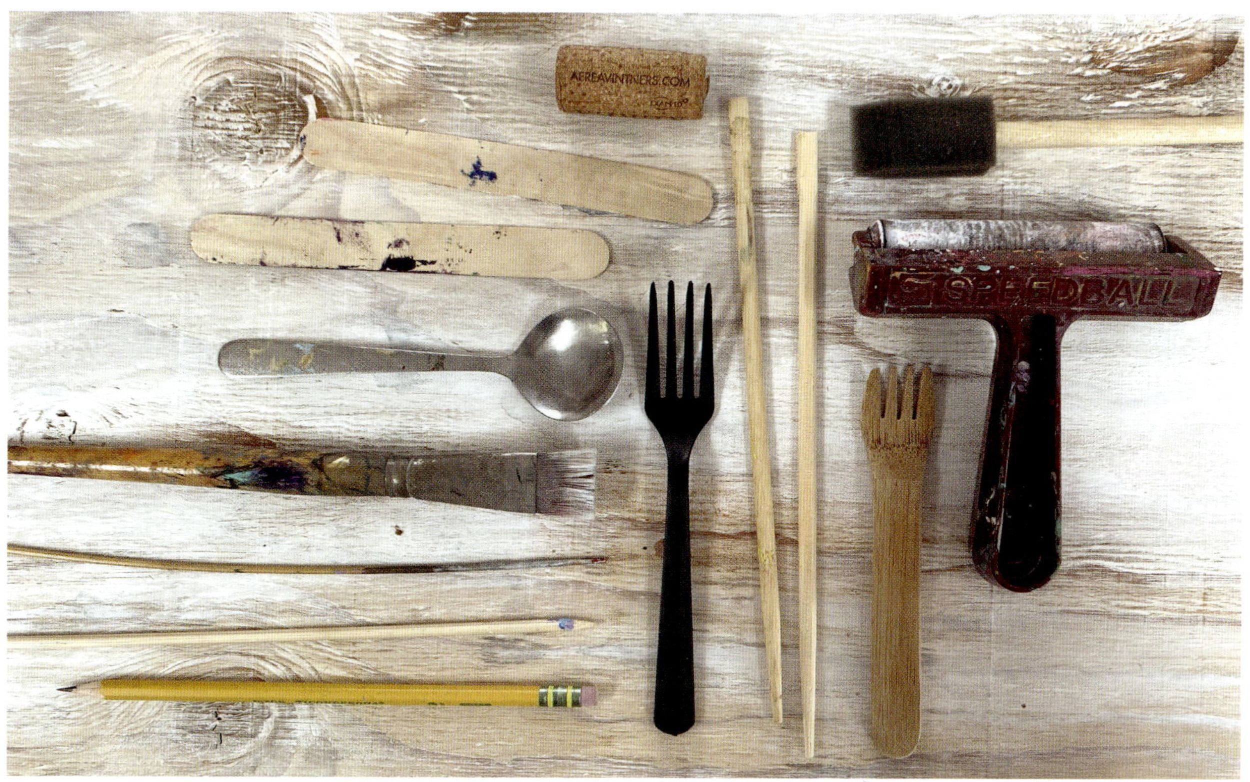

There are so many ways to cover a surface with paint beyond simply using a paintbrush and one flat color. That's a perfectly wonderful option, too, but as you're loosening up and learning to let your intuition run the show, here are some techniques and ideas for making your first marks and layers fun, interesting, playful, and not at all scary!

Techniques

- Use tools found around the house to make cool marks with paint—chopsticks, forks, corks, toothbrushes, pencil erasers, and whatever else you can find that might make interesting marks and shapes.

- Use natural elements to make interesting marks—leaves, pinecones, flowers, grasses, etc.

- Use inexpensive artmaking tools meant for kids (sponges, cheap brushes, stamps).

- Get your hands dirty! Smear the paint with your hands and fingers. What about your feet? (Why not?!)

- Make repetitive shapes like fingerprint dots to contrast flat areas of color and to fill in areas of your background.

- Use a spray bottle with water and create some cool drips in your paint.

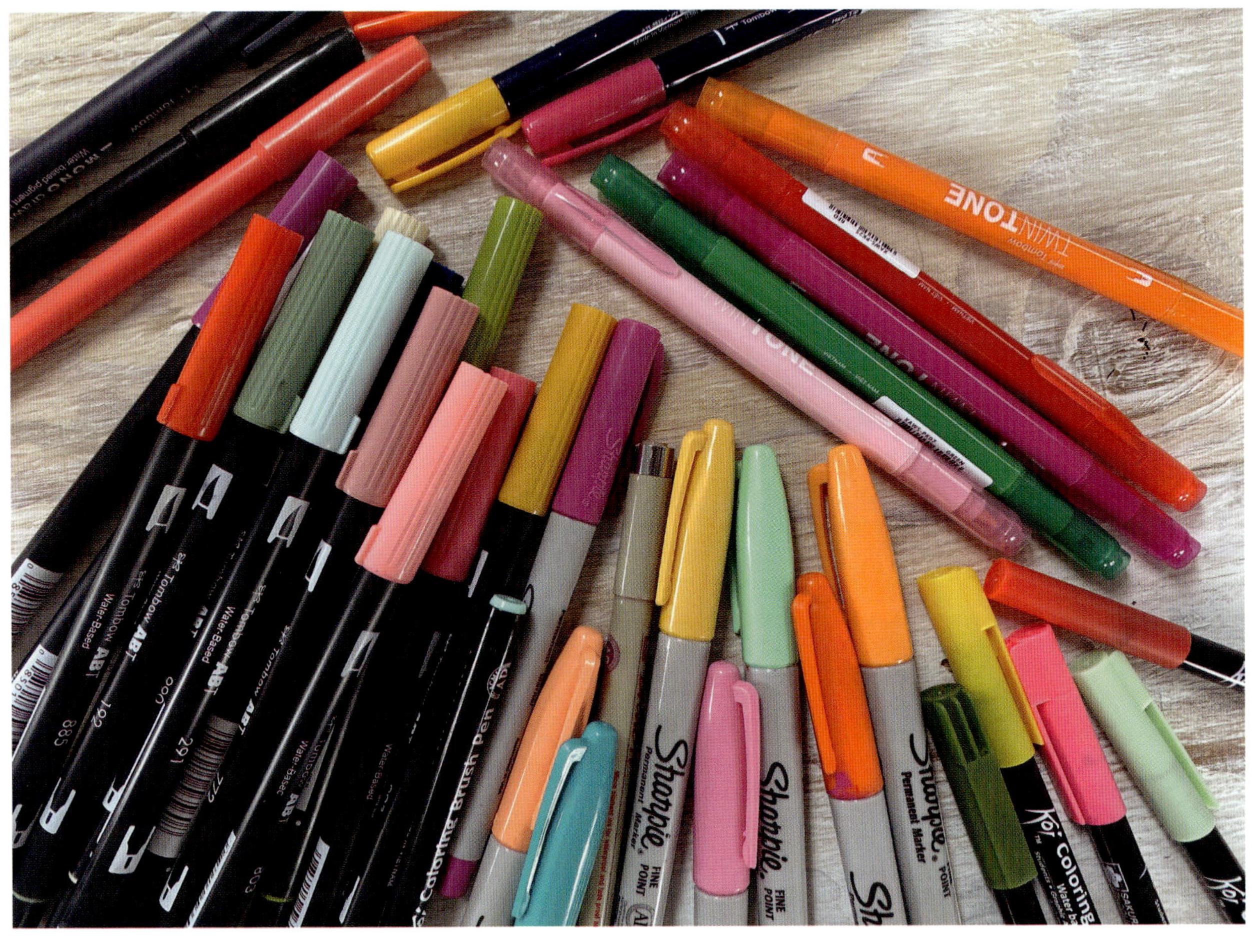

Markers and Pens

Markers are, in my opinion, a super accessible, fun, and satisfying way to make art! The barrier to entry is low—I mean, most of us probably started using markers when we were little—so they're perhaps less intimidating than other types of supplies. Markers are great for people of all ages and skill levels. Sit on the floor and color like you did when you were a kid!

Types

- Water-based brush markers
- Alcohol-based brush markers
- Inexpensive craft markers (like Crayola)
- Paint markers
- Watercolor markers
- Sharpies
- Felt-tip pens
- Gel pens
- Liquid ink pen
- Brush pen (ink)
- Inexpensive ballpoint pen

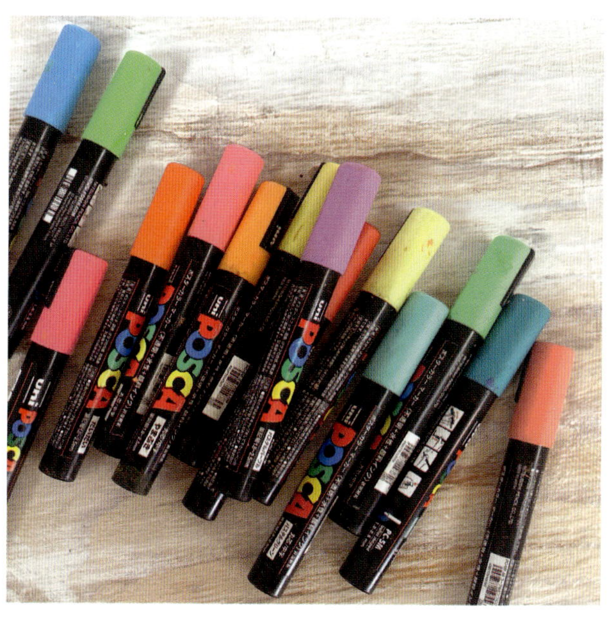

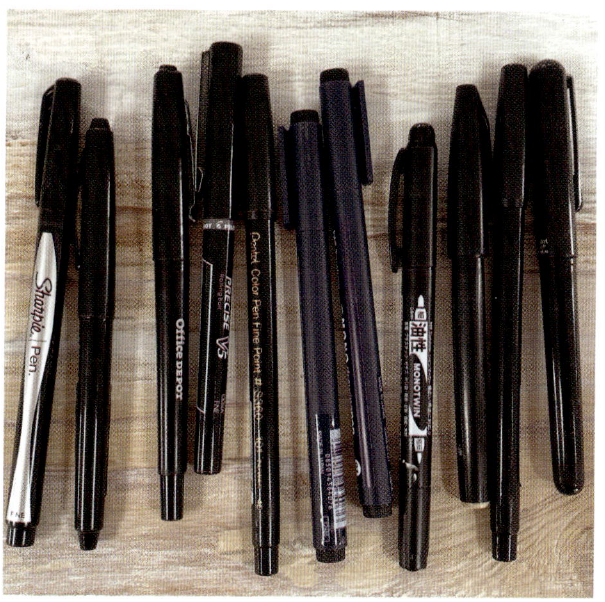

Techniques

- Use a spray bottle with water to make your colors bleed together in interesting ways.

- Use a limited color palette—choose two to four colors and use only those.

- Use a monochromatic color palette, with different shades of the same color.

- Mix different types of markers—Sharpies and watercolor markers, alcohol-based brush markers and gel pens, etc. What sort of interesting effects happen? Play around!

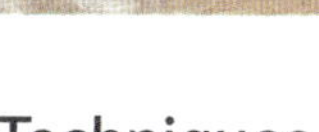

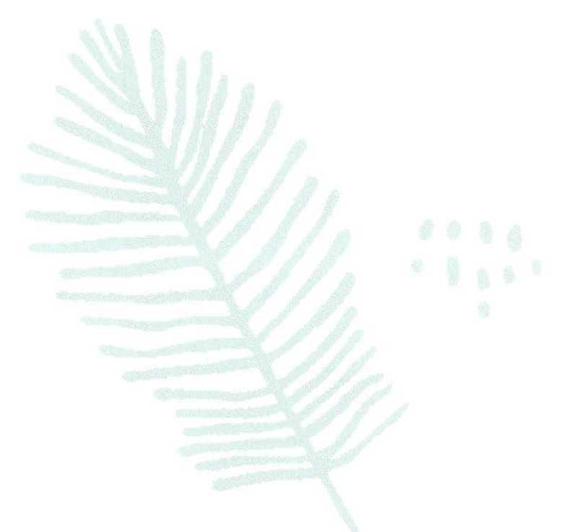

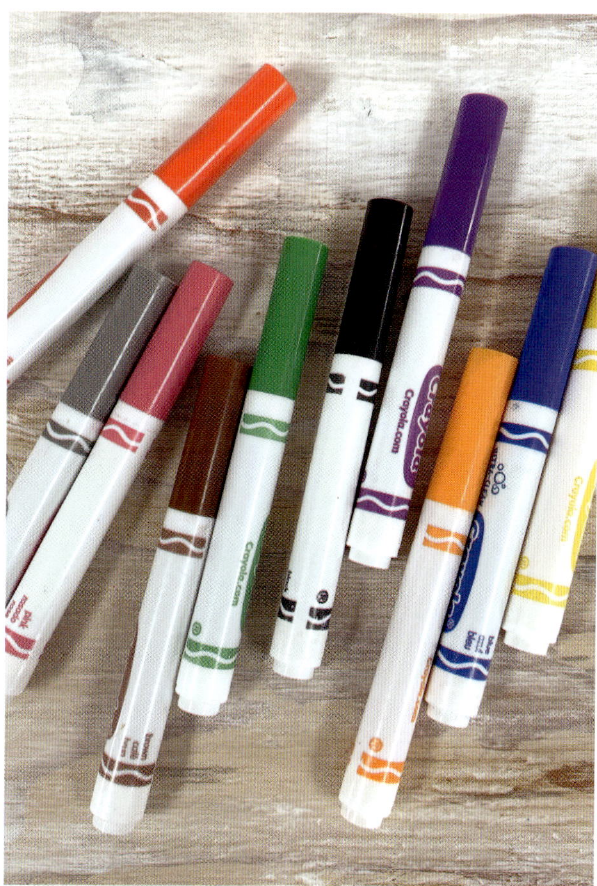

Collage

Oh, collage! I've spent many hours collaging over the years of my creative life. The best part of this technique is that it requires virtually no skill whatsoever and is appropriate for nearly all ages. Pretty much everyone can tear things out of books, magazines, and newspapers and glue them to a page! The more rudimentary and childlike you can make it, the better. Let your inner child come out to play when you're using this technique and see what messages shine through from your inner self.

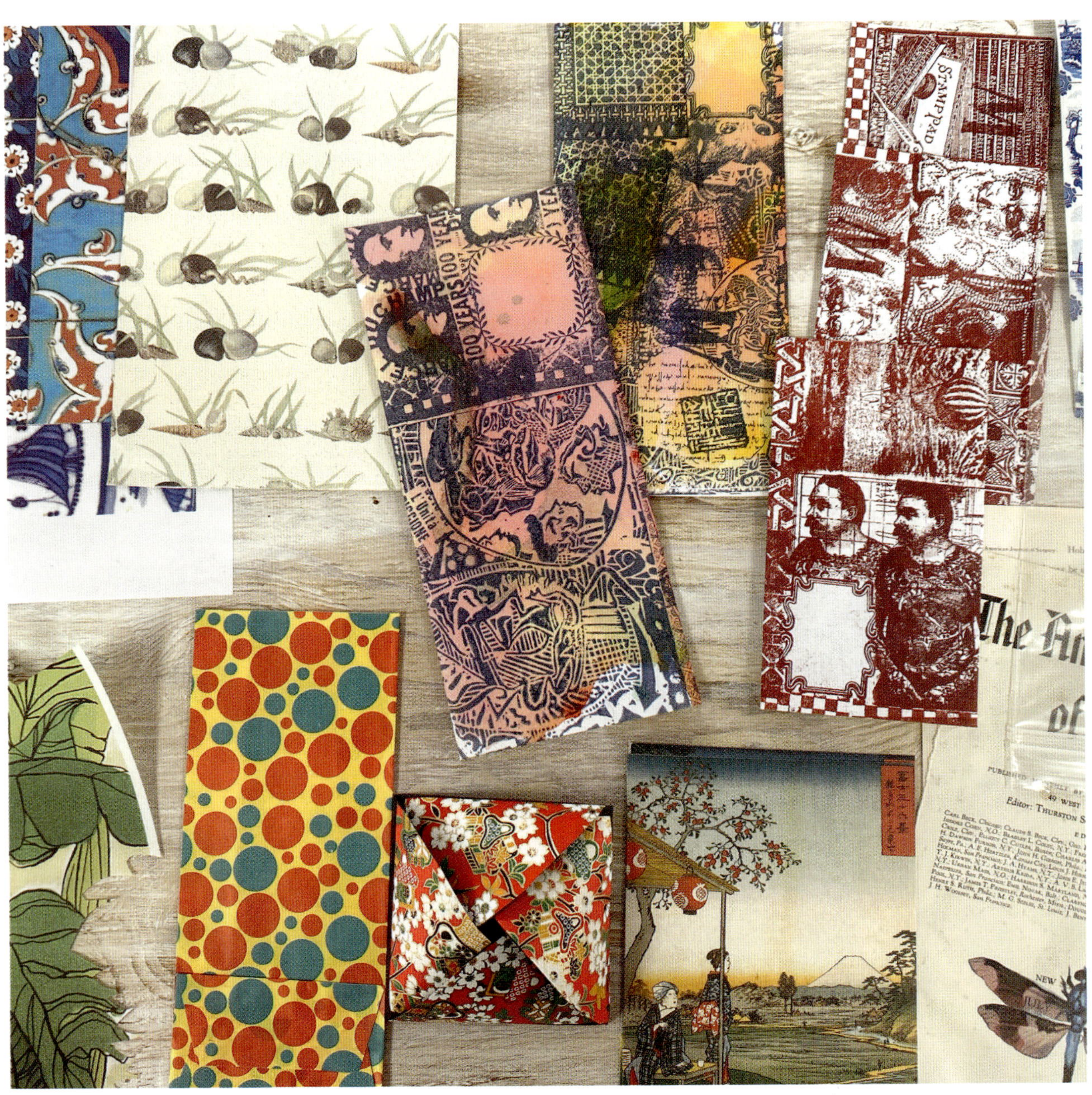

Types

- Magazines
- Newspapers
- Books
- Paint chips
- Origami paper
- Wrapping paper
- Construction paper
- Any patterned paper
- Paper ephemera
- Postcards
- Old greeting cards
- Gift bags
- Basically anything paper!

Techniques

- Without overthinking it, leaf through a stack of magazines, newspapers, colorful patterned paper, etc. Cut colors, shapes, images, and words that feel interesting, moving, or compelling in some way. Use your intuition to choose which pieces to put together and use any kind of glue to attach the pieces to your surface of choice.

- Go to the library and check out books, make photocopies of pages that interest you, and then cut up and use those black-and-white images in your collages.

- Have someone else cut things out for you and use the pile of paper they created.

- Try to combine words and an image together to create some kind of story, narrative, or meaning. Does the story have a message for you when it's finished? (Note: What you create doesn't have to make sense or be real or true!)

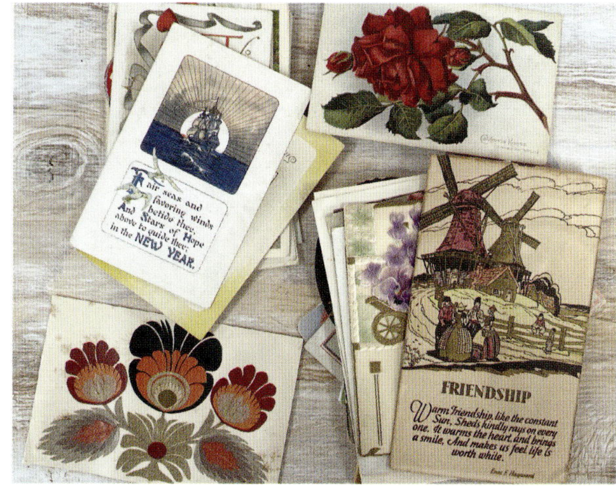

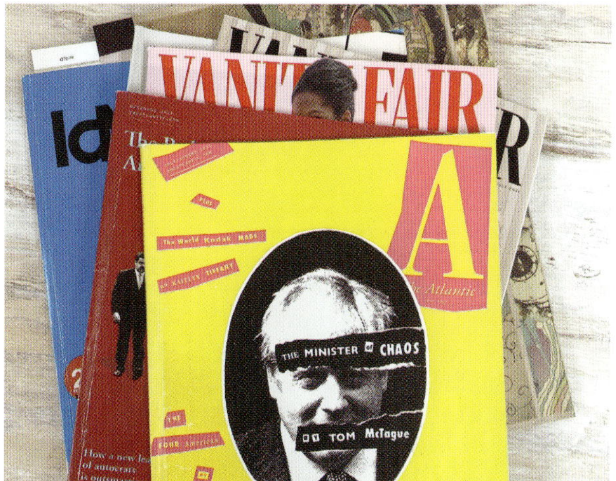

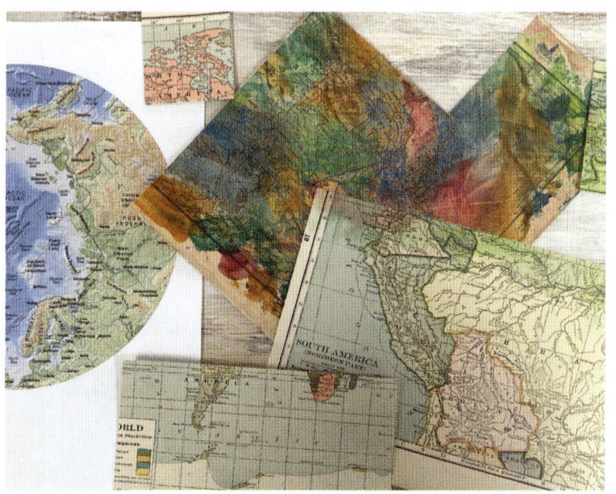

Mixed Media

Mixed media is simply art that's made using more than one type of medium. For example, a piece of art that uses paint, cut paper, and colored pencil together is considered mixed media. Many of my paintings are technically mixed media pieces because I tend to use some combination of acrylic paint, gouache, colored pencil, and paint pens within one piece. Basically, the sky's the limit for how you can combine media, and you certainly don't have to be limited to "traditional" art supplies.

Later in this section I'll demonstrate some ways that I like to combine media and techniques, layering in different textures, colors, and shapes. It's important, though, to keep in mind that my suggestions are just examples and can be used as a jumping-off point for your own creative experimentation and combining of cool materials.

Your creations don't have to be two-dimensional, either—you're not limited to a canvas or piece of paper. What about creating on a cardboard or wooden box? Or a tree stump? Or sticks and rocks? Or attaching three-dimensional objects to a two-dimensional surface? Or what about creating a diorama?

This is where you can get as wild as you want to! Art can be made out of pretty much anything.

Types
- Paint
- Markers
- Pencils
- Pens
- Cut paper
- Wood
- Boxes
- Tissue paper

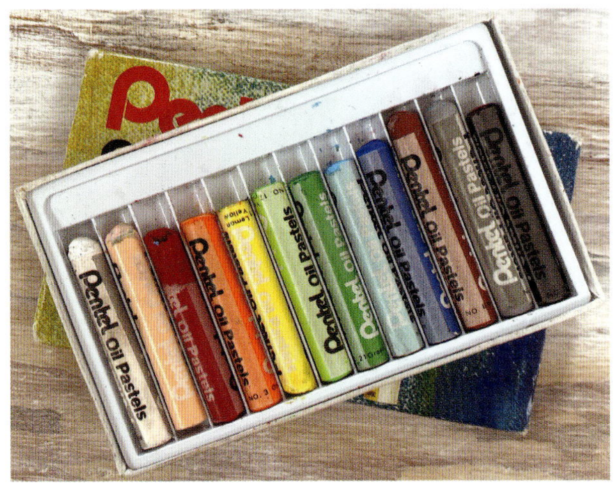

- Glitter
- Mod Podge
- Stickers
- Stamps
- Tape
- Beads
- Feathers
- Ribbon
- Yarn, string, embroidery thread, sewing thread
- Gel medium
- Sequins, faux jewels
- Resin
- Oil pastels
- Chalk pastels
- Spray paint
- Fabric
- Stencils
- Coffee filters
- Found objects
- Natural objects
- Pretty much anything else you want to use. Get creative!

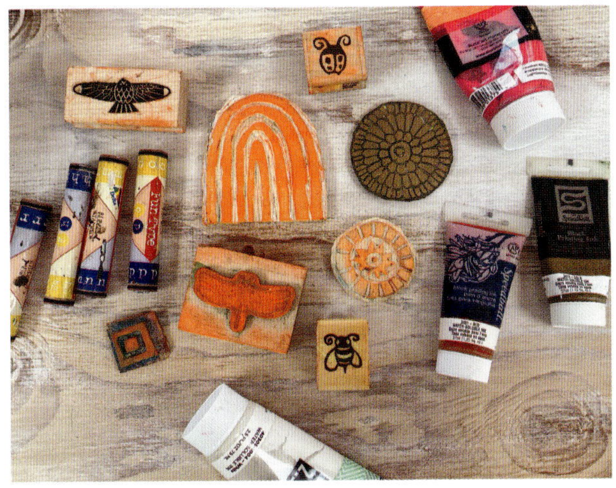

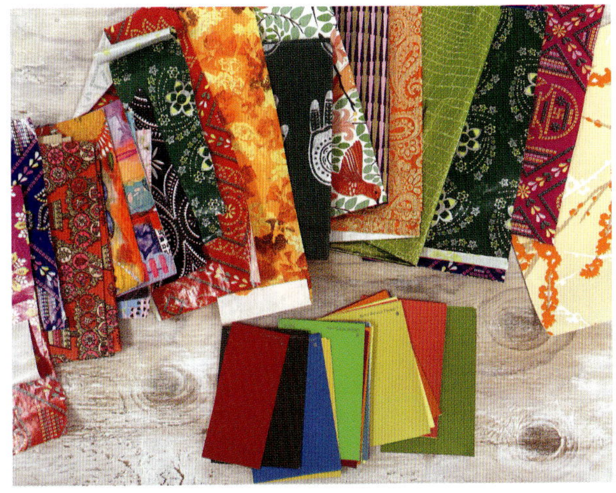

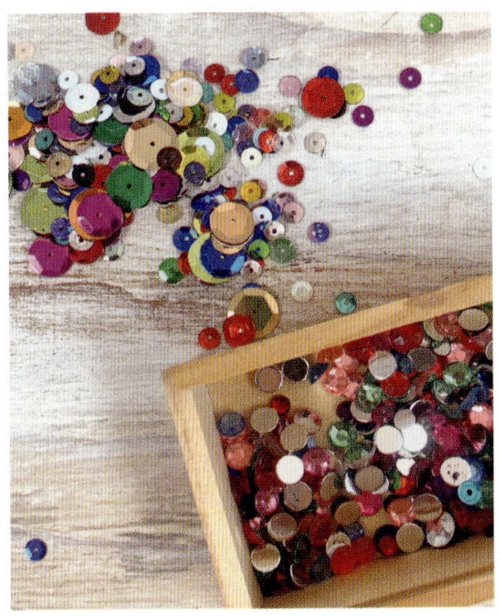

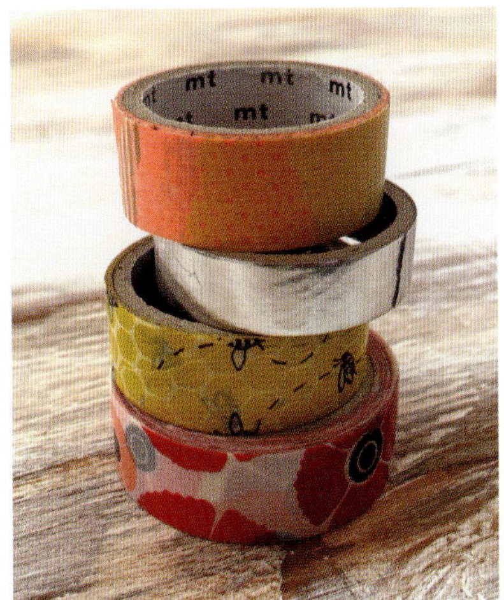

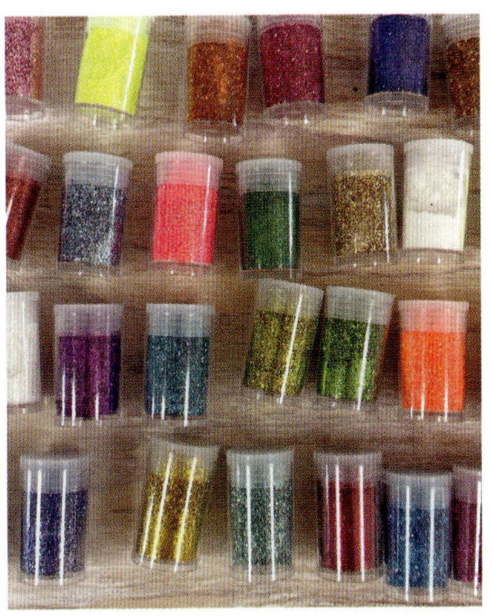

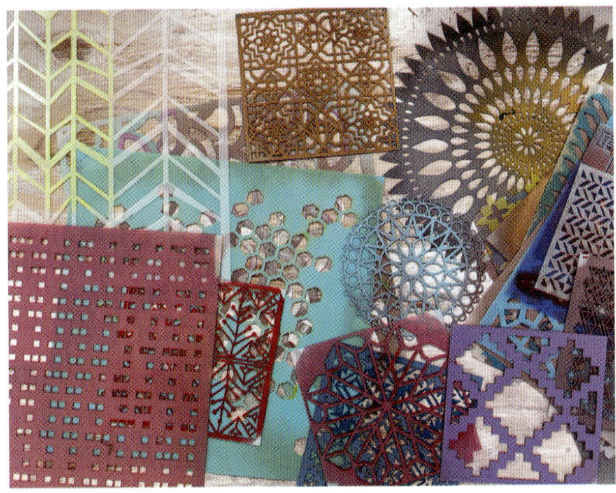

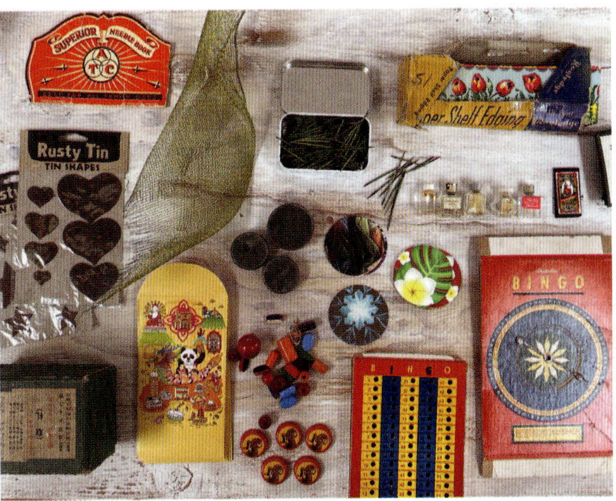

Pencil and Colored Pencil

For Christmas one year when I was a child, I received a giant box of Prismacolor colored pencils from my Grandma Nancy, who was an artist. I have a visceral memory of the moment I opened that gift and the joy and excitement I felt when I saw that glorious box! Those pencils were some of my most prized possessions, and I've loved Prismacolor pencils ever since. I still use them regularly in my work, usually in combination with paint, but sometimes on their own as well. Colored pencils are like markers in that there's not much of a learning curve to using them, and they're great for people of any age.

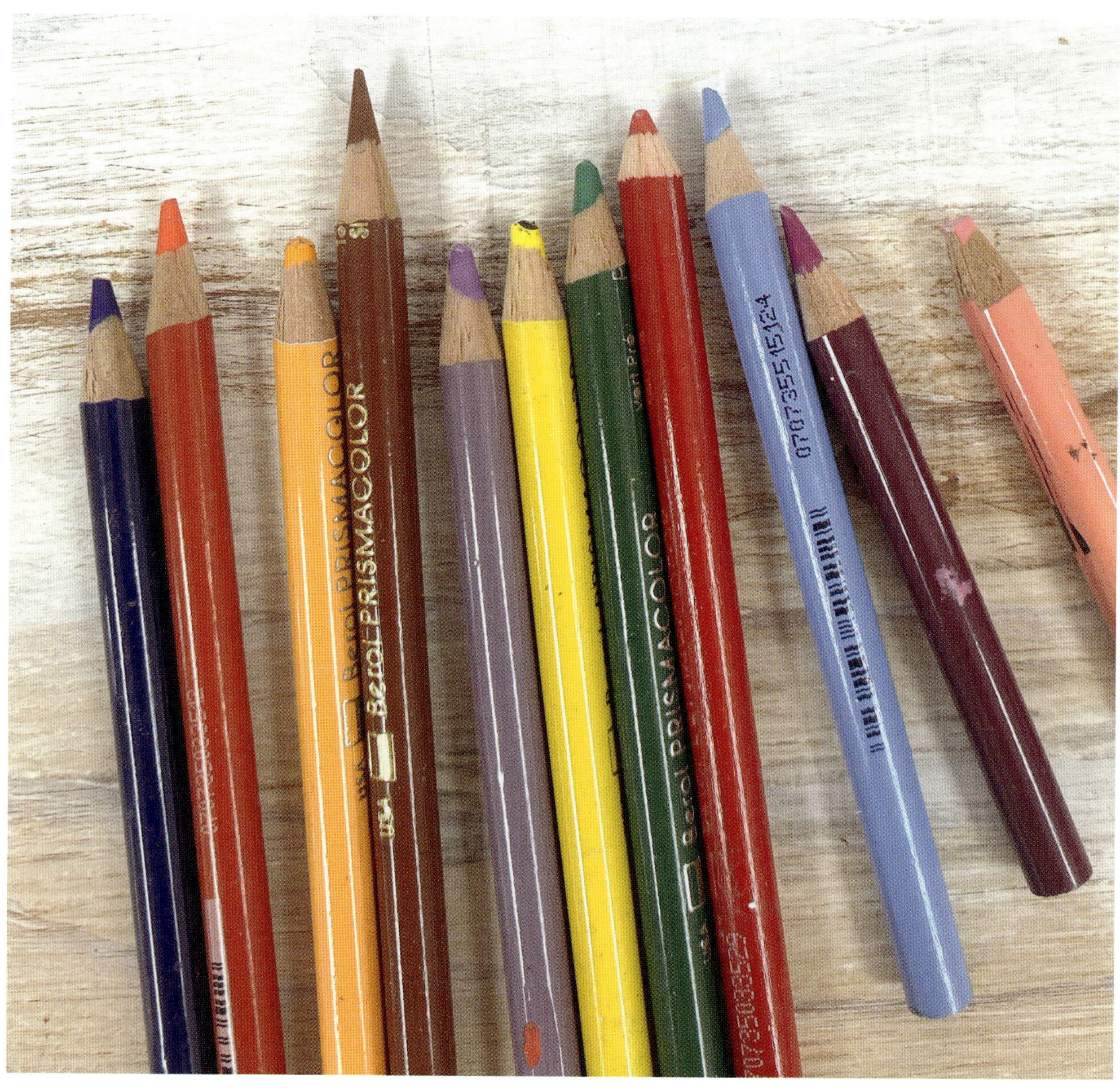

Types

- Wax-based colored pencils (like Prismacolor, Tombow, or Crayola)
- Water-soluble colored pencils
- Graphite pencils

Techniques

- Use a paintbrush wet with water to paint over drawings made with water-soluble colored pencils. The water will make your pencil drawings look like watercolor paintings!
- Use a spray bottle to wet drawings made with water-soluble pencils.
- Use colored pencils and stencils together.
- Use colored pencils on top of painted surfaces.
- Use white and/or light-colored colored pencil on a dark background.
- Vary your pencil pressure to create different lighter and darker, more saturated versions of the color you're using.
- Using a light hand, layer colors to create dimension, depth, and variety.
- Create texture and dimension with cross-hatching—drawing a layer of lines in one direction and then going over that same area with lines in the opposite direction.
- Use a small amount of baby oil or rubbing alcohol on a cotton ball or cotton swab to blend colors together.
- Use just one color (or a graphite pencil) to create a drawing with different shades and textures.

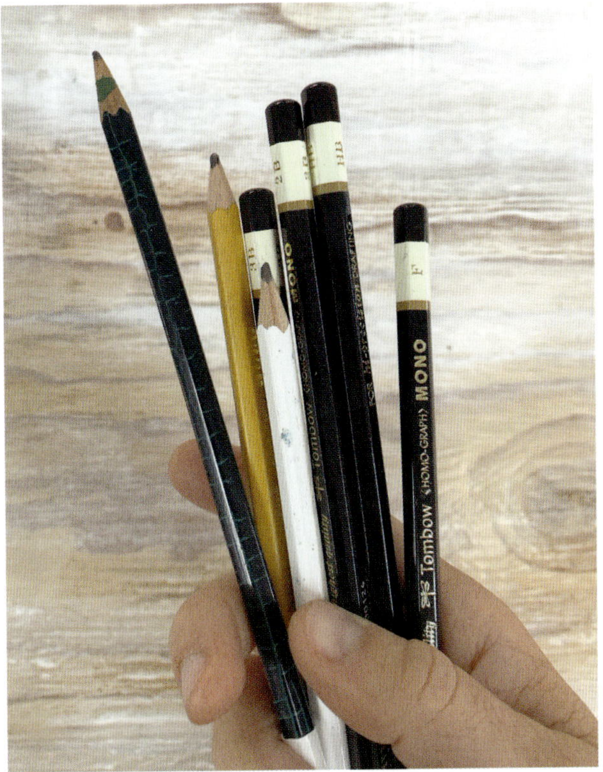

The sky's the limit for how you can combine media, and you certainly don't have to be limited to "traditional" art supplies.

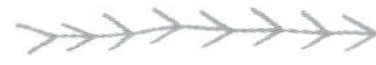

Procreate
Select   Import   Photo   +

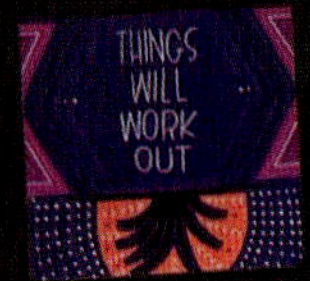
THINGS WILL WORK OUT

YOU KNOW WHAT TO DO

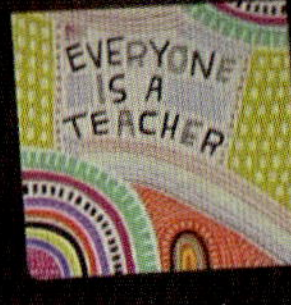
EVERYONE IS A TEACHER

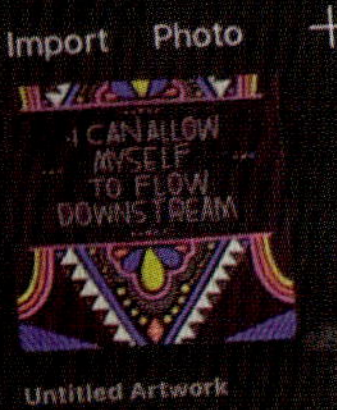
I CAN ALLOW MYSELF TO FLOW DOWNSTREAM

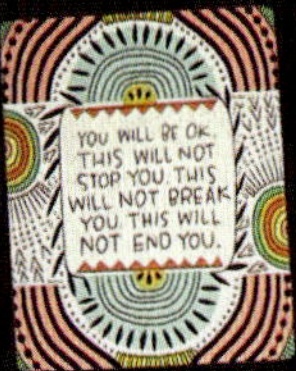
YOU WILL BE OK. THIS WILL NOT STOP YOU. THIS WILL NOT BREAK YOU. THIS WILL NOT END YOU.

YOU WILL SURVIVE THE WILD UNKNOWN

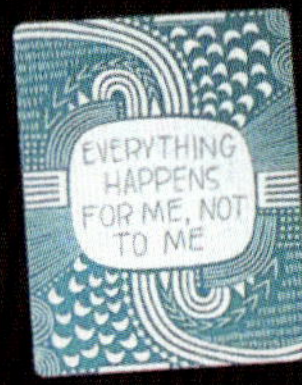
EVERYTHING HAPPENS FOR ME, NOT TO ME

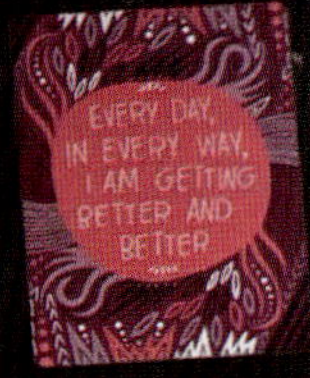
EVERY DAY, IN EVERY WAY, I AM GETTING BETTER AND BETTER

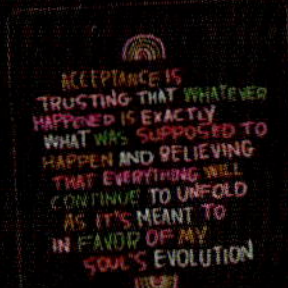
ACCEPTANCE IS TRUSTING THAT WHATEVER HAPPENED IS EXACTLY WHAT WAS SUPPOSED TO HAPPEN AND BELIEVING THAT EVERYTHING WILL CONTINUE TO UNFOLD AS IT'S MEANT TO IN FAVOR OF MY SOUL'S EVOLUTION

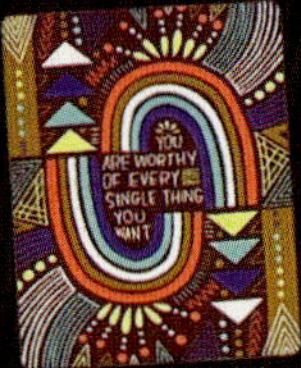
YOU ARE WORTHY OF EVERY SINGLE THING YOU WANT

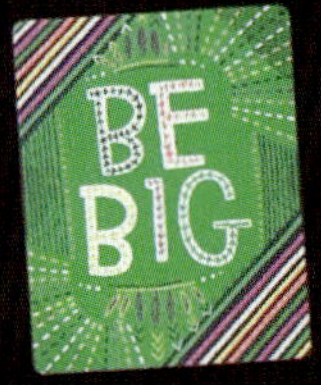
BE BIG

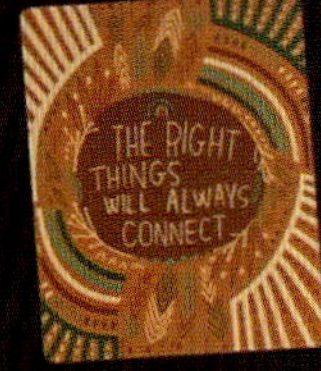
THE RIGHT THINGS WILL ALWAYS CONNECT

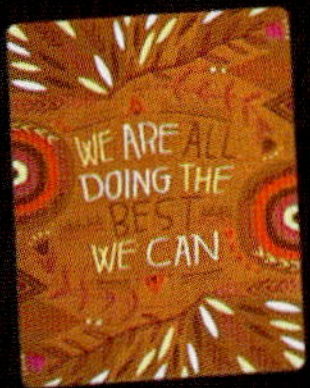
WE ARE ALL DOING THE BEST WE CAN

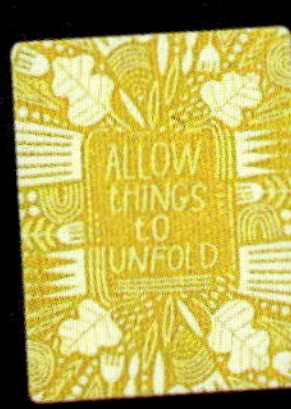
ALLOW THINGS TO UNFOLD

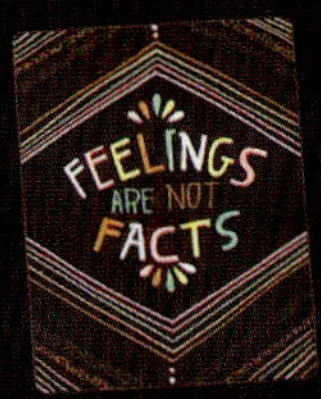
FEELINGS ARE NOT FACTS

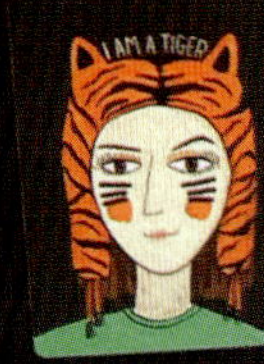
I AM A TIGER

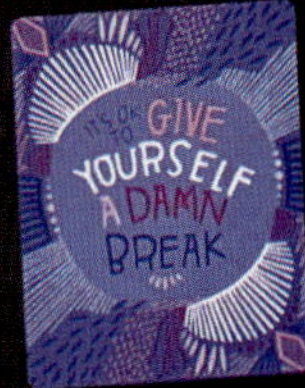
GIVE YOURSELF A DAMN BREAK

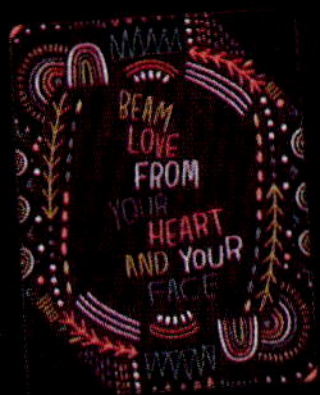
BEAM LOVE FROM YOUR HEART AND YOUR FACE

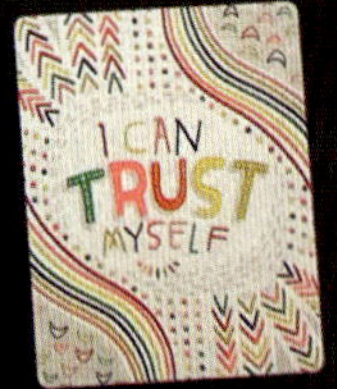
I CAN TRUST MYSELF

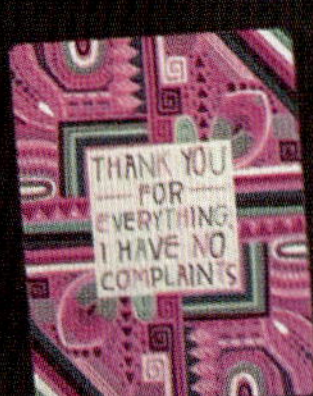
THANK YOU FOR EVERYTHING I HAVE NO COMPLAINTS

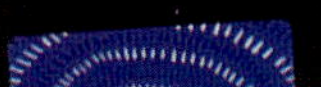

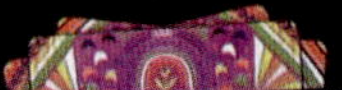

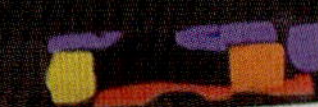

Working Digitally

Creating art digitally is one of my favorite techniques. My love for digital art began in 2006 when I began teaching myself to use Adobe Photoshop and Adobe Illustrator. When I started using an iPad Pro as part of my digital artmaking process several years back, my love deepened even more. The iPad Pro is one of the most useful and versatile digital tools available today; it's portable, powerful, and easy to use once you get the hang of it. That said, do be aware that if you've never tried making digital art before, it can take some time to learn how to use these programs. Many classes are available on platforms like Skillshare and YouTube.

Much of the artwork in this book was created while sitting on the couch or at my studio table, using the Procreate app on my iPad Pro, drawing with my Apple Pencil. Following are some digital artmaking tools and options you might like to try.

Types

- iPad Pro with Apple Pencil
  - Procreate (this is my favorite program to use!)
  - Adobe Fresco
- Adobe Photoshop
- Adobe Illustrator
- Wacom drawing tablet
- Wacom Cintiq

Techniques

- iPad Pro
  - Draw directly into a drawing app like Procreate, experimenting with different brushes to create different effects that you like.
  - Create a photo or painted background non-digitally, bring it into your app of choice, and use that as a background for your digital art creation.

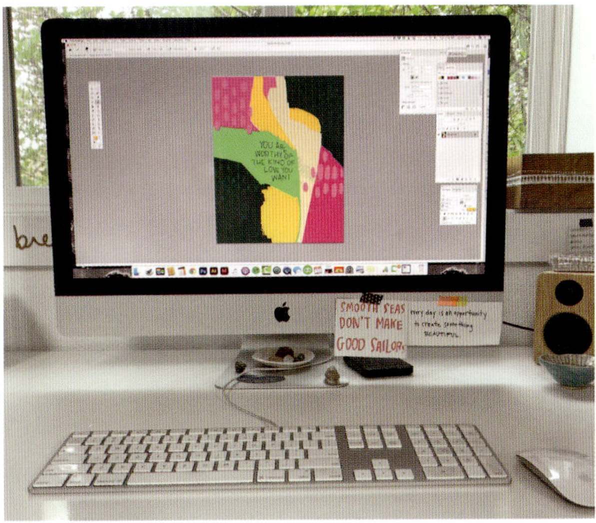

  - Create digital collages by combining photos, textures, words, and drawings.
  - Hand-letter words on top of or within your artwork.
- Photoshop and Illustrator
  - Use a Wacom tablet and a pen to draw directly in the program on your computer screen.
  - Scan photos, textures, drawings, and words into Photoshop to create digital collages.
  - Edit artwork you created non-digitally—erase, blend, change colors, brighten, etc.
  - Use computer fonts over the top of your artwork to create images with art and words.

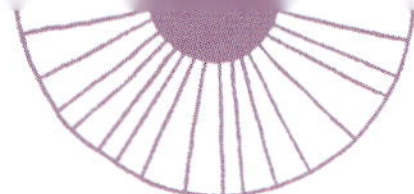

SURFACES TO CONSIDER

WHEN IT COMES to artmaking surfaces, you have so many choices! I mentioned some surfaces in the last section, and this isn't an exhaustive list by any means, but here are some good options and suggestions to think about using. Most of these surfaces are readily available at art supply stores, and you may already have some of them lying around the house. You could even find some of them while out walking through your neighborhood!

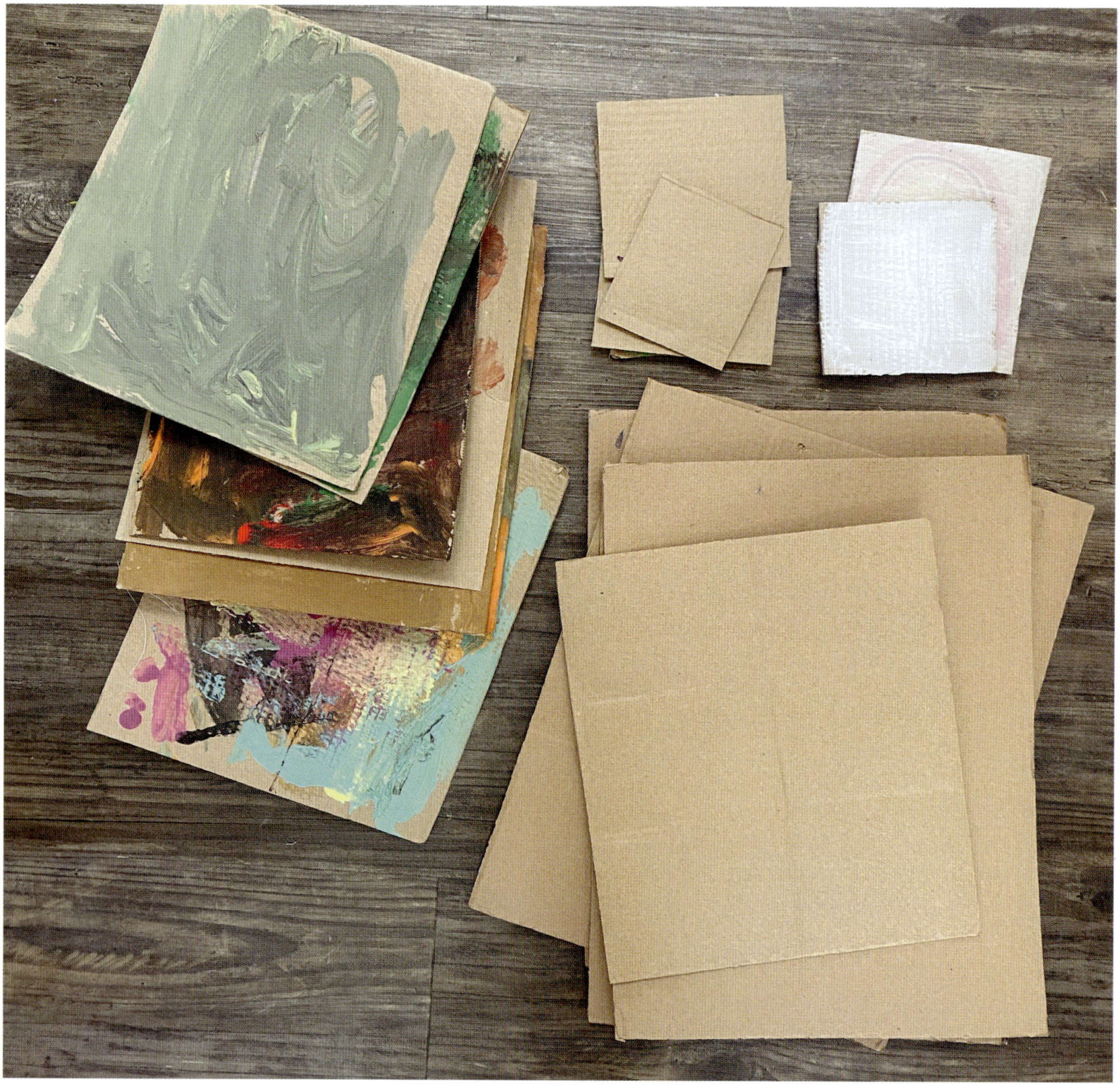

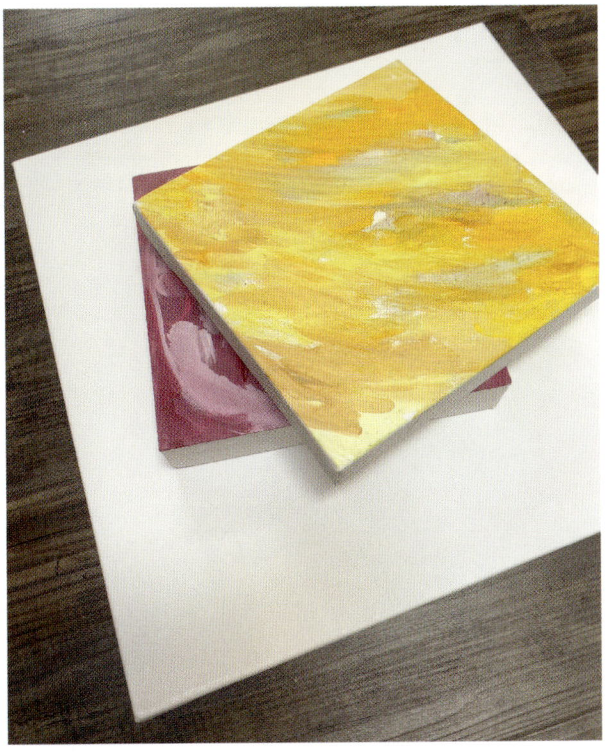

More than any other surface, I've always loved to paint on wood. I've always wanted to be an artist who enjoys painting on paper—and maybe one day I still will!—but wood is the surface that comes the most naturally to me, for whatever reason. I paint on canvas from time to time, but I always come back to wood.

You'll find surfaces that you like more than others, too. Some will feel more "right" than others. Go with it! Try out new things and don't be afraid to say "that's not for me," even if it feels like you "should" be able to make it work. We're all unique and our bodies and minds respond to different stimuli in different ways. You may love the feeling of a paintbrush on paper or a colored pencil on wood, while it may always feel awkward and not quite right to put a pencil tip to paper or a paintbrush to a canvas. Try out a lot of things and stick with what feels the best. That's where you'll make your best, most healing artwork for yourself.

- Sketchbook
- Loose-leaf paper
- Cradled wood panels
- Flat wood panels
- Raw wood
- Canvas
- Cardboard
- Moleskine notebooks
- Watercolor paper
- Poster board
- Cardstock
- Found objects (leaves, sticks, bark rounds, rocks)
- A wall

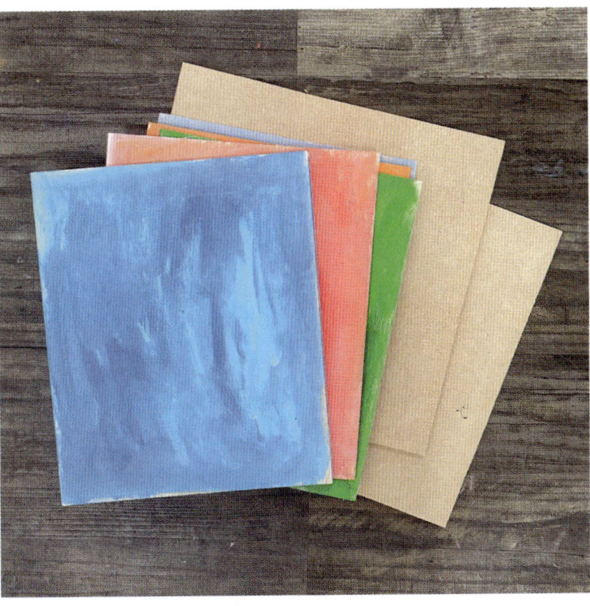

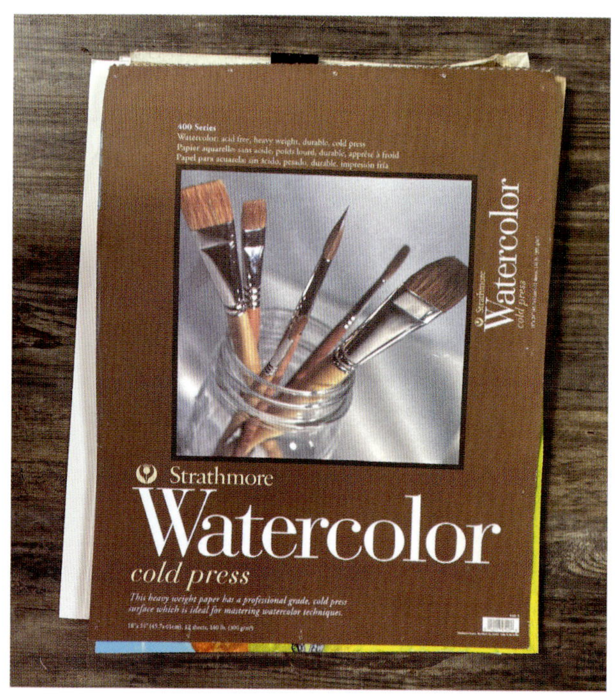

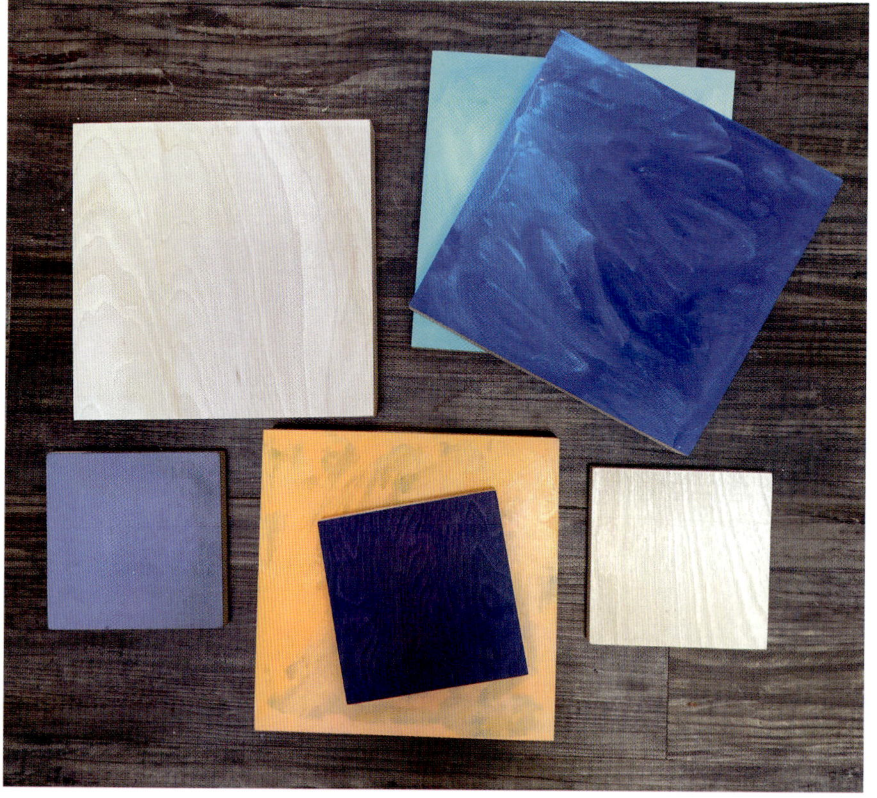

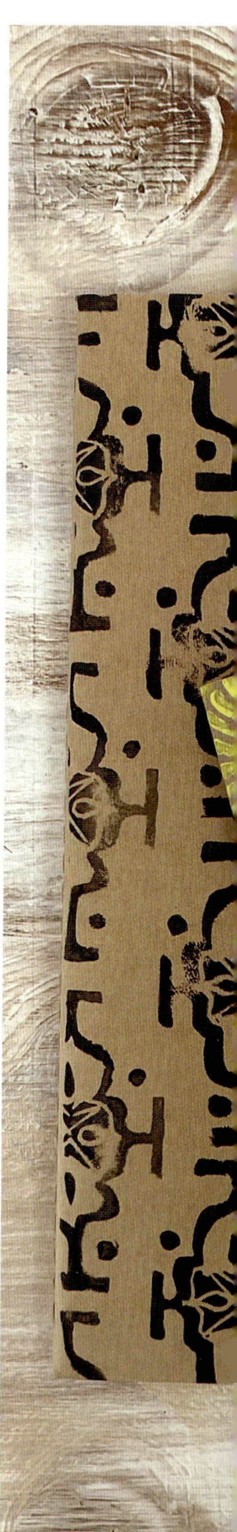

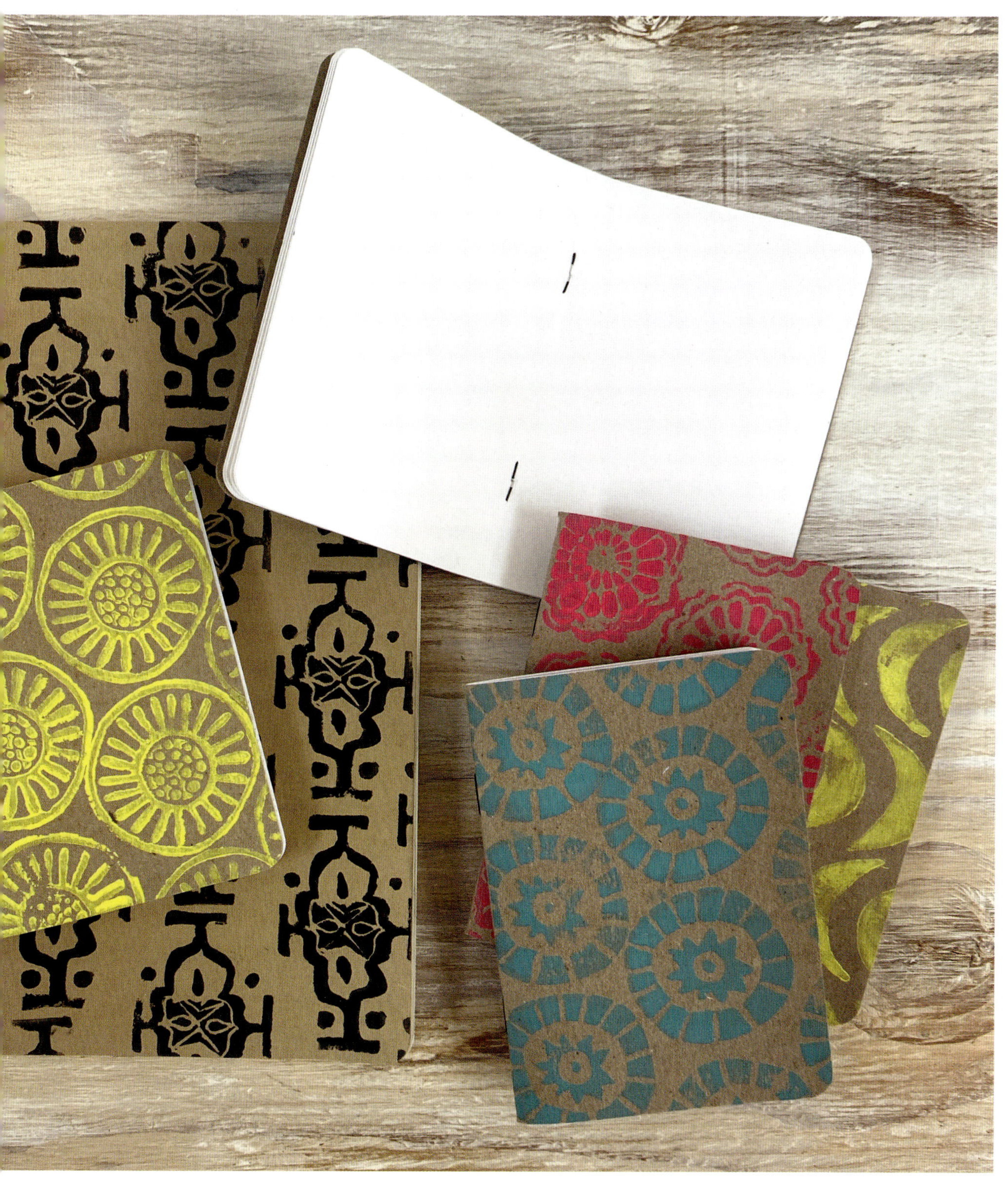

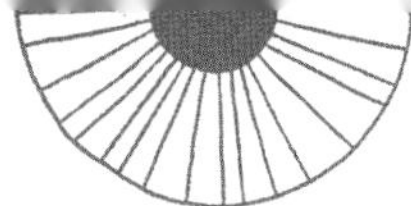

THE PROCESS

IN THIS SECTION, I'll explain the process I use for various media and how I let my inner voice emerge during an artmaking session.

Paints

Options abound when it comes to paint! I use acrylics and acryla gouache, but you might choose to use watercolors, oils, regular gouache (which is slightly different than acryla gouache), encaustic, house paint . . . see? Lots of options!

Painting your intuition-based messages is a bit more of a time-intensive process than, say, using markers or colored pencils. You might have a message in mind already when you start a painting, or you might use the actual act of painting as a way to tune in and listen for a message. For me, painting feels the most satisfying and fulfilling when a message reveals itself as I go along. I like to start without a plan and let the painting and message emerge in their own time. I start by covering my surface with color as a first layer and follow my intuition every step of the way. It tells me what color to use, what shape wants to be painted, what kind of marks to make. Somewhere along the way, a word or a phrase will emerge; it's always something I need to hear for myself in that moment. Some days it's something a bit more generic (like "Say Yes"); other times, it's more specific (for example, "You Are a Wild Thicket"). I trust whatever emerges and incorporate it into my painting in whatever way feels appropriate.

Here, I'll walk you through my typical process for creating a painting using a cradled wood panel, acrylic paint, acryla gouache paint, colored pencils, and Posca paint pens. Use these steps as a starting point, but remember that creating your own unique artmaking processes is what will ultimately fill you up the most and teach you about yourself and your inner world.

Step 1: Cover your surface with paint. I like to use several colors of paint to create a splotchy background, but you could just as easily paint a flat layer of one color. It's up to you!

Step 2: Step back and look at your surface, waiting for an image, shape, color, or word to appear. Trust your inner eye and don't second-guess yourself. Use a pencil to draw your shape(s) on the surface if you'd like, or simply dive in with your paint and go for it! Do this process as many times as you'd like, spiraling in and spiraling out, stepping back to look at the painting and listening to your intuition, and then zooming back in to work on the piece.

Step 3: Add your word(s) whenever they come to you. Intuitively choose where your words will go, how big they'll be, etc. Your inner voice might also tell you that your painting isn't supposed to have words but instead the message will be communicated solely through images—that's great, too! Trust it.

Step 4: Fill in areas with decorative elements like dots, dashes, fingerprints, lines, or anything else you wish. Remember not to be precious with your work! Imperfections are beautiful and make a painting unique.

Step 5: Listen for an internal "Stop! This painting is complete." Do your best not to go past this point to make things more perfect!

Step 6: Spend some time writing about your message to deepen the process for yourself and to integrate your message fully.

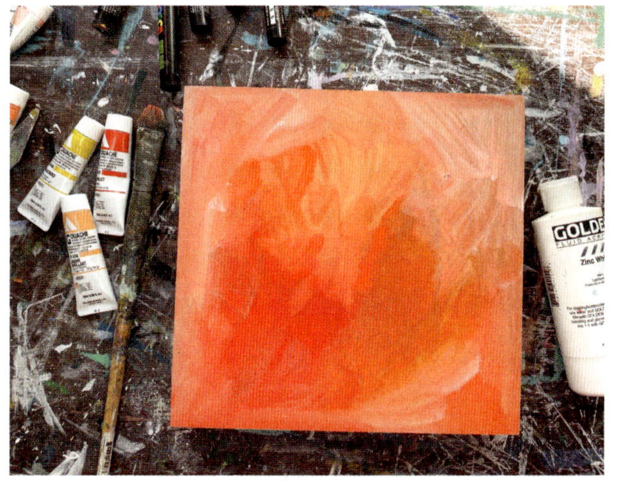
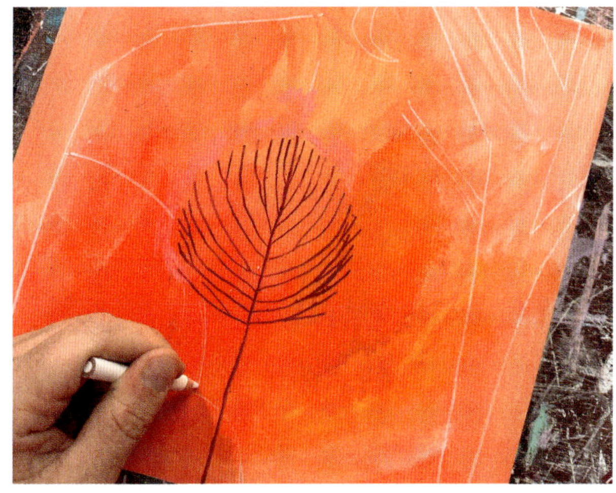
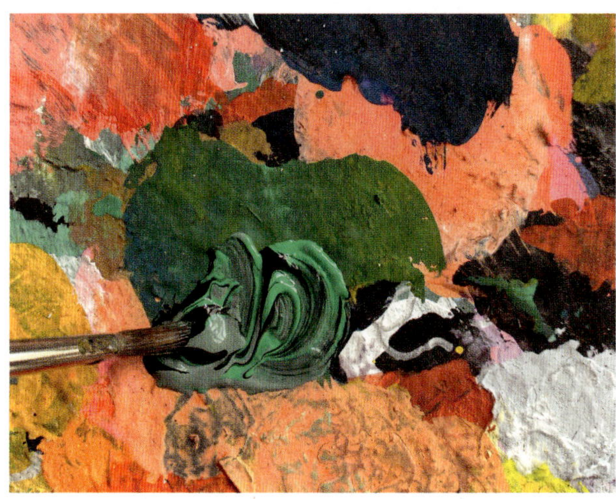
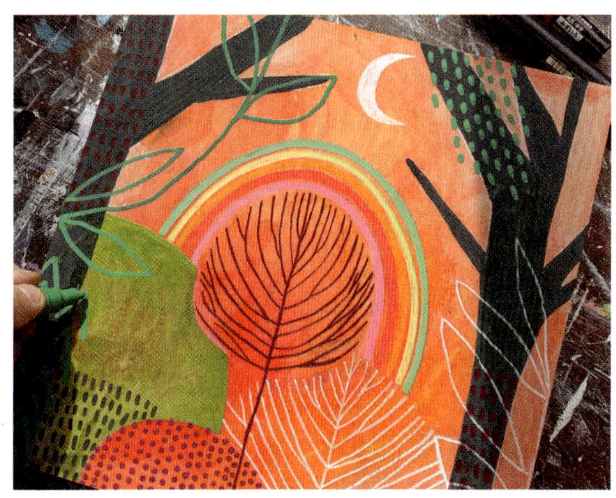
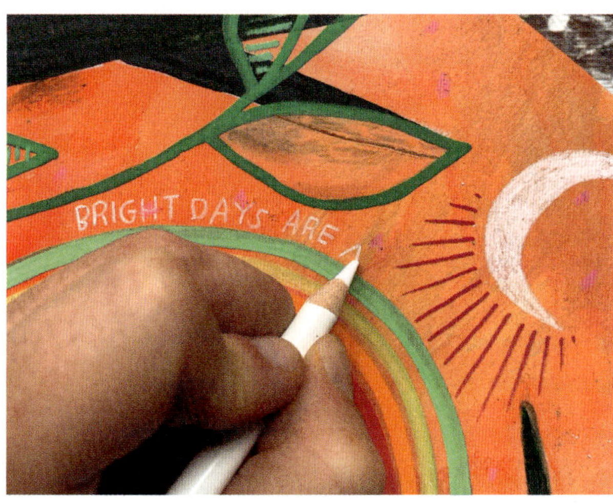
BRIGHT DAYS ARE
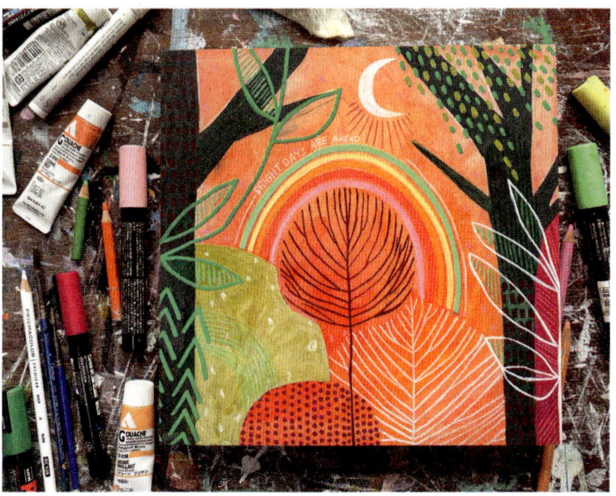

Here are some of my finished paintings that I created using the techniques outlined in this book. You'll see that some are more word-heavy, some are more focused on the images and the words are much smaller, and some actually have no words at all (but are infused with a personal message nonetheless)!

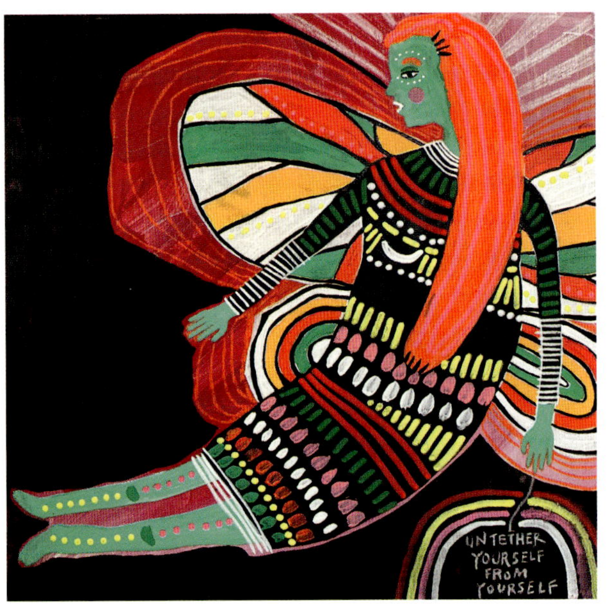

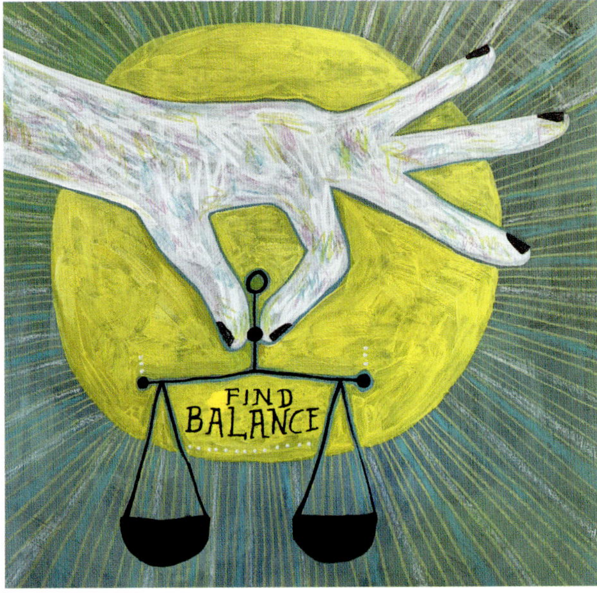

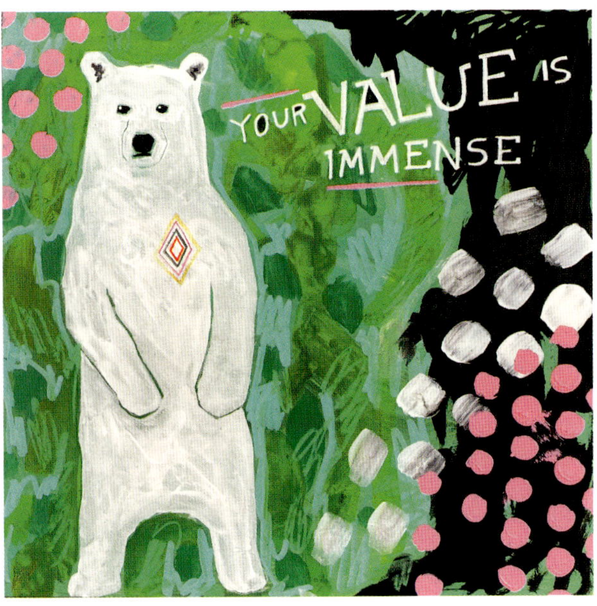

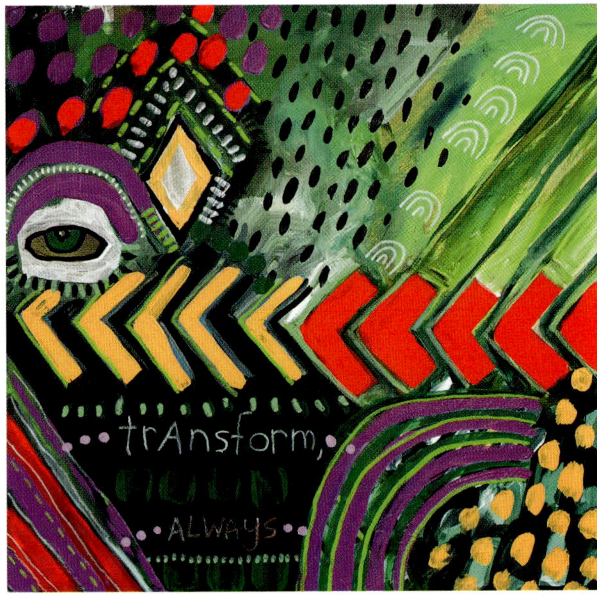

For me, painting feels the most satisfying and fulfilling when a message reveals itself as I go along. I like to start without a plan and let the painting and message emerge in their own time.

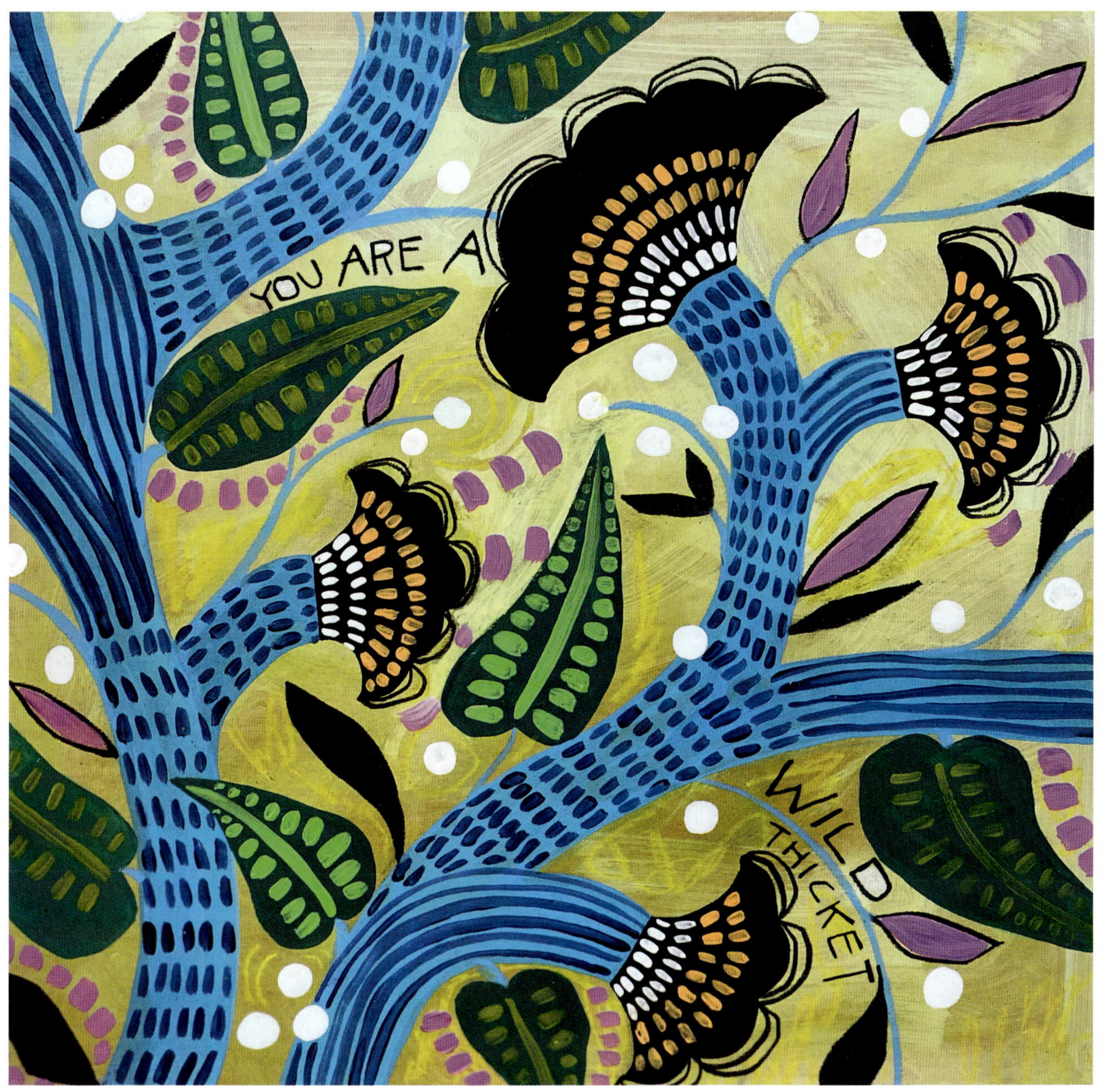

YOU ARE A
WILD THICKET

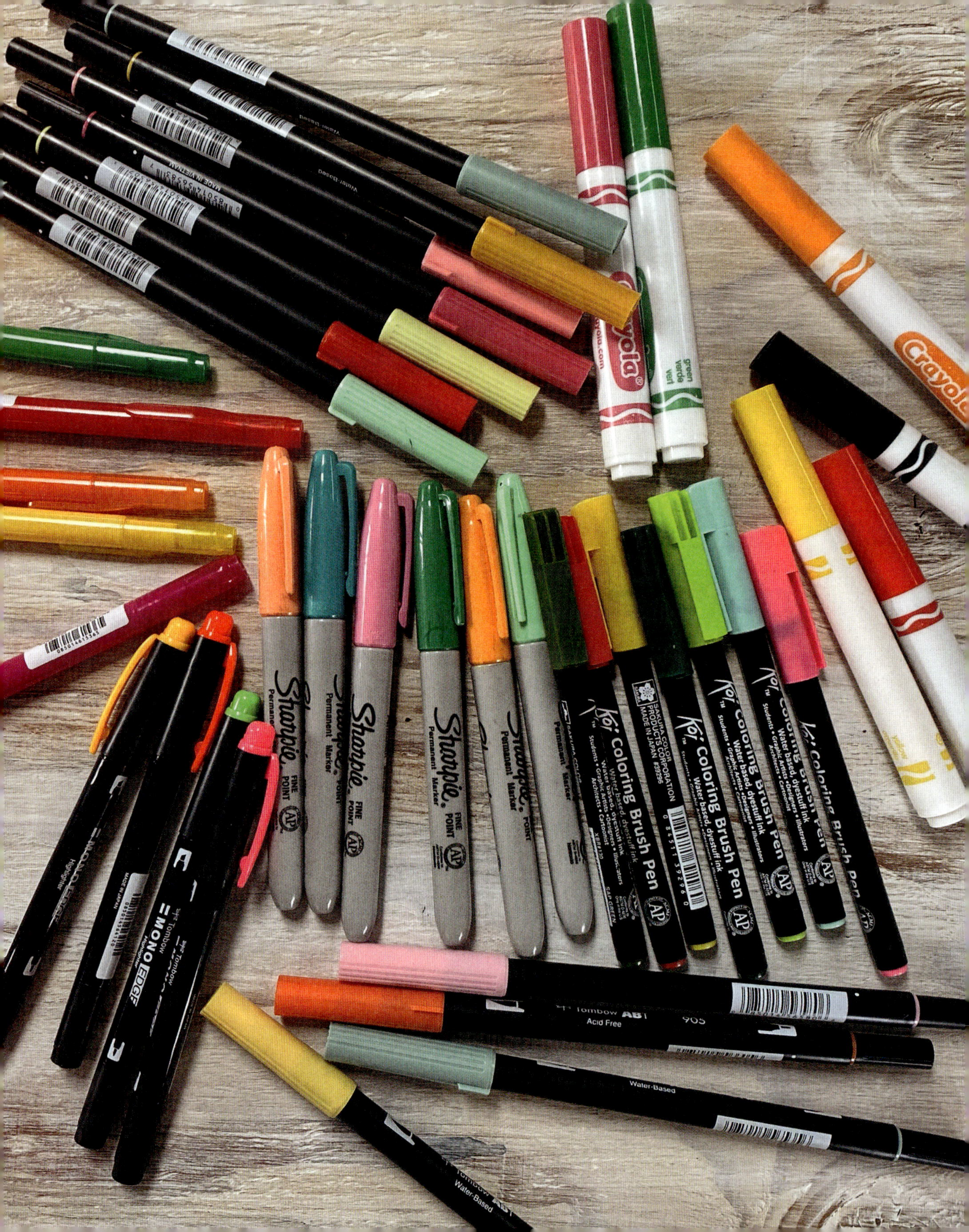

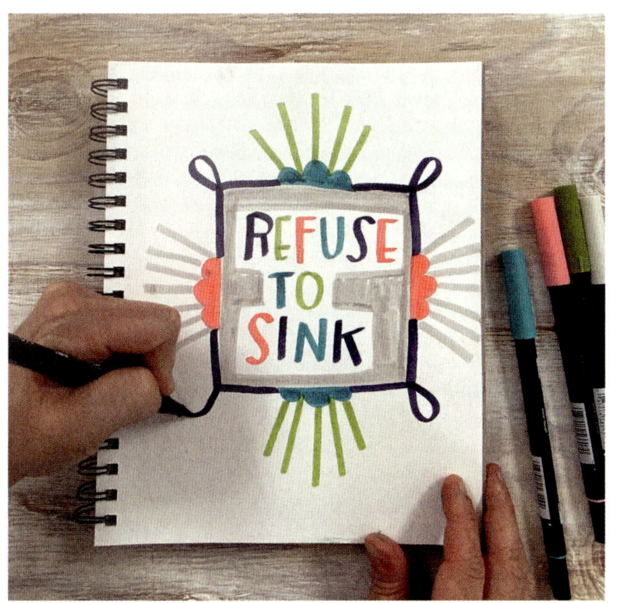

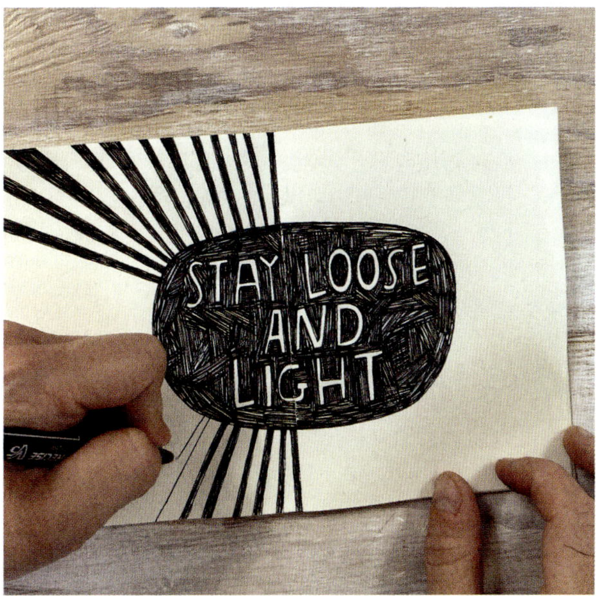

Markers and Pens

Any type of markers, pens, and paper will work for this technique. Your supplies can be as fancy or as inexpensive as you'd like! My favorites to use are Tombow Dual Brush Pens and a Canson Mixed Media Sketchbook with nice, thick paper that doesn't bleed through. There are lots of other options, too—Crayolas, Sharpies, Gelly Roll pens, highlighters, felt-tip markers, or whatever other variety of markers or pens you have around. You can choose to use a lot of colors, or maybe just a few colors (a limited palette often creates lovely, striking drawings and can be a nice parameter to work within), or even just a simple black marker. For paper you could try inexpensive loose-leaf computer paper, a spiral-bound sketchbook, Moleskine, cardboard, cardstock, watercolor paper . . . You get the idea. Anything goes! There are no limits here. Which supplies are you intuitively most drawn to? Start there!

Step 1: I usually start with hand-lettering the words of my message when I'm using markers, and then decorating and filling in the page from there. Sometimes I begin with a shape—an animal, a flower, a motif—and move on from there, adding the message somewhere along the way. Sometimes the words are the main focus of the drawing, sometimes they're just a small piece.

Step 2: Get familiar with hearing the messages your inner voice is sharing with you. It will also guide you in other ways. It'll tell you which color to choose next. Which shape to draw. Where the words should go. What symbols to incorporate. What the next right step is. When your drawing is finished.

Step 3: When you feel stuck, you can simply get quiet and wait for guidance about what to do next. It's always there!

Here are a few examples of my finished marker drawings, all created using Tombow Dual Brush Pens in my Canson sketchbook. I tend to work quickly when using markers so I don't get stuck in my head and start overthinking or overworking anything. My goal is to simply keep my hand moving; keep my mind open; and fill the page with color, words, or some combination of the two. It's always a surprise to see the finished drawing, as it's usually not what I expected but is deeply satisfying for my inner self!

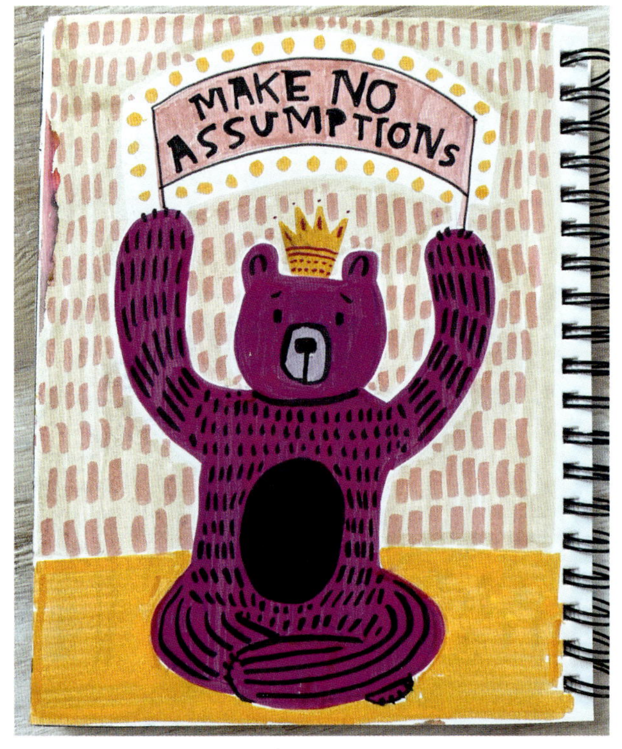

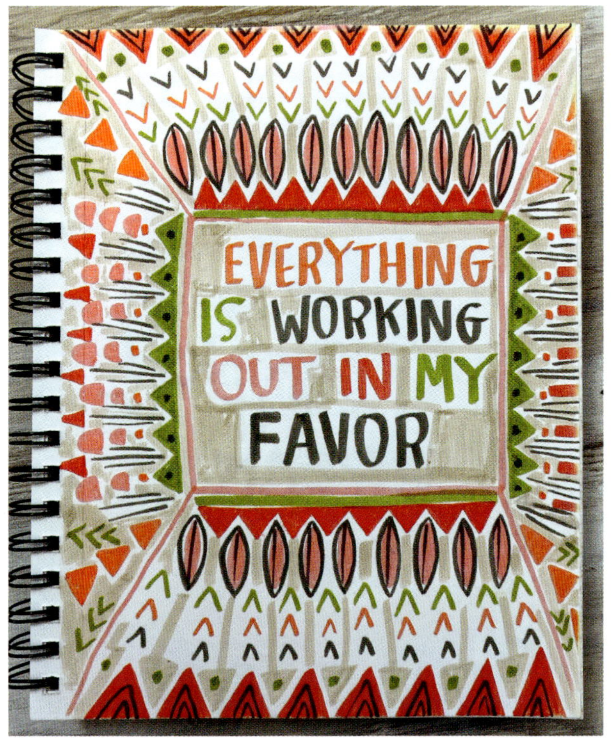

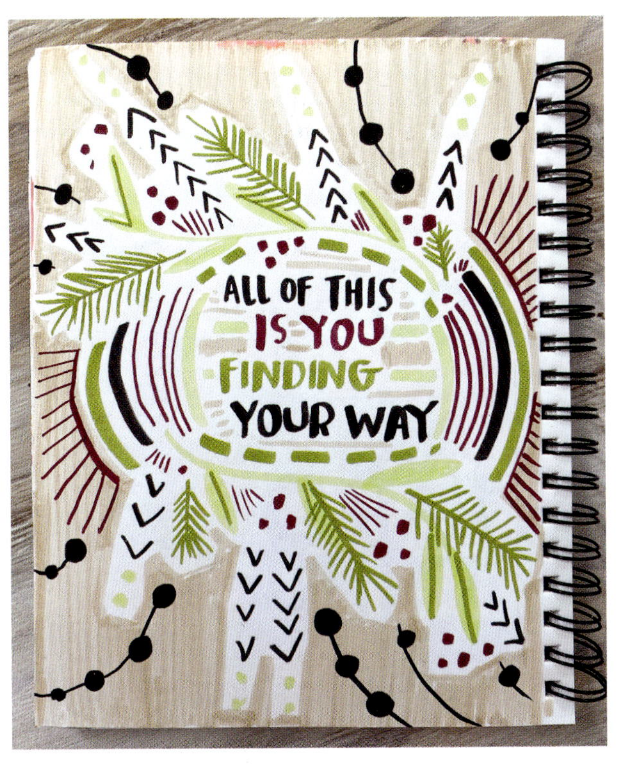

ALL OF THIS
IS YOU
FINDING
YOUR WAY

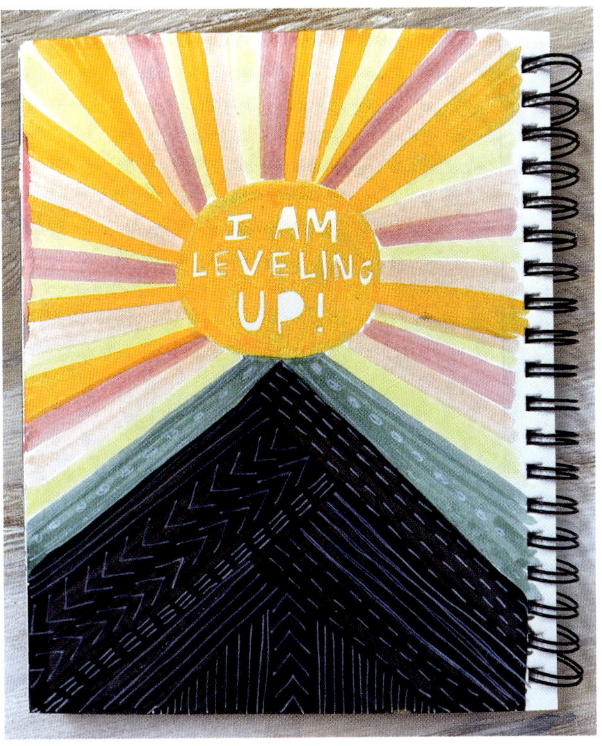

I AM
LEVELING
UP!

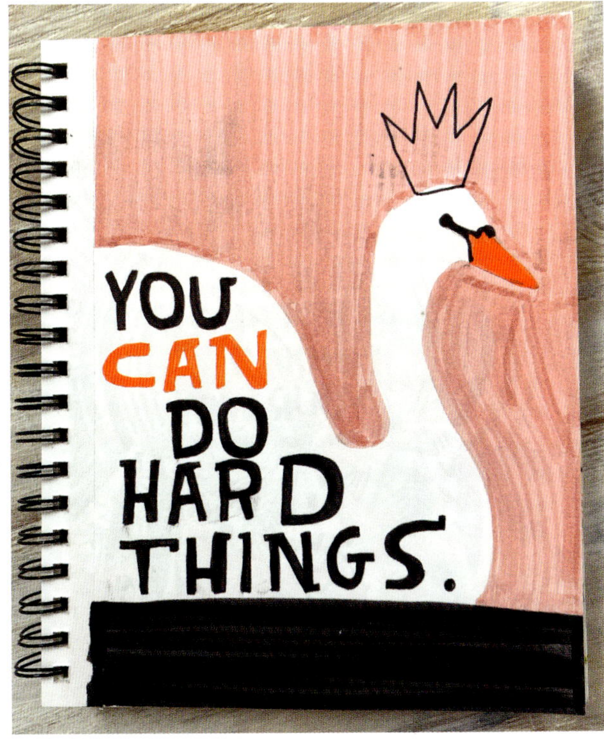

YOU
CAN
DO
HARD
THINGS.

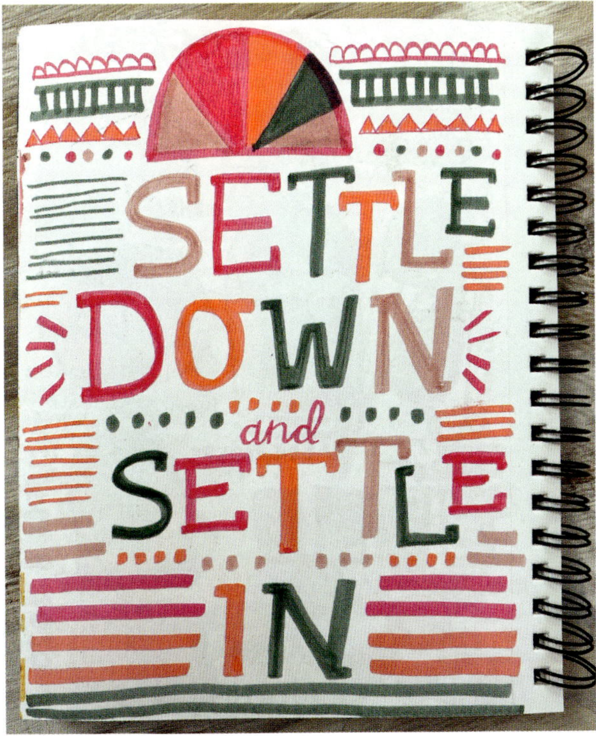

SETTLE
DOWN
and
SETTLE
IN

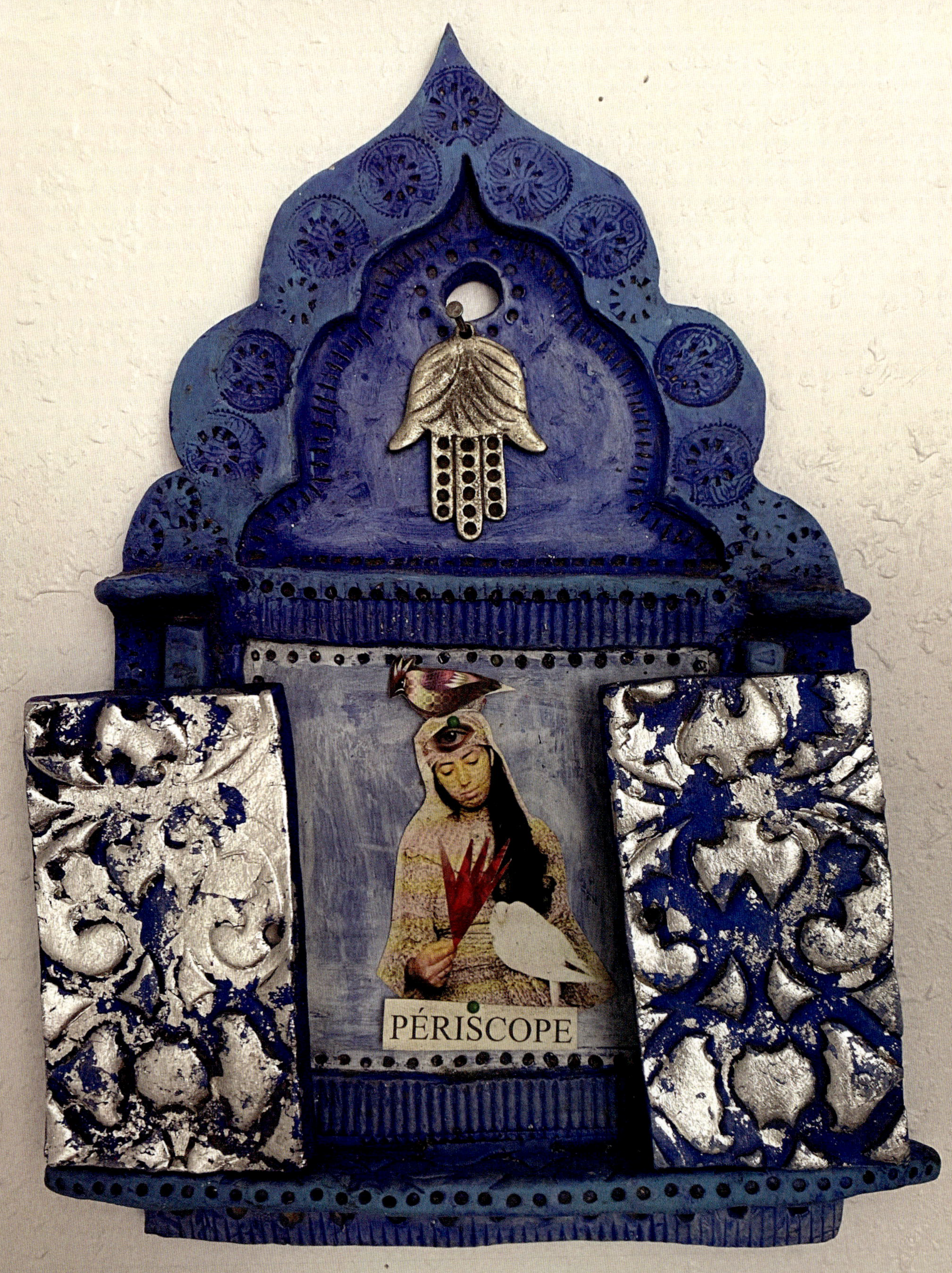
PÉRISCOPE

Collage

One of my favorite collage memories is from an artist retreat in Morocco that I went on in 2014, led by my creative clay artist friend Caroline Douglas. We tore colors, images, and words out of Moroccan magazines as a way to loosen up our creative minds, and I created the little "Periscope" collage, pictured here, that I've treasured ever since. This is one of those techniques that can be more powerful than you might expect; I think it somehow allows your subconscious mind to come to the forefront and your thinking mind to pipe down a little bit as you're cutting and tearing and searching through magazines and papers for things that light you up.

Here I'll explain the process for creating a collage in my sketchbook using magazines, colorful patterned paper, and a basic craft glue stick; you can do the same, or use any other surface and materials that you'd like.

Step 1: Spend some time tearing words, images, colors, and shapes that you like from a stack of magazines, books, newspapers, and/or catalogs.

Step 2: Spend some time moving your pieces around. You don't have to use every single thing that you tore or cut out, so don't be afraid to eliminate pieces. Trust your gut! Listen for messages that want to come through as you're arranging. Stop when you get to an arrangement that causes you to feel an internal YES.

Step 3: Glue the paper pieces down to your surface.

Step 4: Admire your creation! Spend some time writing about the meaning of the message to deepen the experience.

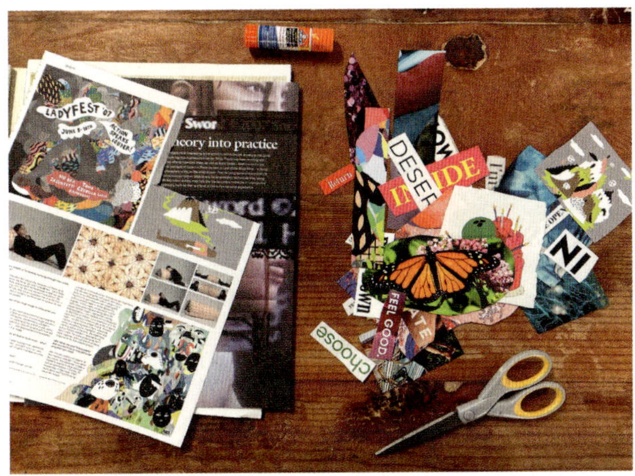

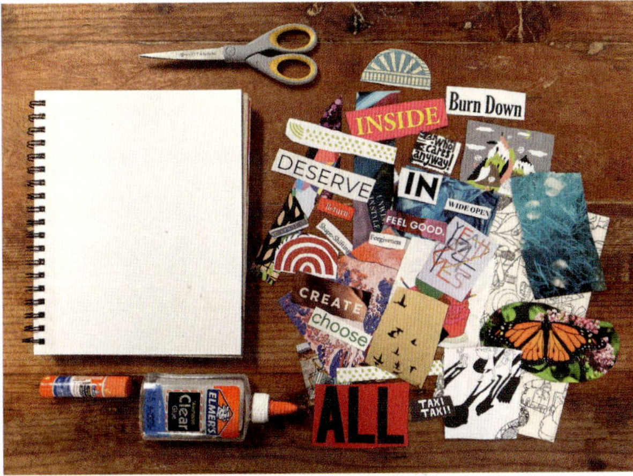

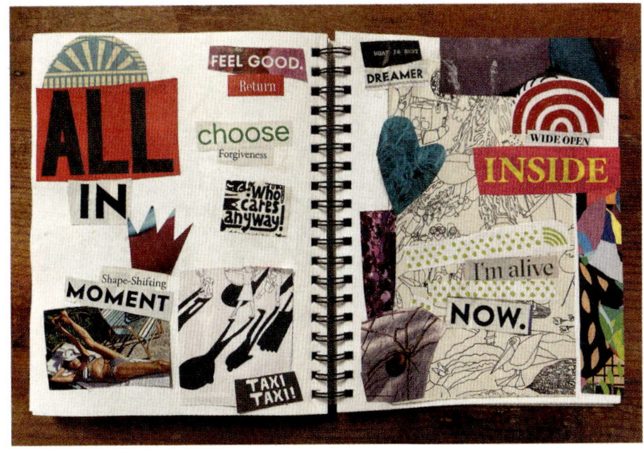

Here are some examples of finished collages I've done over the years, all made in sketchbooks. Some have more words, some have less, some are more image driven, others are unified by some sort of color theme . . . every creation and every day is different. Collage is fun because there's no way to know what you're going to create when you start out; the message and the vibe make themselves known the further you get into the process. It's a great, simple, fun way to practice diving in and trusting your inner voice in your artmaking!

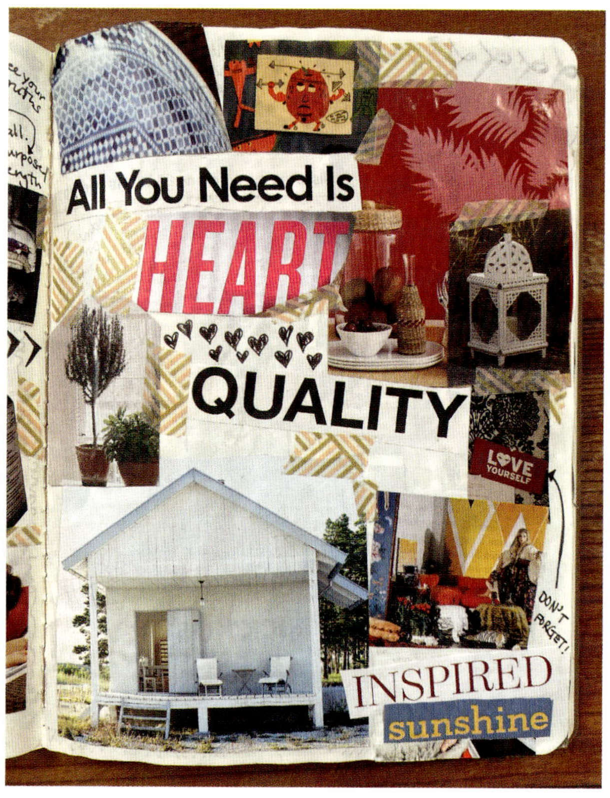

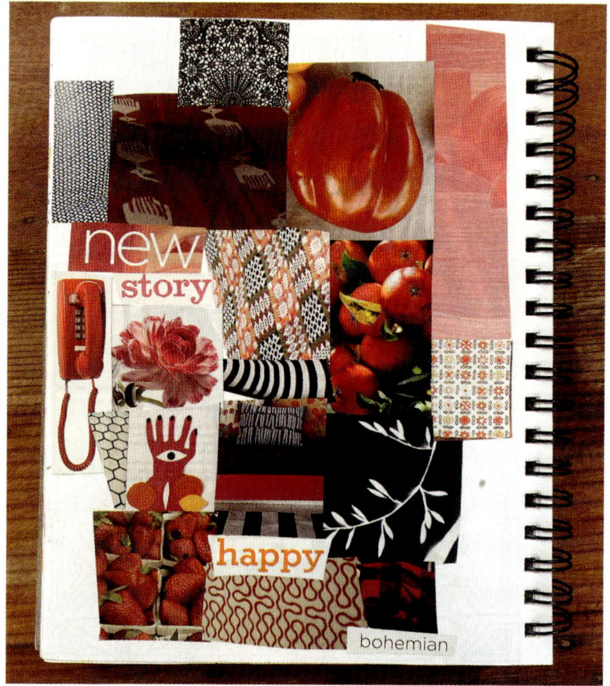

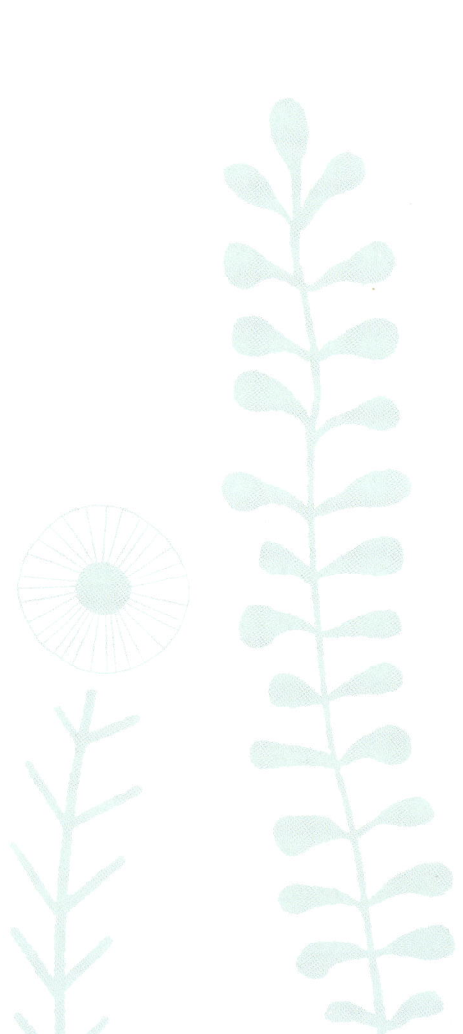

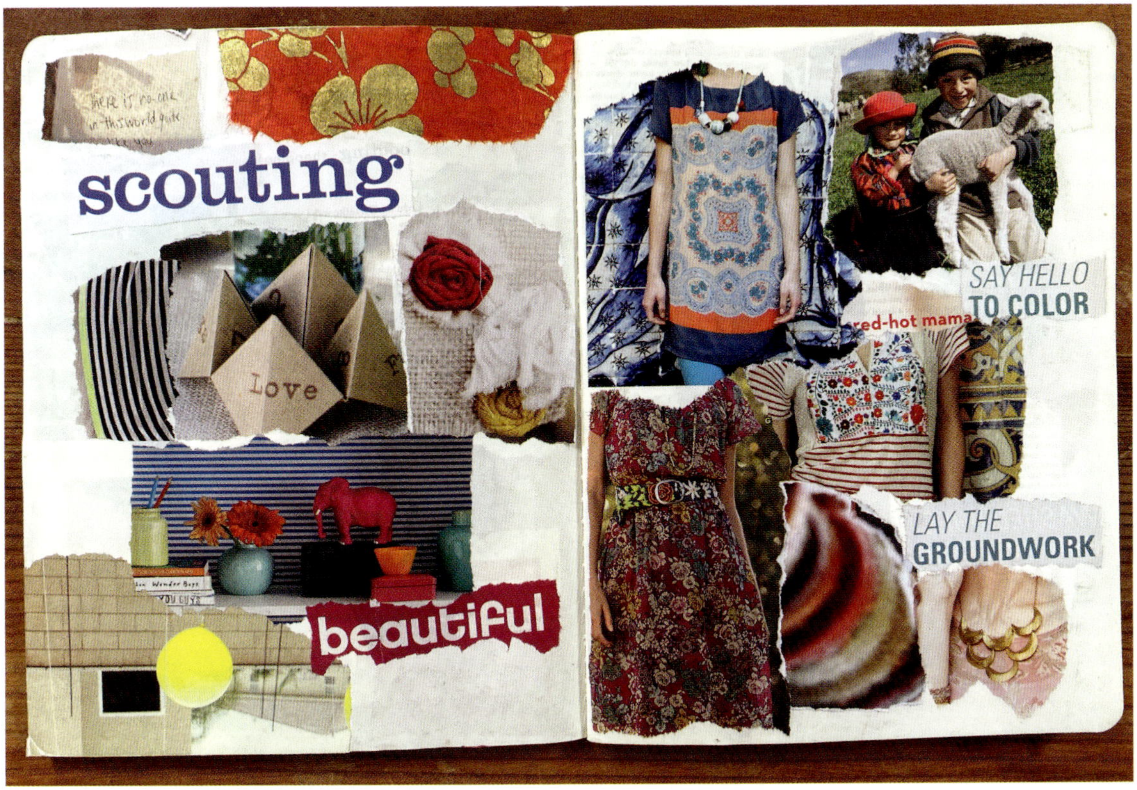

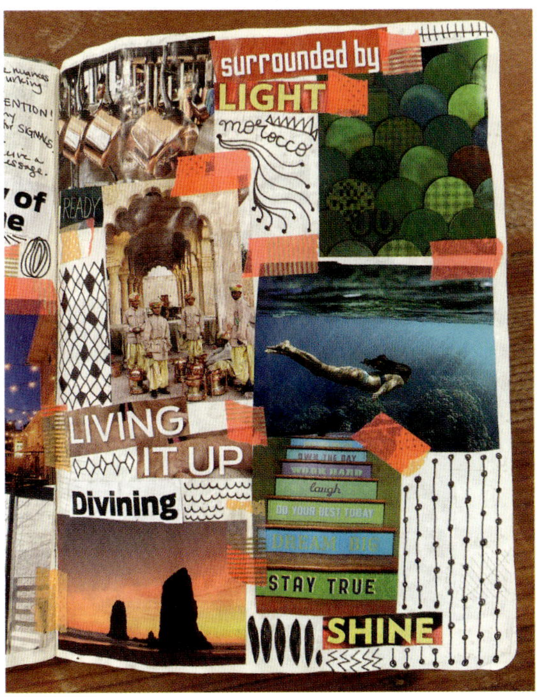

surrounded by
LIGHT
morocco
READY
LIVING
IT UP
Divining
OWN THE DAY
WORK HARD
laugh
DO YOUR BEST TODAY
DREAM BIG
STAY TRUE
SHINE

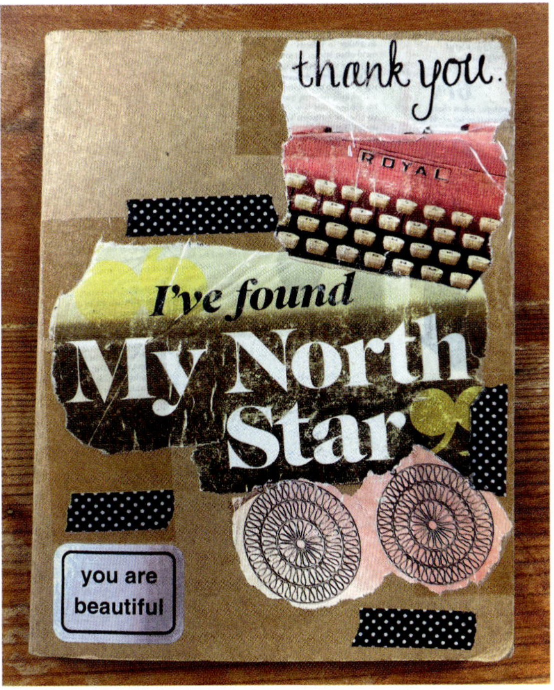

thank you.
ROYAL
I've found
My North
Star
you are
beautiful

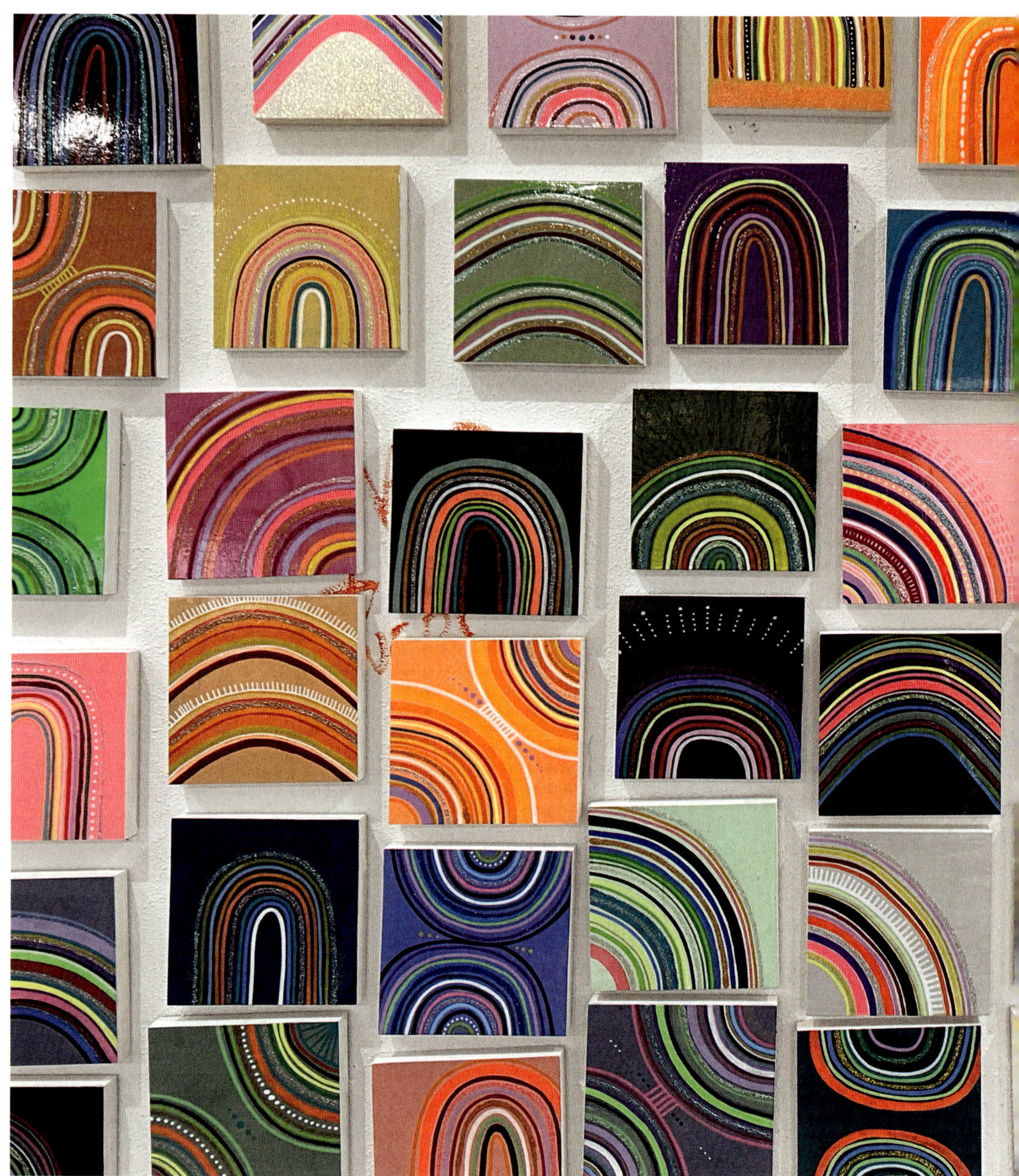

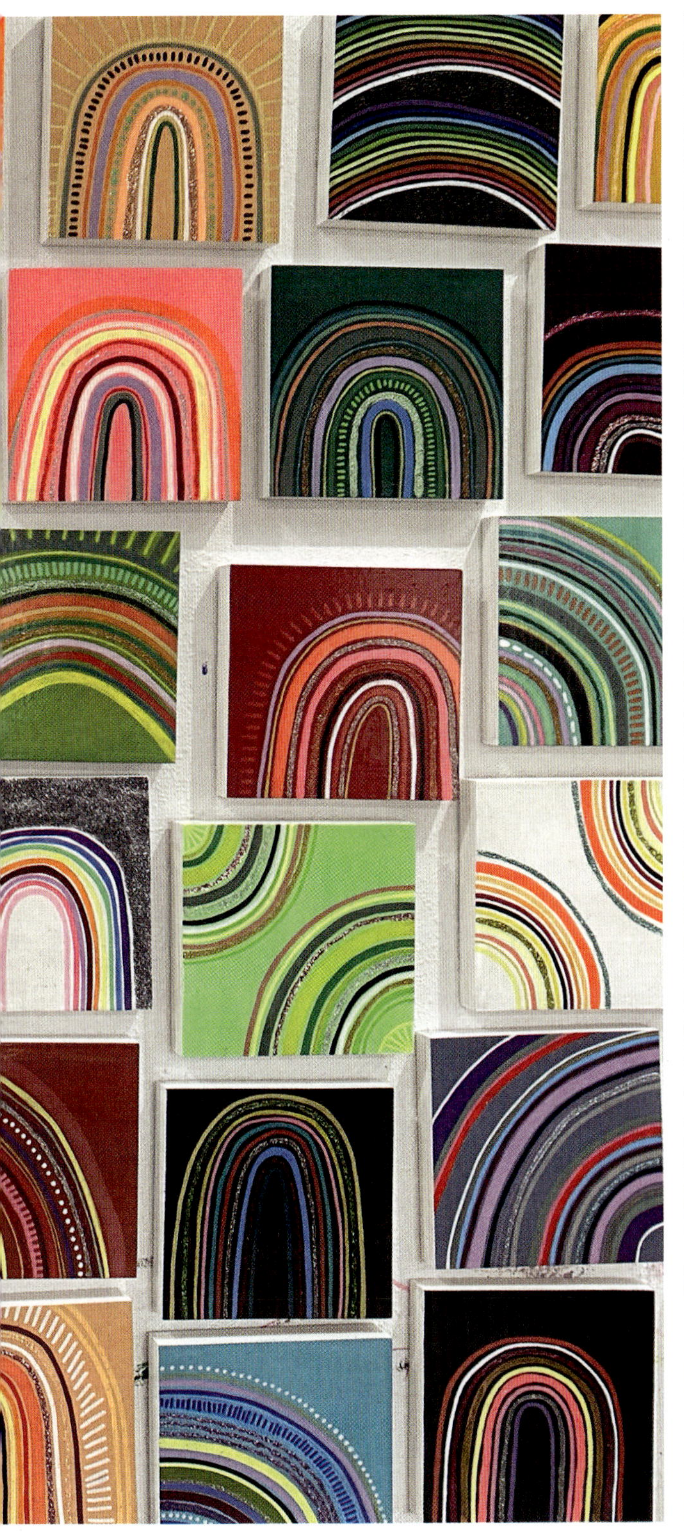

Mixed Media

If there's a technique that embodies the idea of there being no rules and making up your own, mixed media is it. Basically, anything goes here. The term "mixed media art" spans so many different materials and techniques that it's impossible to tell you what you should do or how to do it! Whether you choose to make your art on paper, wood, cardboard, or something else altogether, using paint, pens, markers, colored pencils, cut paper, stamps, stencils, or whatever else your creative inner being has in mind for you, you can really let your creativity loose. Everything is fair game!

I approach this style of artmaking similarly to my paintings, in that I use the process as a way to uncover a message from my intuition. I begin without a plan and intuitively choose colors and materials to use, listening internally for a word or a phrase that wants to come through. The words are typically the last piece that I add to the artwork— the final layer—but this is not a rule by any means and certainly might not be the case for you in your own process. You can incorporate your message at any point in the process, whenever it feels right.

I love combining supplies! I created a series of 100 mixed media rainbow pieces using paint, glitter, paint markers, and colored pencils, which you can see here. When I first got the intuitive hit to use glitter in the paintings, my mind immediately thought, *No. No one will buy a painting with glitter on it; it's too juvenile! I like it, but no one else will.* But thank goodness I knew to listen to my inner voice and not my fear voice that was trying to run the show! I ended up using glitter in the paintings, and they're some of my favorite pieces I've ever made. AND, bonus, they all sold, and my fear voice was wrong! It always, always pays to listen to your intuition.

In my example here, I chose to create my artwork on a small cradled wood panel. I intuitively felt like I wanted to create a little jewel of a piece, and the small size felt like the right choice. I used acrylic and acryla gouache paint, a stencil, spray paint, paint markers, colored pencils, glitter, sequins, cut paper, glue, and stamps.

Step 1: Cover your surface with paint to create your background layer. One color or multiple colors will work equally well.

Step 2: Use spray paint and a stencil to spray a pattern onto your background layer.

Step 3: Cut shapes out of paper and glue to the surface in whatever kind of arrangement you like. Use markers, paint, glitter, sequins, or whatever you want to embellish your piece, using your intuition as a guide for what colors to choose and what lines to draw. Tune in to your inner voice as you create, listening for words or messages that catch your attention and feel like they might want to be part of the piece.

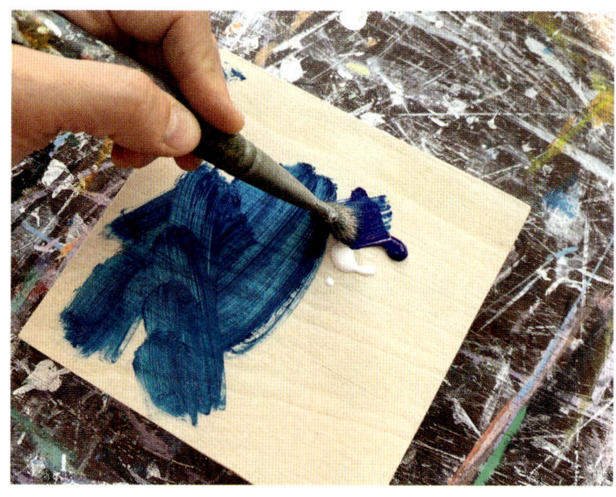

Step 4: Cover over or change anything you don't like as you go along. Be bold! As you can see here, I ended up covering some of the marks I made the further I got into creating the piece.

Step 5: Keep adding new layers and elements. Consider where your word(s) might go as you're working and decide whether or not to leave a little space for it.

Step 6: As a final layer, add your word(s). I chose just one word as a lovely and simple reminder to myself. Yours might be simple, too, or it might be more complex. Remember, you make the rules!

Step 7: If you choose, coat your finished piece with spray varnish, Mod Podge, or gel medium to protect your finished artwork.

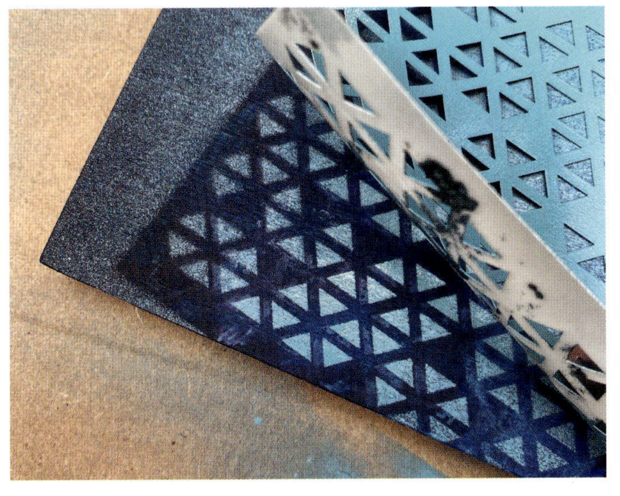

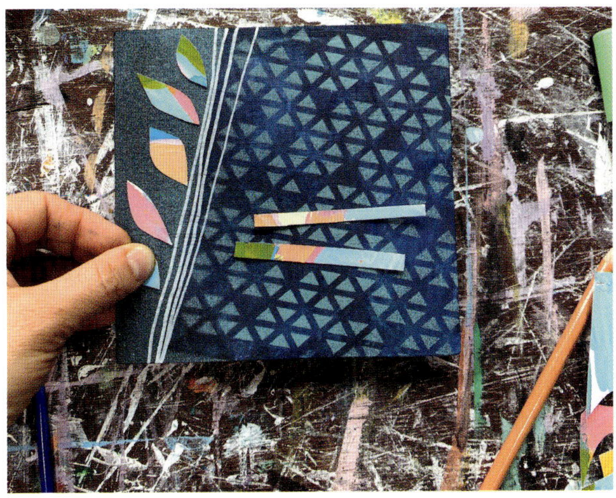

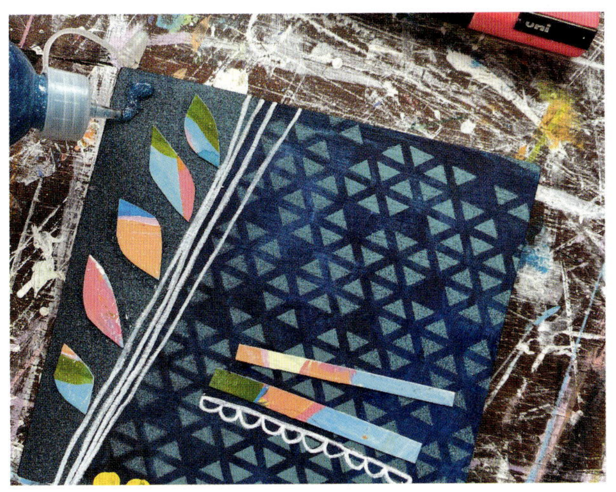

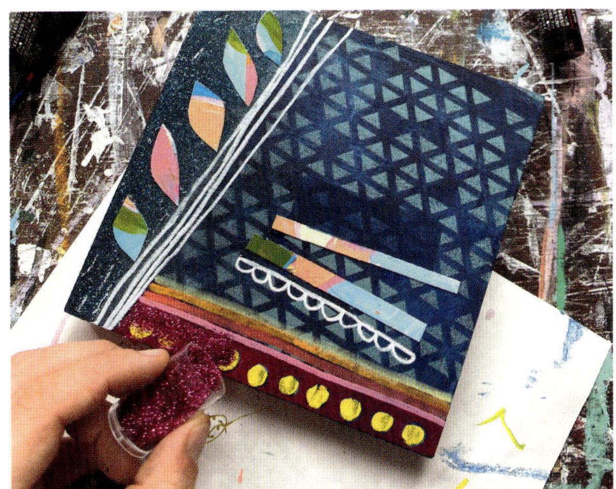

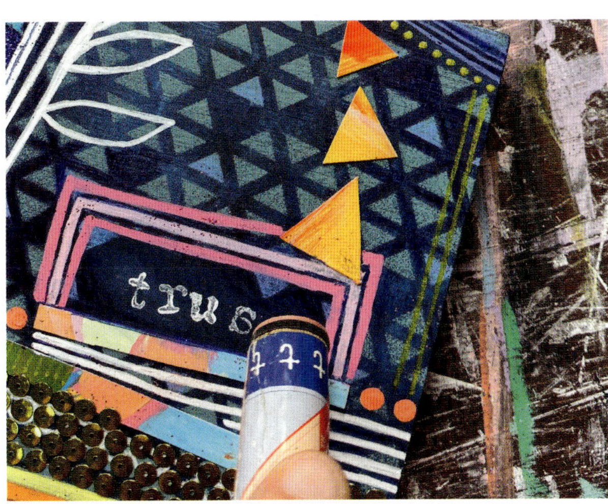

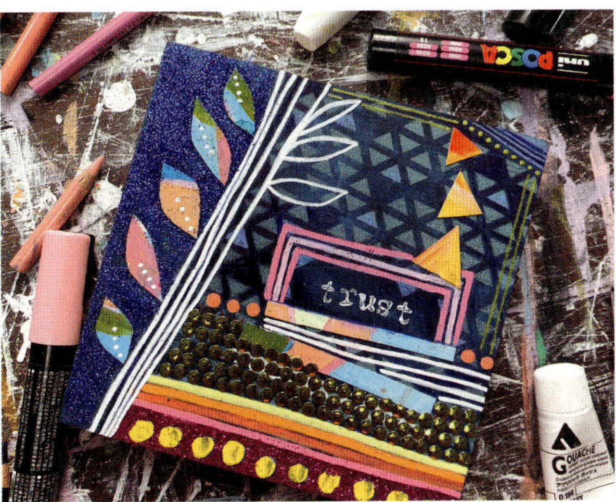

Working Digitally

Since Procreate is probably the most popular iPad drawing app (and my personal favorite and what I use most often), that's what I'm demonstrating on these pages here. I use Procreate pretty simply with a lot of flat color because that's my style and what feels best for me, but you could very well be different. There are dozens of different preloaded brushes built into the app, and you can buy countless more on websites like Creative Market and Gumroad. You can learn to emulate the look of gouache, oil paint, pastel, marker, and basically anything else within Procreate. It's pretty amazing! This is a glimpse into my simple intuition-based artmaking process within the app. I hope it'll inspire you if you're interested in digital art and serve as a jumping-off point for your own digital explorations within Procreate and beyond!

Digital images are versatile and can be used in many ways—you can turn them into art prints, greeting cards, or calendars; you can get them printed on all varieties of surfaces through print-on-demand companies like Society6 and Printful; you can use them as a wallpaper for your computer or phone; and you can easily make edits and color changes if you need to. And it's not at all messy, which is sometimes a big bonus!

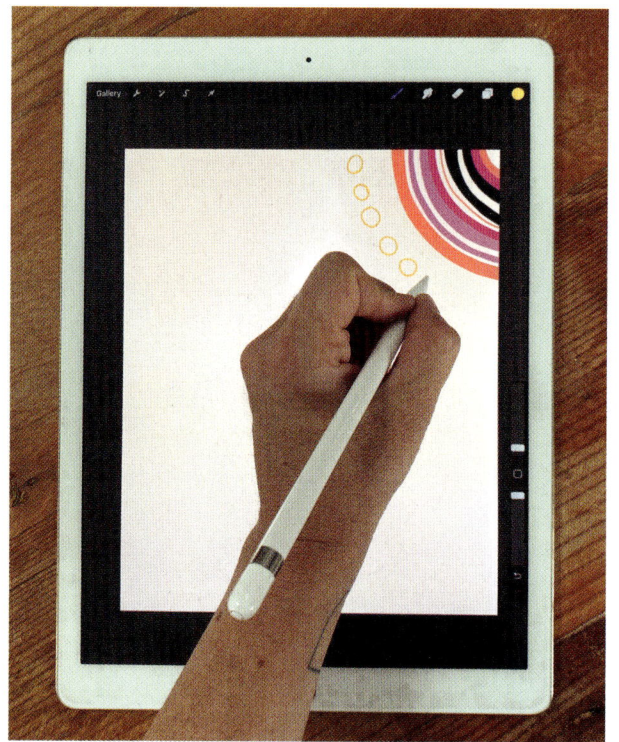

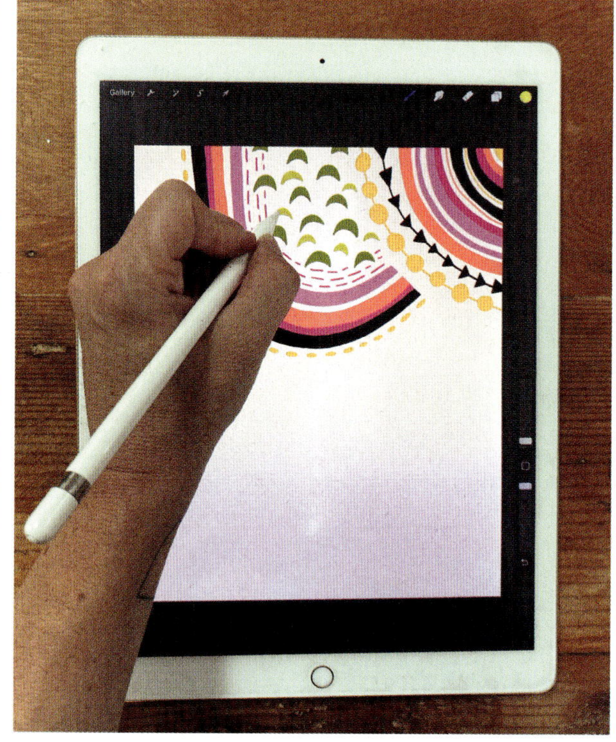

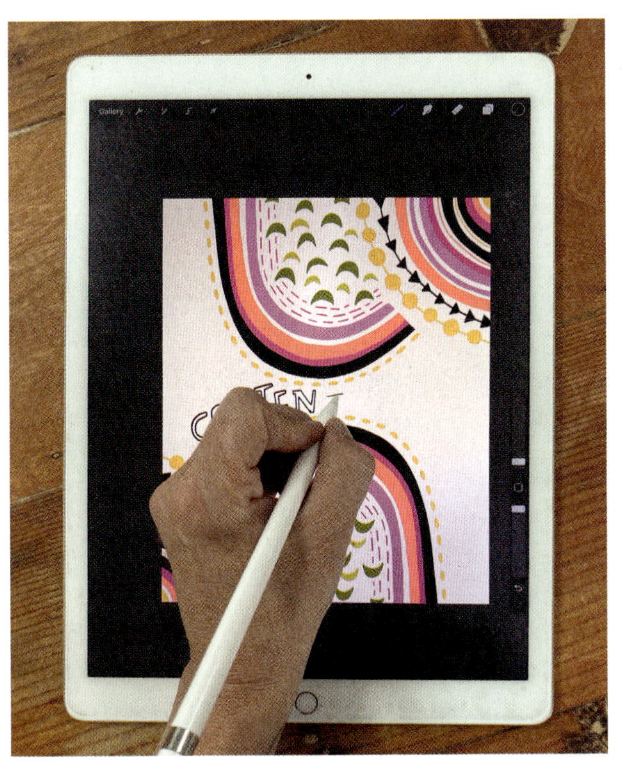

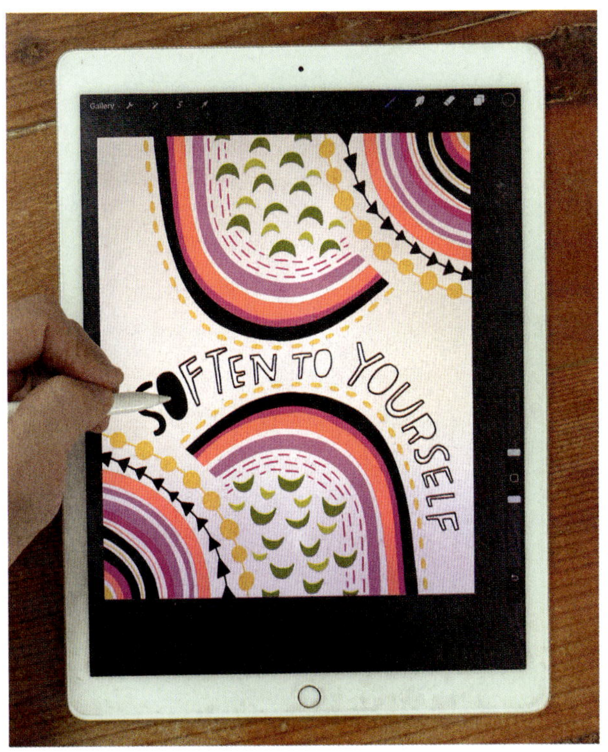

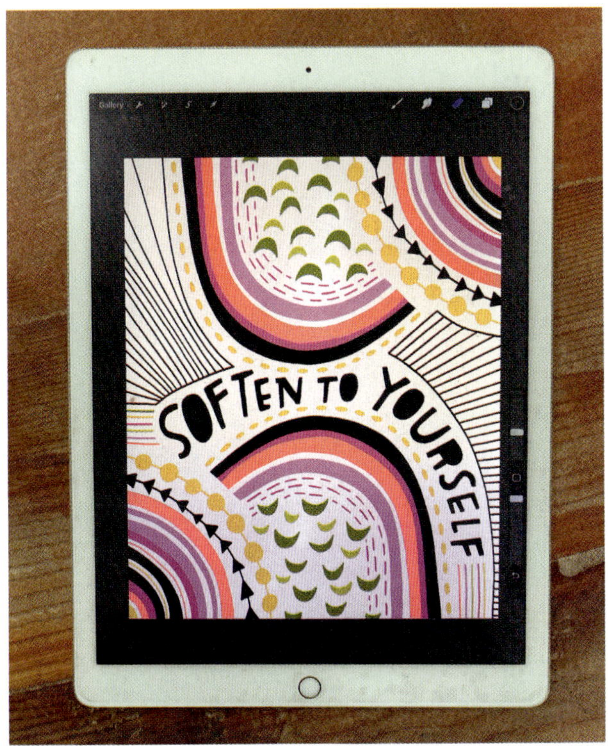

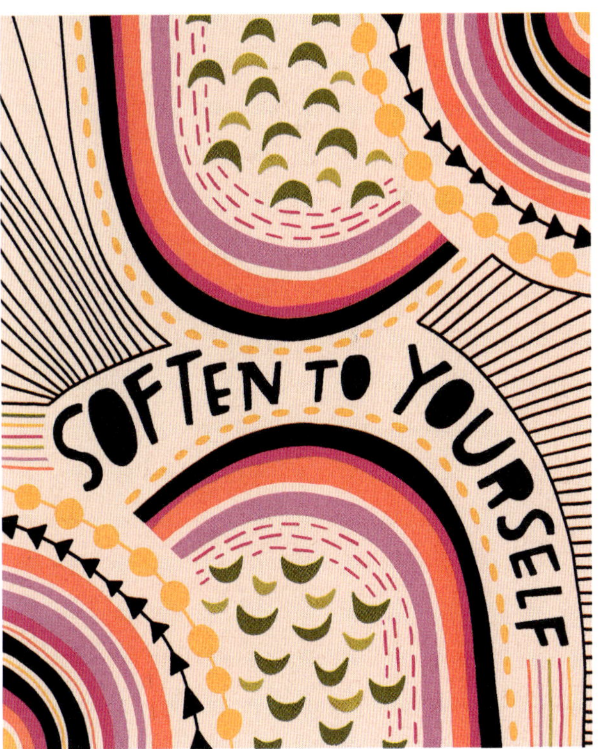
SOFTEN TO YOURSELF

As I mentioned earlier, a lot of the artwork in this book was created digitally. Here are a few examples of images I created specifically using the Procreate app on my iPad Pro, exactly as I demonstrated here in this section.

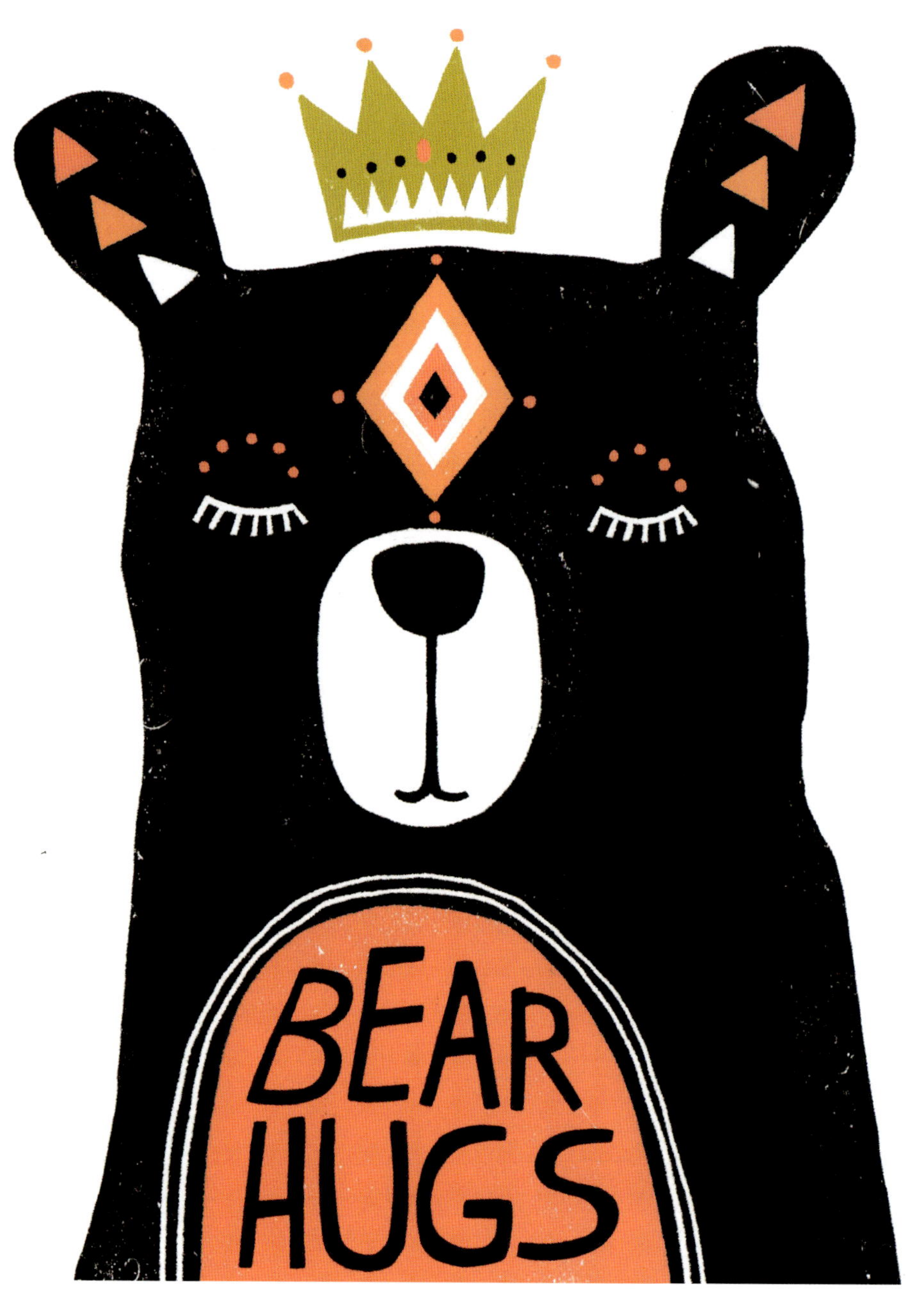

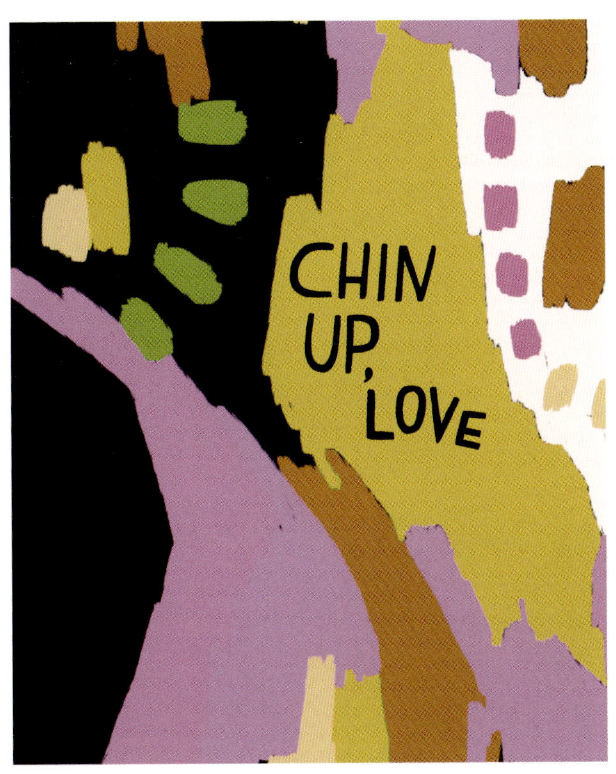

CHIN UP, LOVE

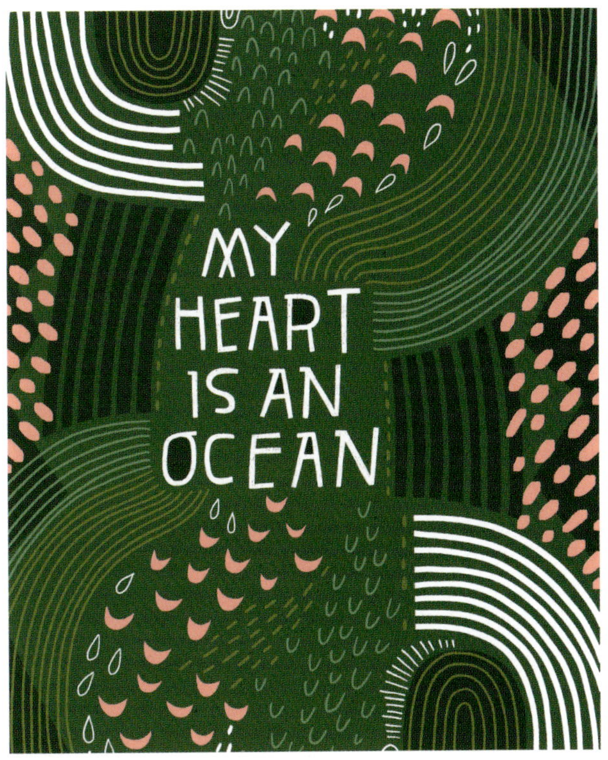

MY HEART IS AN OCEAN

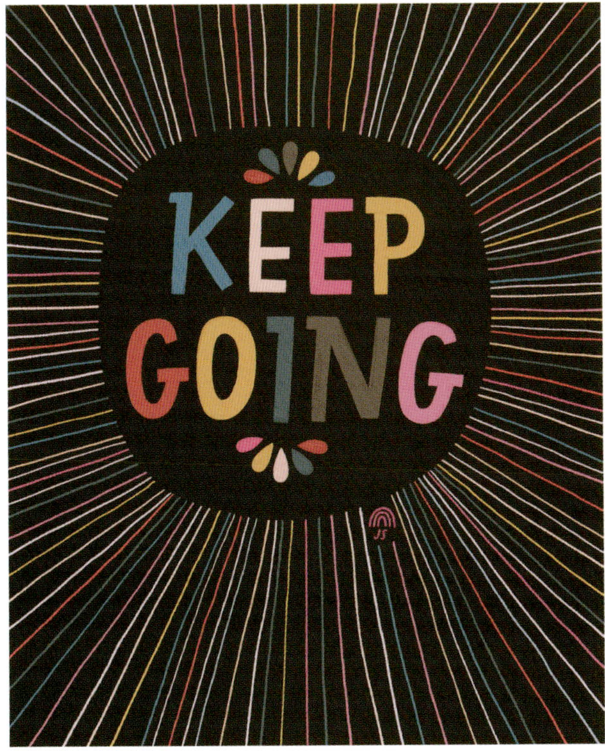

KEEP GOING

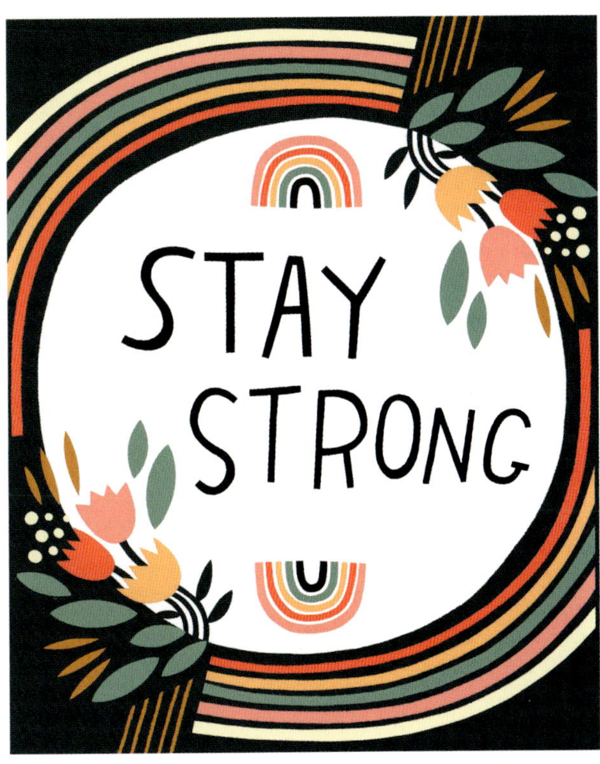

STAY STRONG

Pencil and Colored Pencil

Any type of colored pencil or graphite pencil
will work here. This technique is super basic.
Sometimes keeping things simple is an excellent
way to quiet down and hear your inner voice.
For these drawings, I used Prismacolor pencils and
a very un-fancy "teacher pencil," as my kids call
them. The colored pencil drawing is in my Canson
Mixed Media Sketchbook, and the pencil drawing
is in a little pocket-size Moleskine. But really,
anything goes!

Step 1: I generally approach this straightforward
technique similarly to the way I use markers in
that I've already got a message in mind before I
begin, and I want to hand-letter those words as
the main focus of my image.

Step 2: If hand-lettering intimidates you, I
encourage you to just give it a try. Your letters
don't have to be perfect or straight, and they
don't have to look amazing. The quirkier
the better!

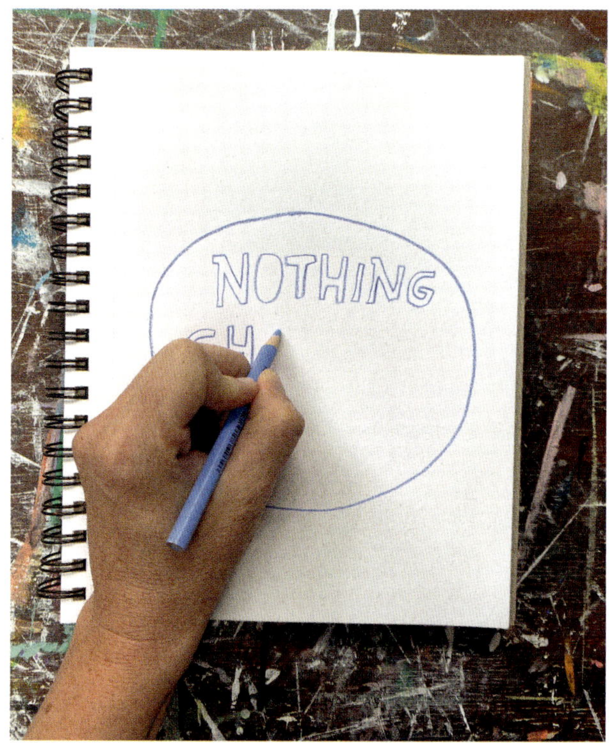

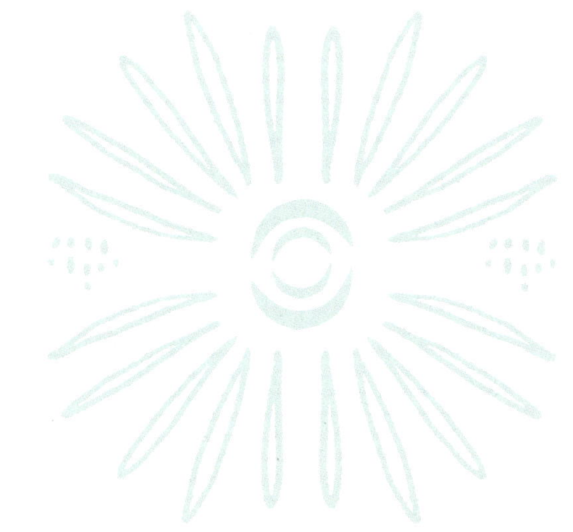

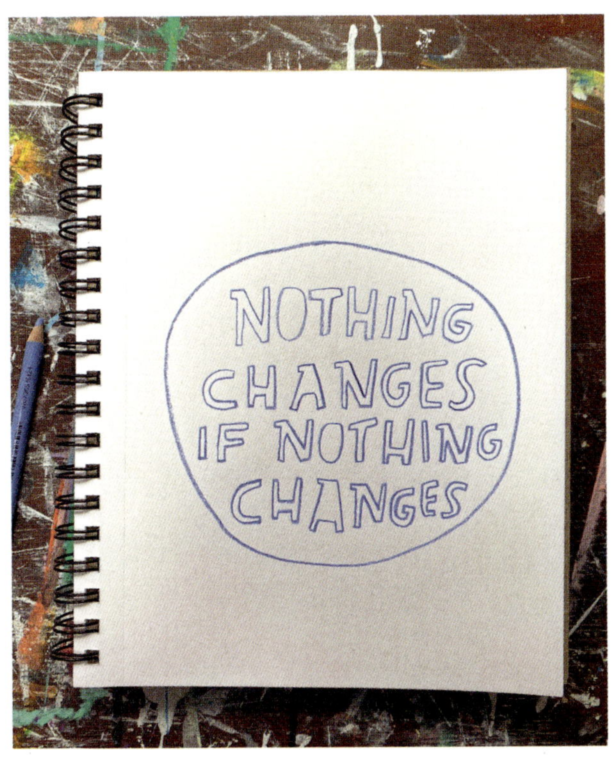

NOTHING CHANGES IF NOTHING CHANGES

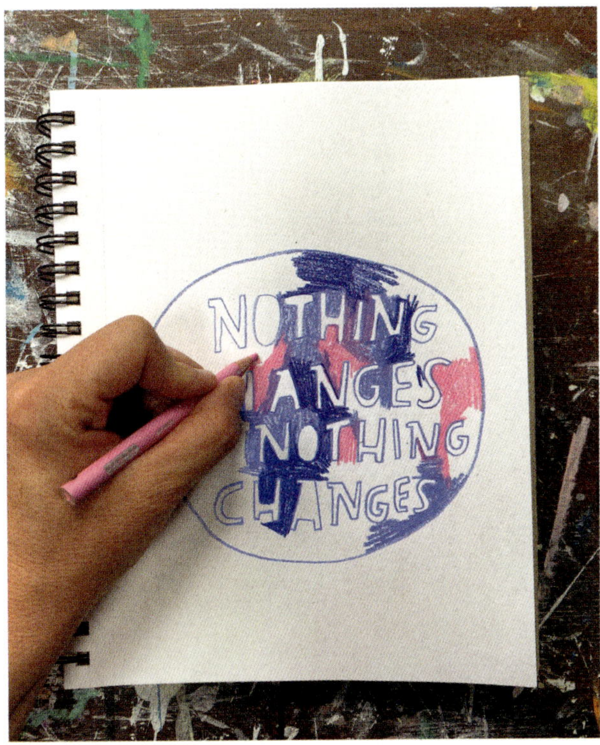

NOTHING CHANGES IF NOTHING CHANGES

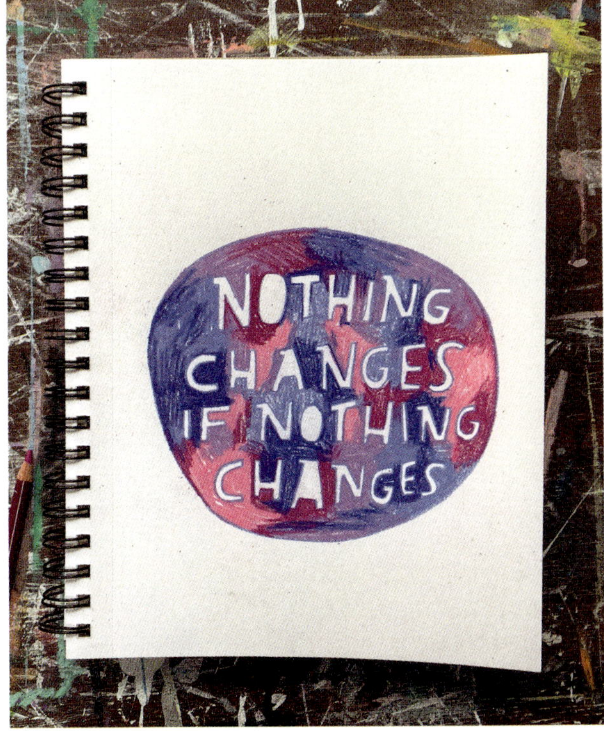

NOTHING CHANGES IF NOTHING CHANGES

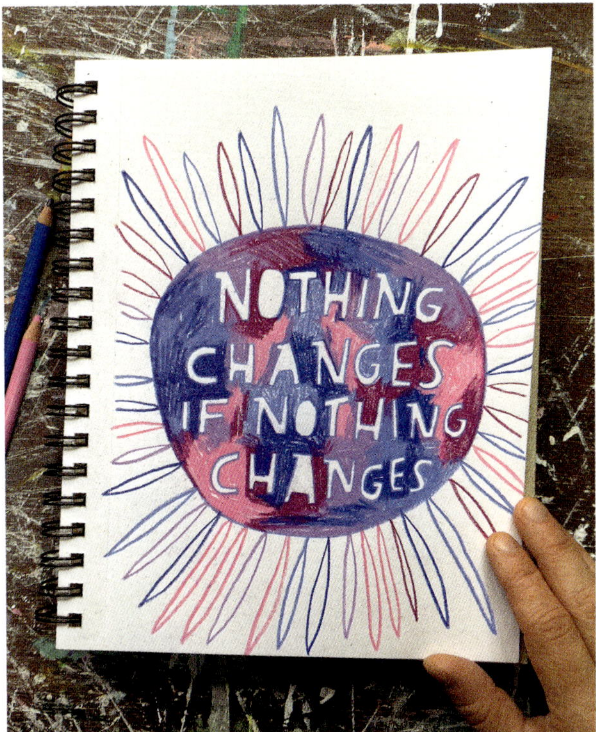

NOTHING CHANGES IF NOTHING CHANGES

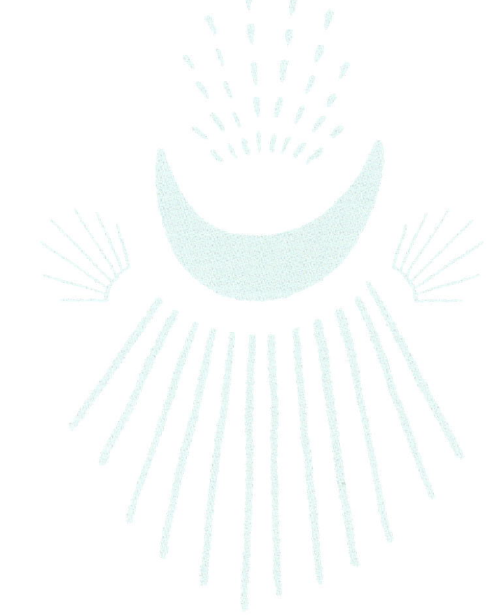

Remember, the aim here is not a beautiful end product, but a beautiful relationship with your inner self. Hand-lettering is something that will get easier with time and practice, so do your best not to judge yourself and just have fun making letters and shapes and playing with colors!

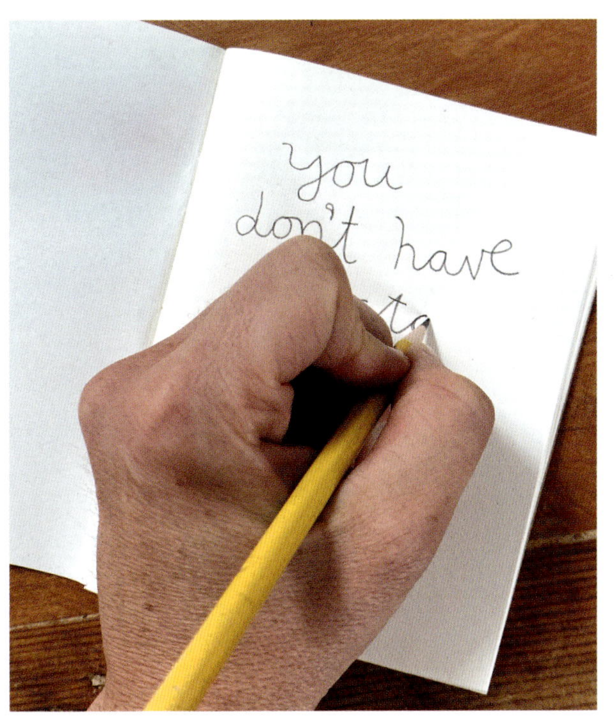

you
don't have

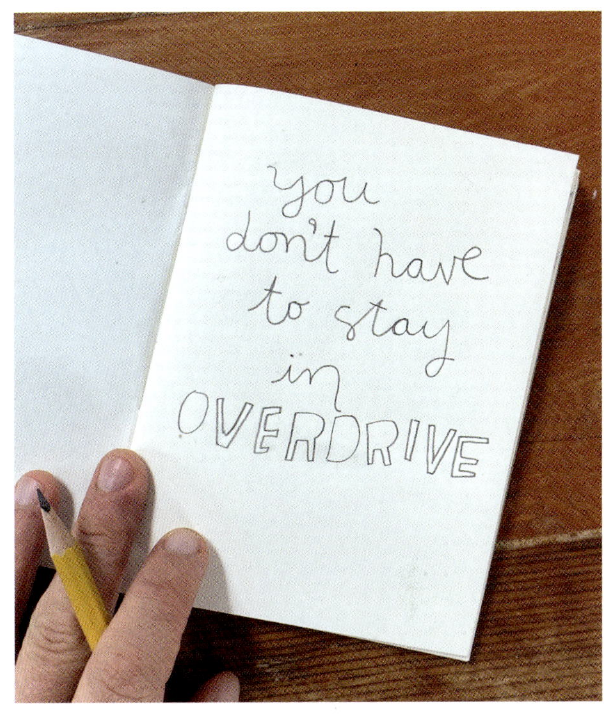

you
don't have
to stay
in
OVERDRIVE

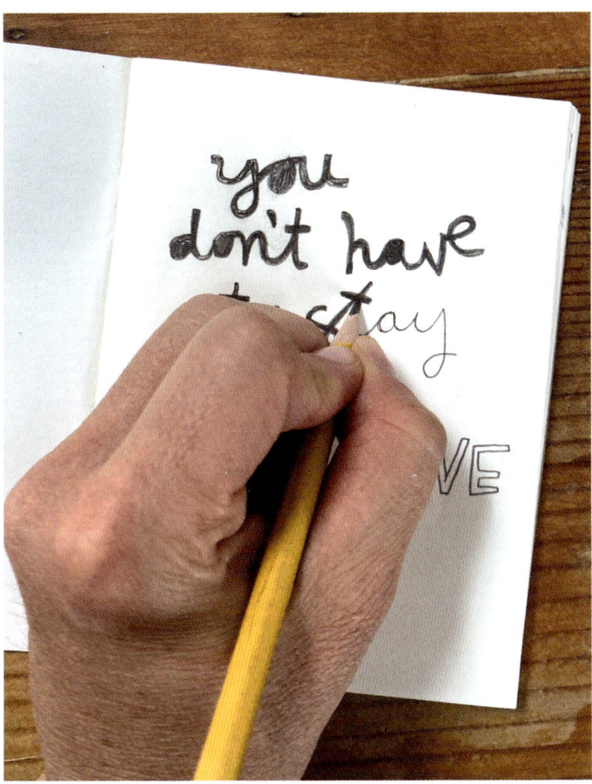

you
don't have
stay
VE

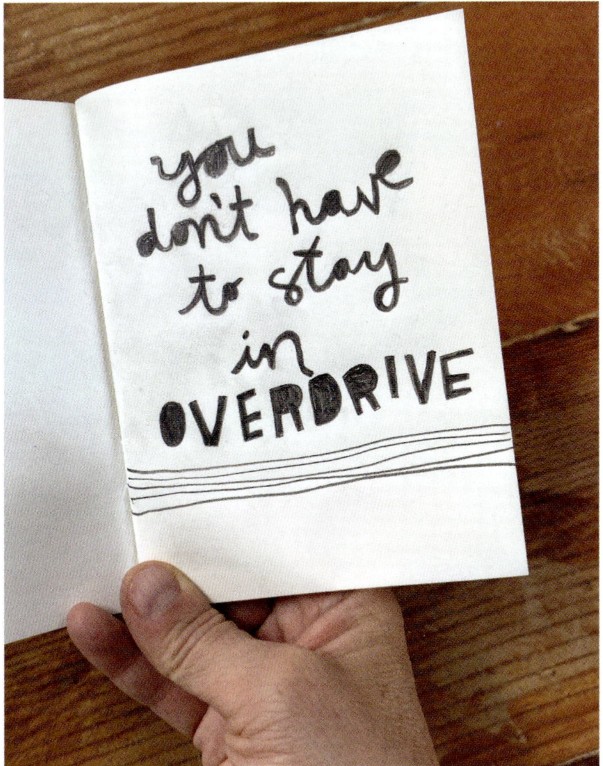

you
don't have
to stay
in
OVERDRIVE

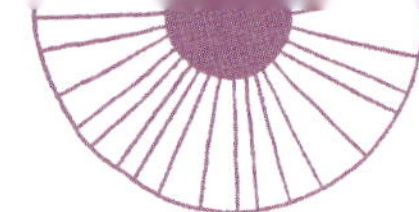

FINDING VISUAL INSPIRATION

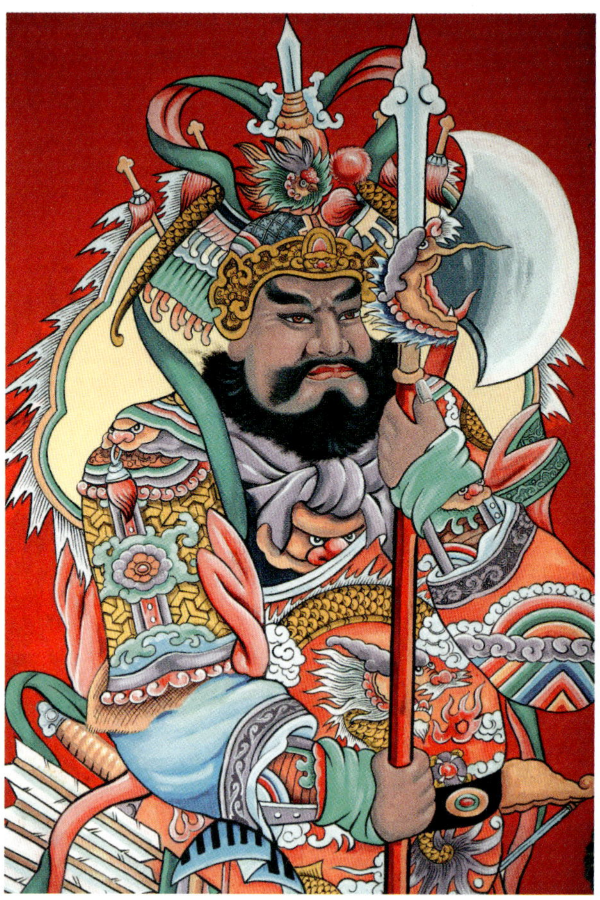

THE WORD *INSPIRATION* comes from the Latin word *inspirare*, which means "to breathe into." Inspiration, then, is what breathes life into your creative process. It's something that moves you into the act of creating. Inspiration can come from all sorts of places, and I encourage you to use your own imagination and visual imagery that already lives inside you as your most potent and reliable source of inspiration.

Of course, it's also vital to get outside yourself to bring some new energy into your creative practice. Looking for inspiration in your outer world allows you to incorporate new ideas into your artmaking and to integrate them into your process in your own unique way.

Given that you're reading this book, I imagine you're a visual person, which means you'll probably be inspired by other artists. This is completely natural, but it's important to remember not to copy. I use this helpful reminder for myself: **Don't regurgitate; innovate.** Imagine you're a filter and picture running the images that inspire you through your filter. Try to distill what it is about the image(s) that inspires you rather than simply copying what you see. When you know what it is that inspires you, how can you express that idea in your own way?

Visual inspiration can be found in both expected and surprising places, and it's important to keep your eyes and senses open as you make your way through the world. The internet is an easy and obvious place to find visual inspiration these days. There are billions of images literally at our fingertips whenever we want or need them! While there are many wonderful advantages to having the internet and endless inspiration at our fingertips, it also means that many of us are looking at the same images, feeling inspired by the same things, and there's a lot of regurgitation and copying that happens because of it. It's a great tool, but it's also super important to find inspiration outside of the internet.

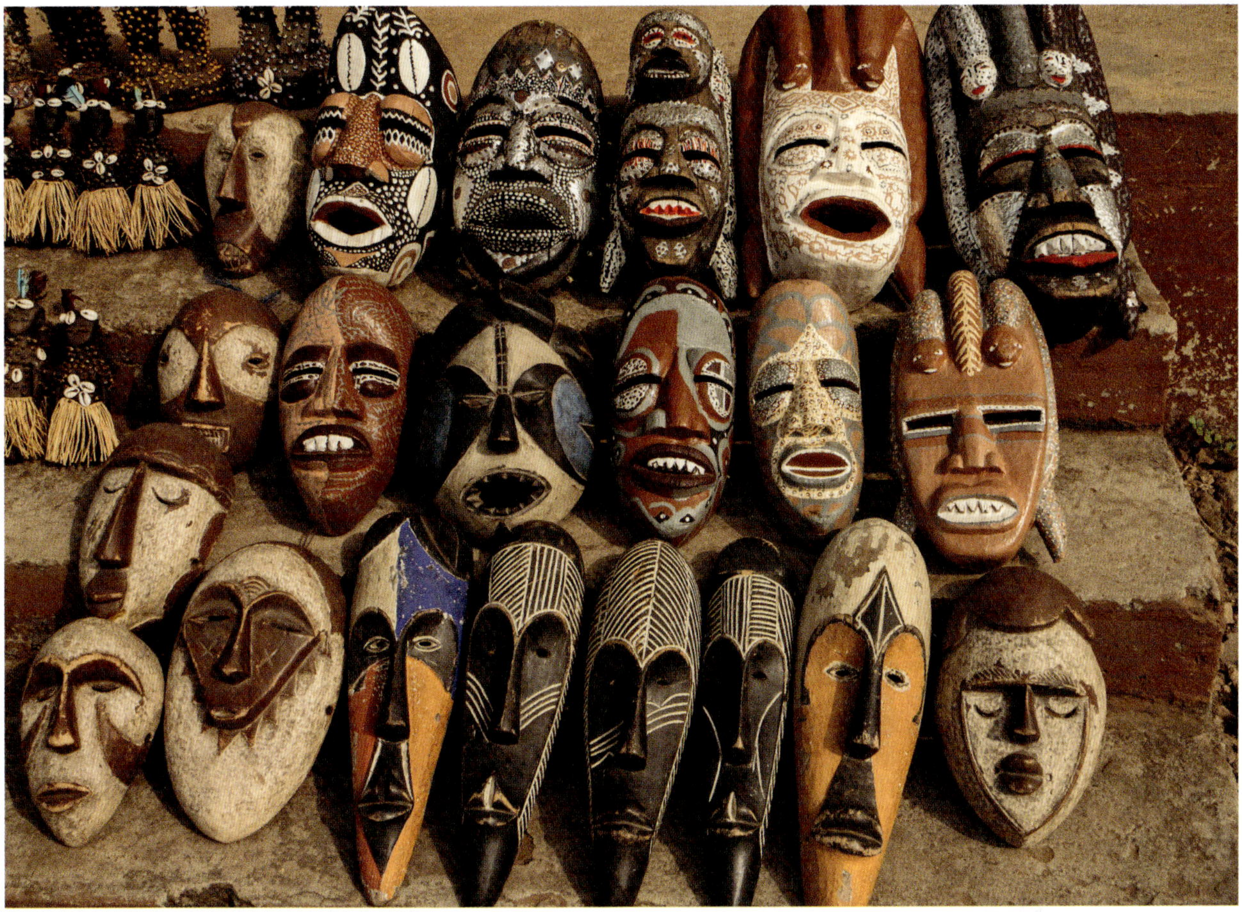

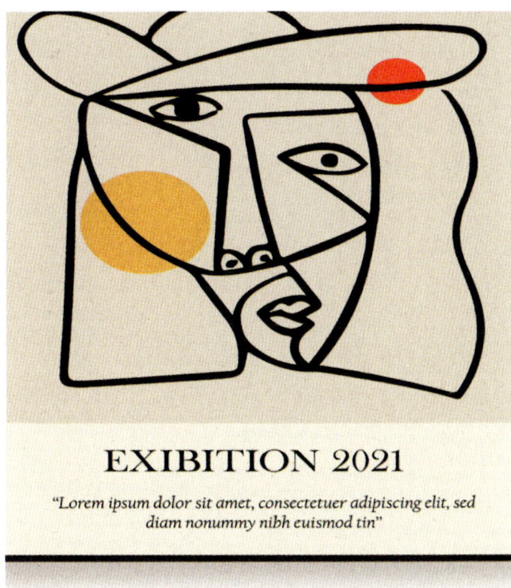

EXIBITION 2021
"Lorem ipsum dolor sit amet, consectetuer adipiscing elit, sed diam nonummy nibh euismod tin"

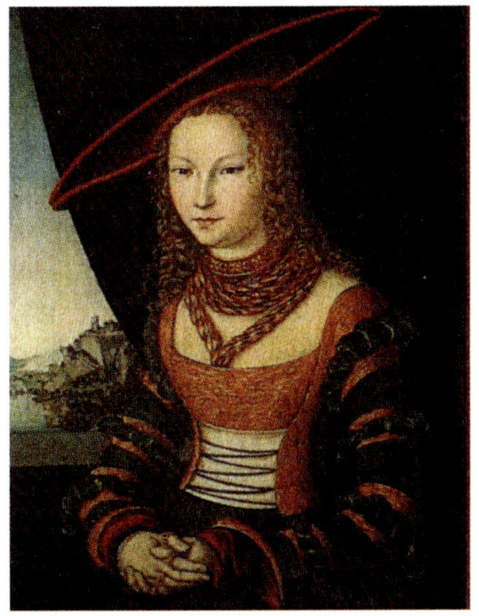

Albert Einstein famously said, "Creativity is the residue of time wasted." Get out there and do something unproductive! The times when you loosen up and disrupt your usual patterns are often times when inspiration flows in effortlessly. (If this feels scary or indulgent to you, believe me, I get it. "Be unproductive?! But that's irresponsible and ludicrous!" This is how my mind responds to the idea. But you might be surprised if you give it a try . . .)

Get outside! Go for a walk in the woods. Sit by a river. Examine trees, bugs, birds, plants, and flowers. Lay in the grass at night and look at the moon and the stars. Go to a bookstore and look at beautiful books. Go to the library and find books about things you find fascinating; make photocopies of your favorite images to use as references later. Go somewhere brand new, take a different route when you're driving home, take a walk and use your intuition to give you directions on which way to go, lie in the grass and watch the clouds, go to a flower shop, a botanical garden, or a museum. Go window shopping in stores you love and stores you wouldn't normally choose to go in. Read poetry, watch documentaries about creative people; take a class and learn something new. These are just a handful of suggestions; inspiration can spark and flow in so many ways. Keep your mind and all five of your senses open! Here are some other ways to notice sources of inspiration:

- A sound or a smell could cause a memory or an image to float into your mind.

- An overheard snippet of a conversation could create a flash of insight.

- An unusual color combination on an advertisement or a billboard might compel you to try out some new colors in your own artmaking.

- The shape of a leaf, flower, or bug might inspire a new idea or become an important new motif in your work.

- Someone's outfit or hairdo or facial expression might catch your attention.

- A handwritten sign tacked to a telephone pole might be exactly what you need to see in order to get you out of a creative slump and back into action.

- A pattern in nature might inspire you to make marks in a different way.

The point is, you just never know where inspiration is! Assuming it could be anywhere and everywhere, walking through the world with all your senses open and engaging with your life will put you in inspiration's path.

Look for shapes and color combinations that intrigue you. Carry a camera with you, or a little notepad, or use your phone. Breathe in and capture all that you can from your actual surroundings. Then run it all through your filter so you can thoughtfully and authentically express what's true and real for you in your unique and magical way.

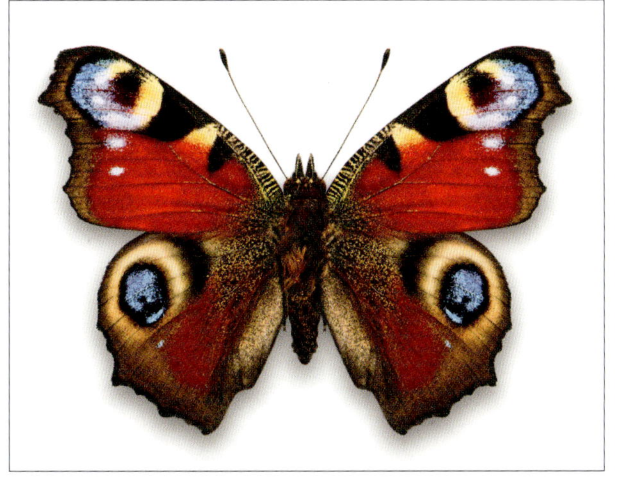

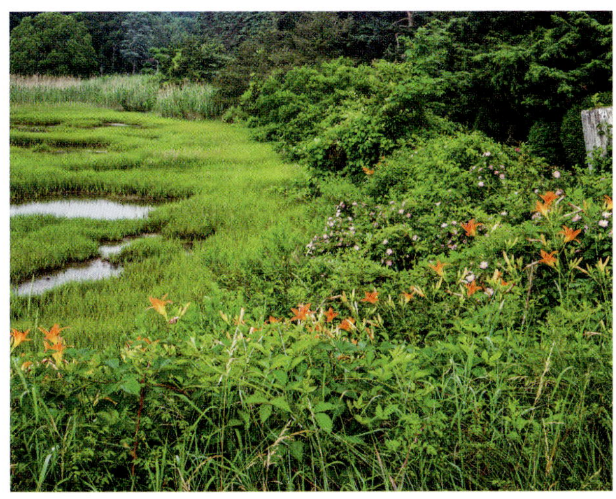

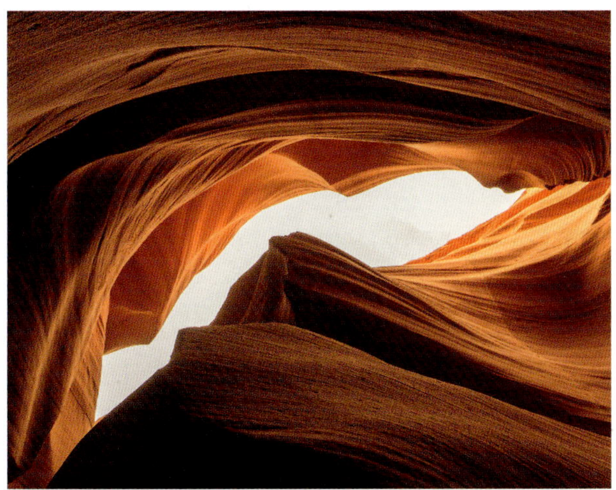

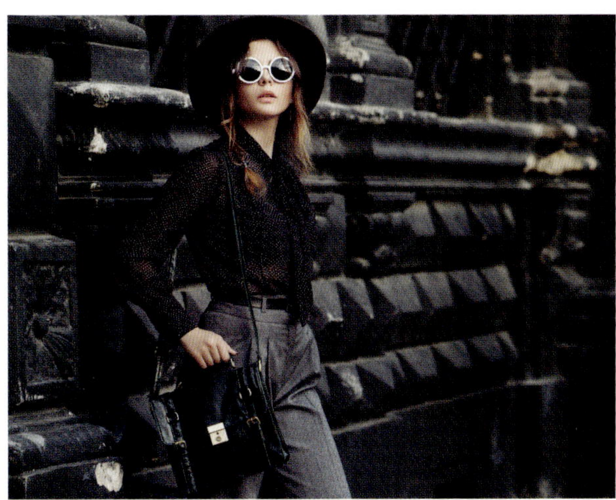

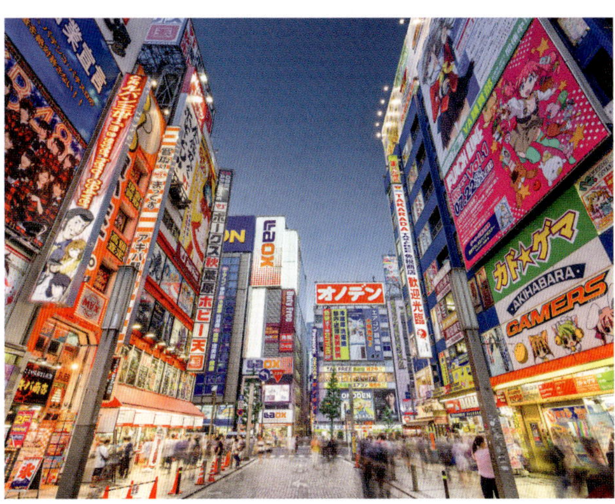

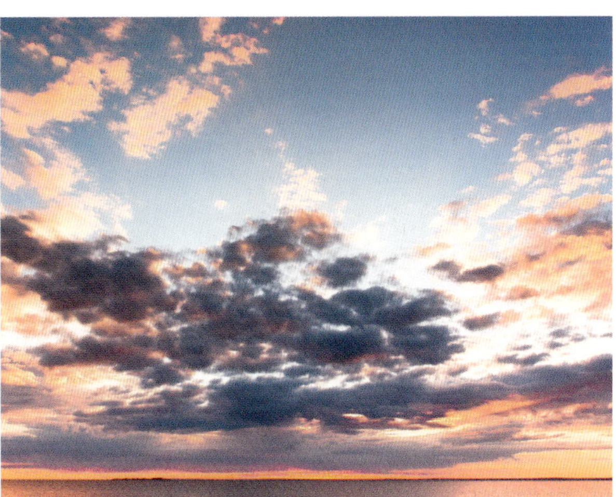

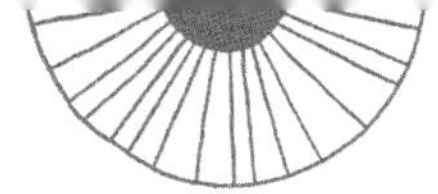

INCORPORATING PERSONAL SYMBOLS

WHEN MAKING ART, laying down the first mark is often the hardest. Starting with something familiar can take some of the pressure off. Sometimes when I don't know where to start, I begin with a familiar motif.

You might already feel an affinity with some symbols or motifs. We connect to images and make meaning out of them in all kinds of ways, and we regularly use images to express ourselves. Sometimes people are even so connected to certain images that they tattoo them on their bodies (I did!).

A handful of important symbols are meaningful for me and make regular appearances in my creative work. My connection to these symbols evolves as time goes on and sometimes their meaning shifts and grows. I've used some symbols for decades—for example, birds wearing crowns, which represent hope, resilience, and self-love. Some motifs, like snakes, are relatively new in my visual world, symbolizing rebirth and shedding layers to become who I truly am.

I understand the meaning in my connection to some symbols and ideas more than others; some simply feel right when my hand is creating them. But incorporating personally meaningful images is a regular part of my artmaking practice.

Using important motifs also allows me to add layers of meaning in my artwork without having to use words all the time. It's almost like using a different type of language. It doesn't matter whether anyone else understands the importance of these symbols; what matters is the power they hold for you and you alone. Sometimes motifs can replace words altogether and can represent the messages you hear from your inner voice. Between images and words, there are a lot of ways to honor and express the messages you receive!

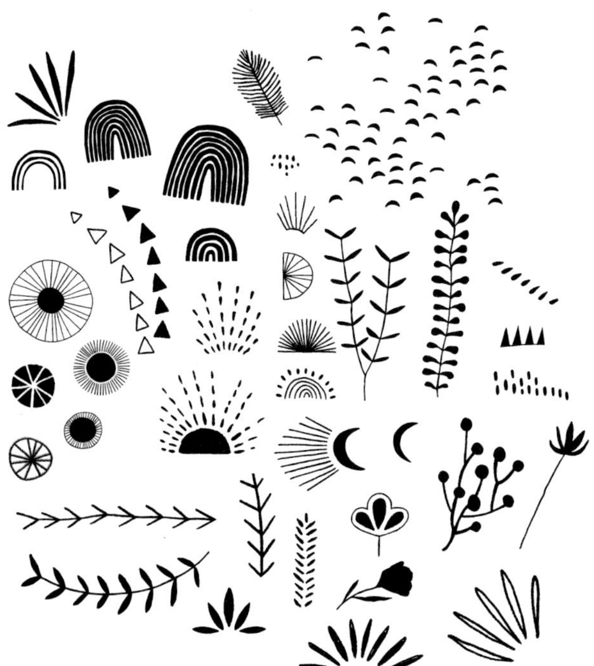

What Symbols Do You Feel Connected To?

What images give you a sense of comfort, power, hope, or motivation? Are there certain motifs, shapes, or marks that just *feel* right to you in some way?

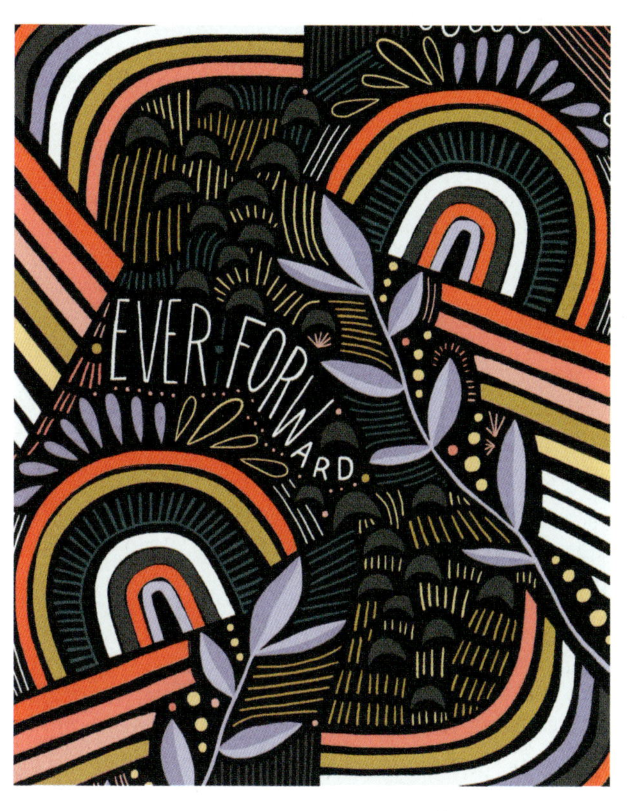

EVER FORWARD

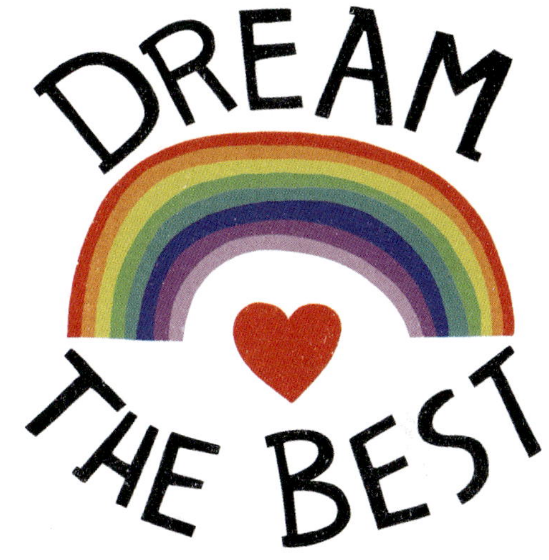

DREAM
THE BEST

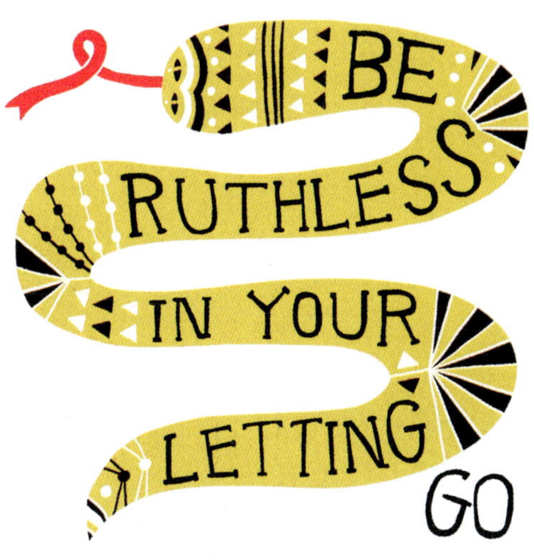

BE
RUTHLESS
IN YOUR
LETTING
GO

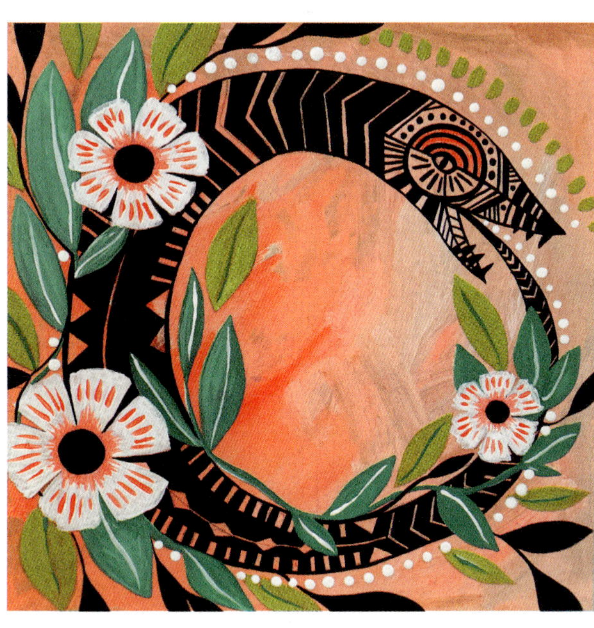

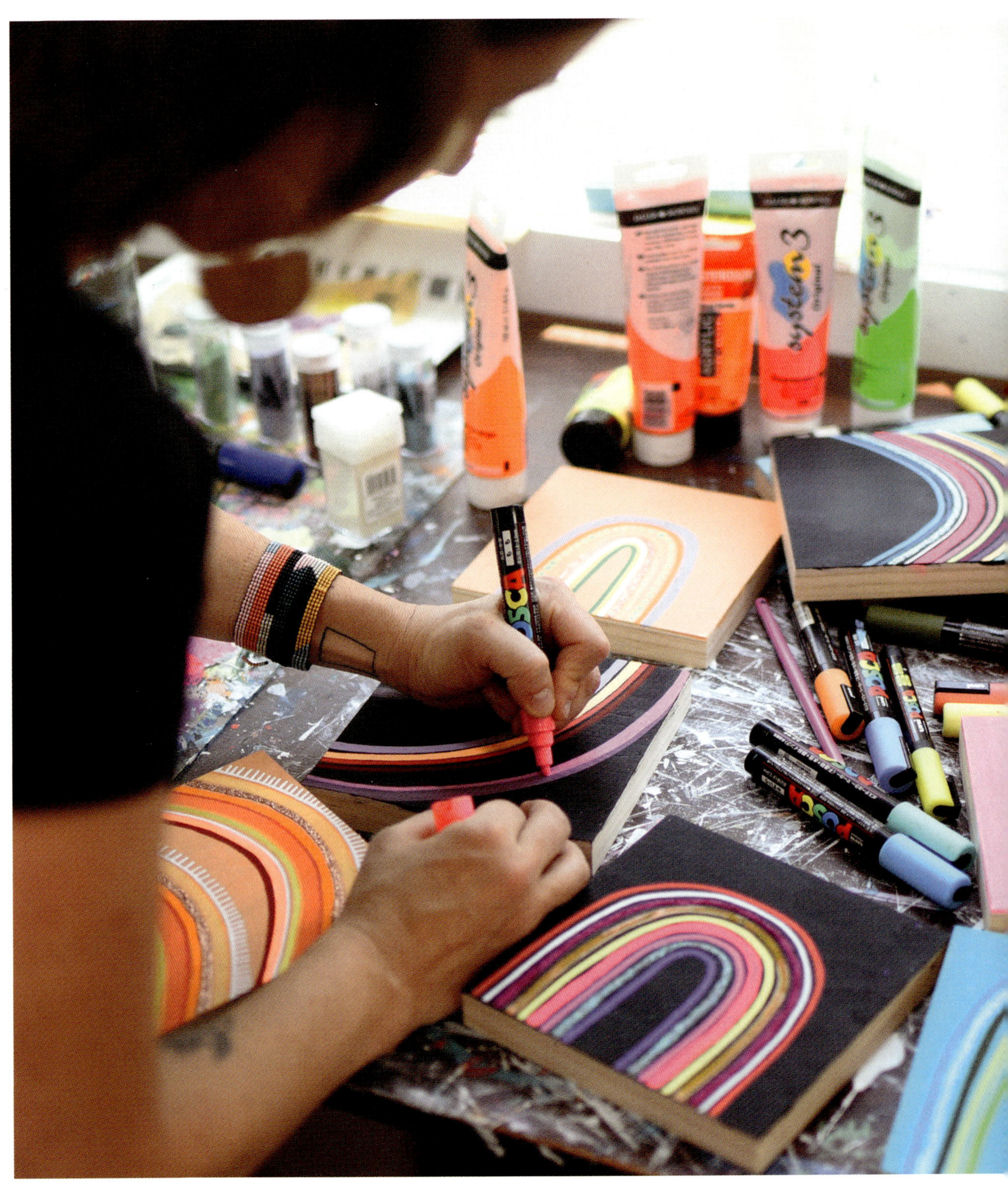

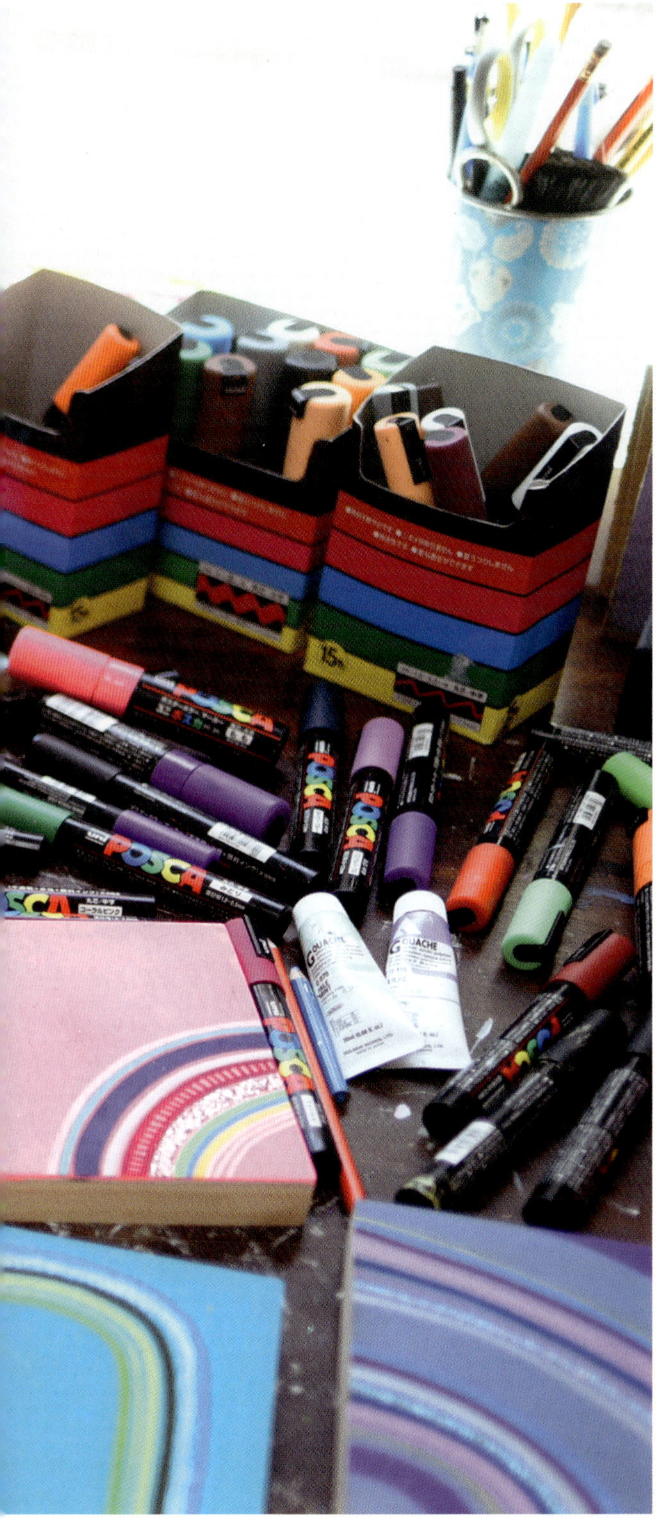

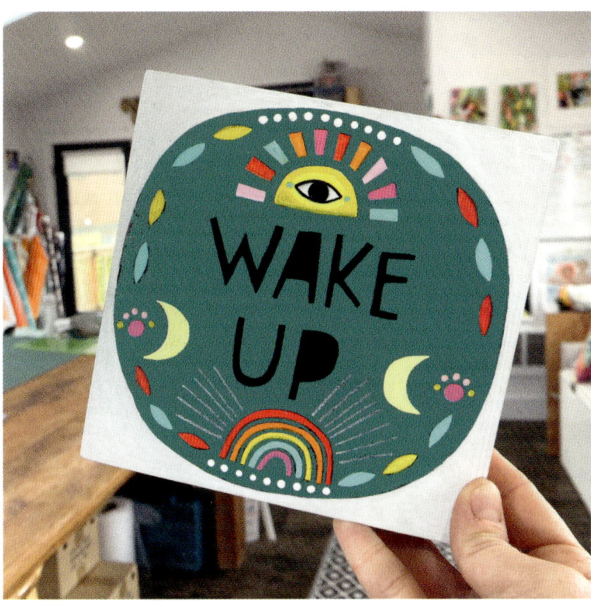

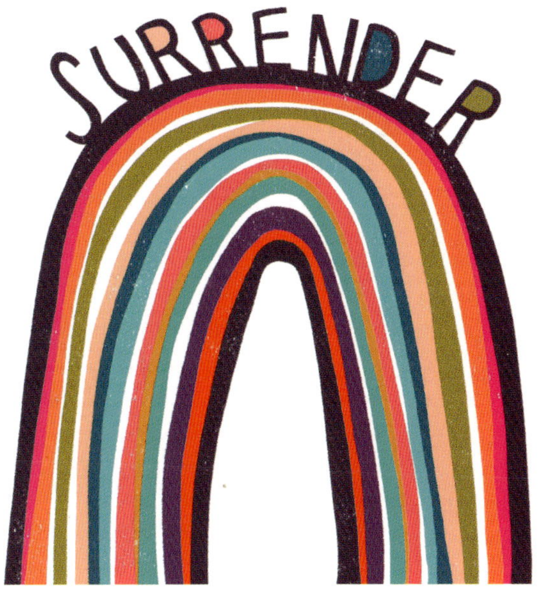
WAKE
UP

SURRENDER

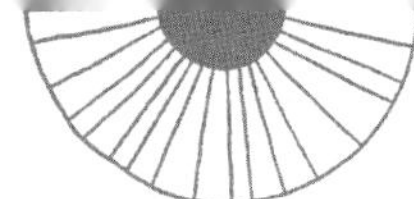

THERE ARE NO RULES

I'VE SAID IT countless times throughout this book so far, and I don't want to sound like a broken record, but I'll say it again: This process has absolutely no rules! There's no right or wrong way to listen to your intuition, to make art to soothe your own soul, or to using creativity as a tool for wonderful self-care. Or perhaps a better way to say it is that there are a lot of right ways. Infinite right ways!

You have an opportunity in this process to give yourself radical permission to do things your own way, according to you and no one else. This might feel scary, it might feel liberating, or it might feel like a mix of both. Think about this: No one else in the entire universe sees the world through your eyes. No one else is experiencing life the way that you are. It blows my mind a little bit when I can really sit with this idea. Why do we ever let ourselves believe that other people know better for us than we do, when no one in the world is inside each of us but our own selves?! It's absurd . . . and it's so common! And of course, there are so many reasons. We all have different reasons for and varying degrees of learning not to trust ourselves and ignoring our intuition.

When you're meandering on an unknown path, creating your own personal artmaking process, following what feels good is an excellent north star. Following what feels good will move you forward in your own unique way, and you'll arrive at your own unique destination, making art in a way that's just for you. Your process and your art will be uniquely your own.

When I say there are no rules, I really mean there are no rules. You don't have to follow anyone else's rules, *and* you don't even have to follow your own. If you do something one day that feels good, that doesn't mean you're stuck doing things that same way forever. You're free to change your mind whenever you darn well please! You're free to make mistakes, mix it up, and start over as many times as you want to.

Your unique process can be as systematic or as free-flowing as you want, or anywhere in between. Perhaps you'll find you have a little ritual that helps you settle in and focus—drinking a cup of tea, saying a quiet little prayer to yourself, doing some jumping jacks . . . anything! Maybe you'll find you like to have your supplies set up in a certain way that makes you feel ready to create. Maybe you'll have a certain series of steps that feel good to go through each time you sit down to create. Perhaps the opposite will be true and simply showing up as you are and doing things in whatever way feels right in the moment is what's going to work best for you. I have no idea what the right way will be for you! But following what feels good is the key. And then whenever something starts to not feel good anymore, change it. Make it all up as you go along! No one is holding you back in this process except you. Read that again: No one is holding you back except YOU!

The wild reality is that all you really need to do is get out of your own way and everything will flow naturally. We get in our own way with all our stories and judgments and fears, and all those thoughts do is muddy up the clear channel that allows you to hear your inner voice. Quieting

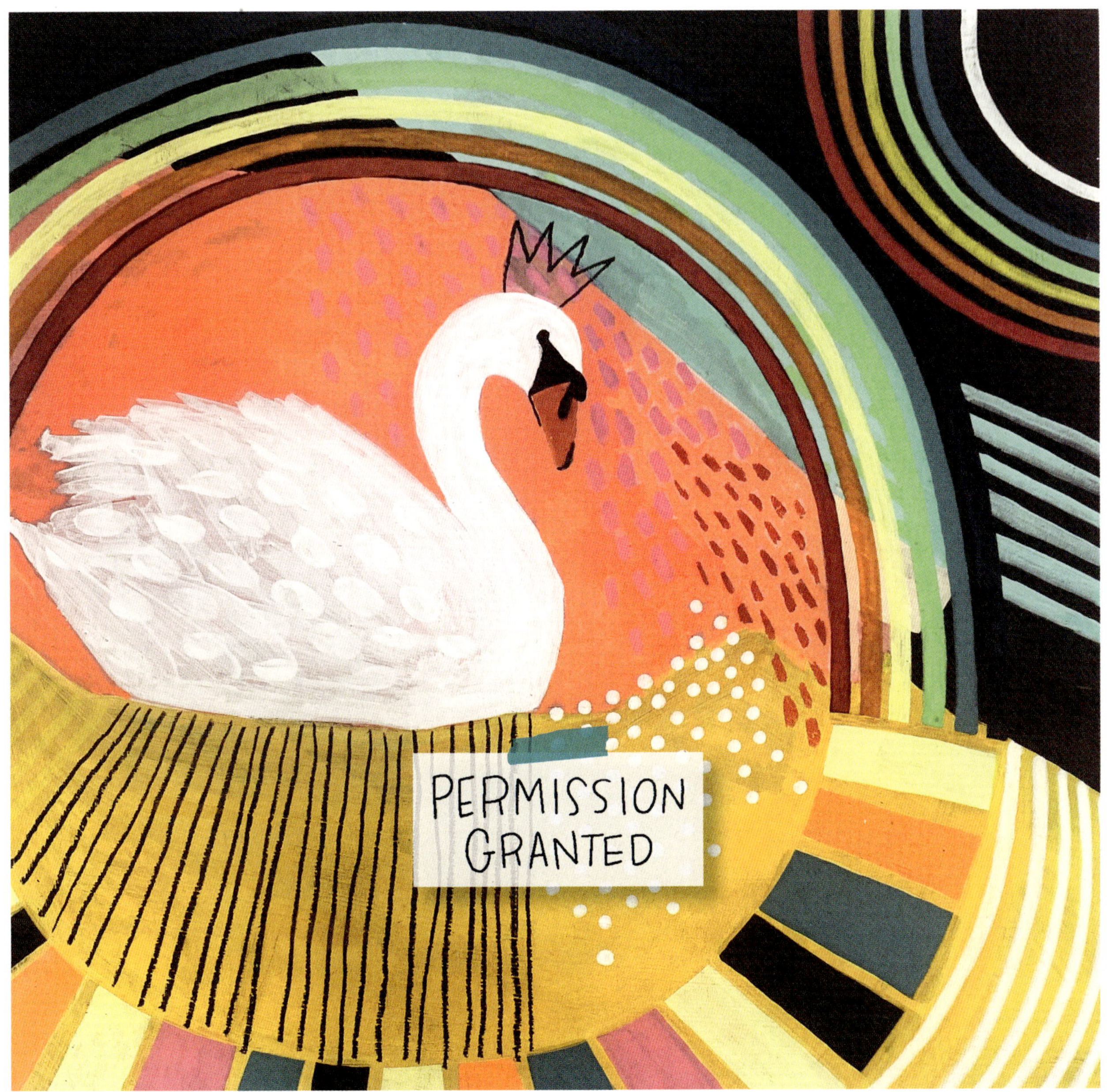

those noisy thoughts and creating calm space inside yourself will allow you to easily connect with what feels good in order to create an artmaking practice that fills you up and helps you take good care of yourself. The wisdom to do things exactly as you're meant to is already inside you; you already have all the answers as well as the map. All you have to do is get quiet, listen, and follow the guidance from deep within yourself.

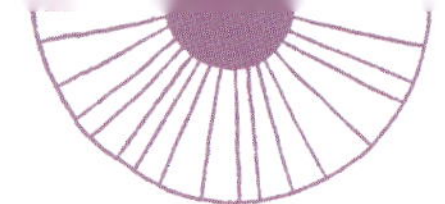

SHOWING UP

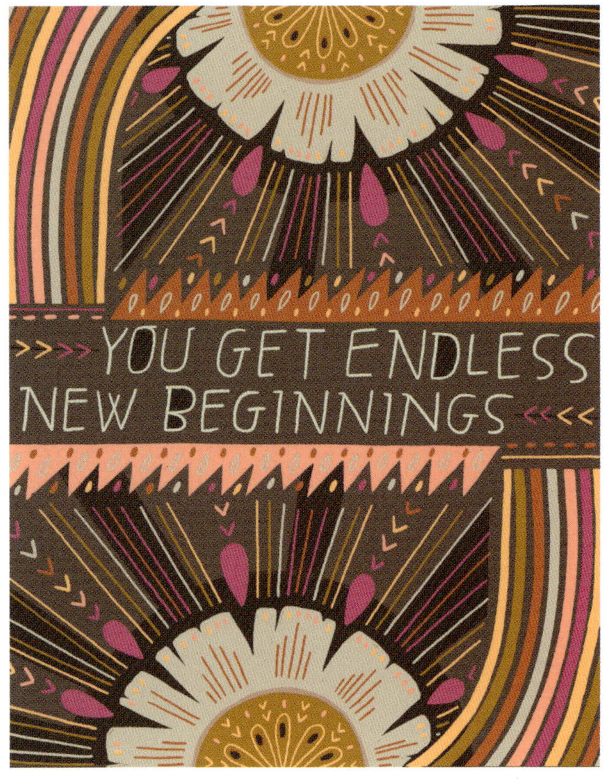

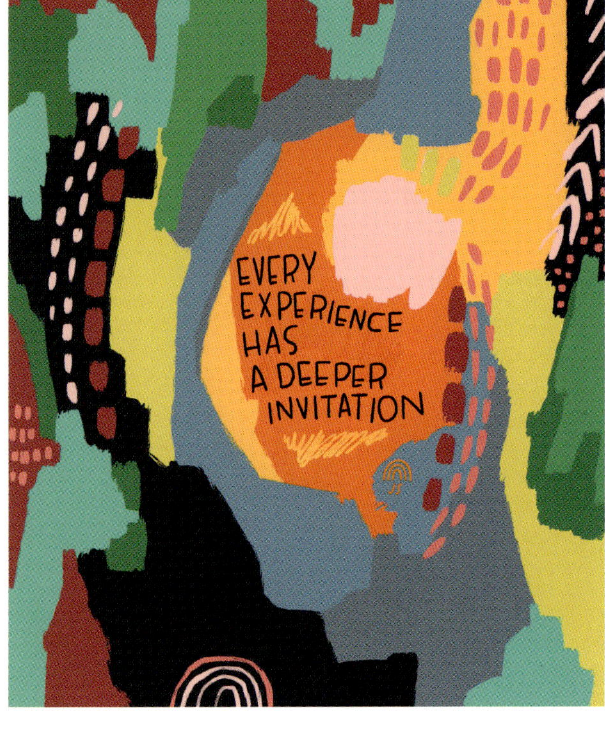

LIFE IS ALWAYS trying to wake you up in order to help you grow.

Every moment is asking you to step into your wisdom . . . the wisdom that already exists inside you. That invitation inward is always there, and you have endless opportunities to say yes to it.

Sometimes you're not going to want to show up and make time and space for your artmaking practice. And in those moments you'll have a choice. Will you keep your word to yourself, or won't you? Will you grow, or will you stay the same? Will you explore your inner world, or will you tune it out? (This is totally normal, by the way!)

There are no right answers here; some days you'll choose to show up, and other times you won't. And that's all perfectly okay and normal! Please don't expect rigid perfection from yourself. You're a human, not a robot! Gentle inquiry and loving care are what we're after here. When you feel judgmental toward yourself, turn that around and get curious. What's going on inside of you, and why?

Showing up for yourself means checking in with what's true for you in the moment. If you're paying close attention, you'll discover that every day and every moment are different. Some days you might be exhausted but making art will be exactly the thing that feels good at the end of a long day. Other days you might be exhausted and going to bed early or taking a long hot bath might be the best choice for you. Some days tuning in and making art will relieve a bit of anxiety bubbling inside you; other days a hike or a run might be what you need to get that anxious energy out. Some days going out and gathering some visual inspiration will be what you need; other days, motifs, images, and words might fly out of your imagination. It's exciting to show up and see what you're working with each day! Every day is brand new.

I'm a big fan of giving yourself some leeway and some wiggle room when it comes to your artmaking practice. Simply acknowledging the fact that you know you're not going to want to show up every day will take some of the pressure off. When those days come around, you can ask yourself things like:

- Is this really one of those days where I just don't have it in me to show up?

- Is fear, laziness, or self-sabotage getting in my way?

- How will I feel if I don't show up and keep my word to myself today?

- How will I feel if I do keep my word to myself today?

- How can I be gentle with myself right now?

- What does my inner voice have to say right now?

Getting to the root of why you're resisting artmaking can be very useful. Some days the right choice might legitimately be to skip it. But my hunch is that many days your inner voice will tell you the best move is to show up on the page or at the canvas even if you don't want to.

Keeping your word to yourself teaches you that you can trust yourself. It teaches you to know that when you say you'll do something, you know you'll do it. Keeping your word to yourself in your artmaking practice will help you keep your word to yourself in other areas of your life as well, in both your inner and your outer worlds. Showing up to the page helps you show up to your life. Showing up to your life helps you show up to the page. It's all intertwined.

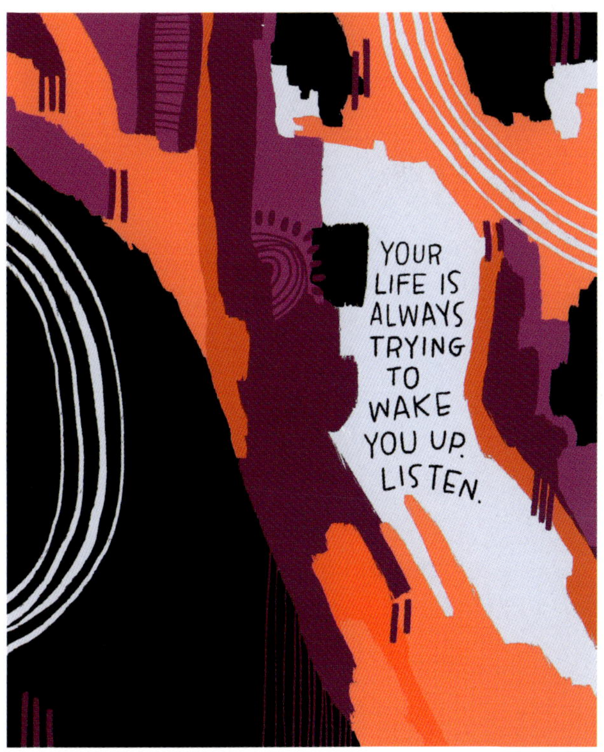

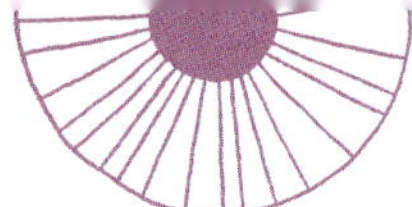

FOCUS ON THE PROCESS

I WANT TO reiterate here that while there's obviously an important visual component to this artmaking process, the most important thing to focus on is your internal experience. Expanding your ability to tune in, cultivating a relationship with your inner self, and learning to navigate your inner world are at the heart of this way of making art. The final product and how your image turns out is honestly not that important at all. While it's a wonderful bonus to create something you love, the artwork that you feel ho-hum or even extremely negative about might hold the most powerful and transformative gifts for you.

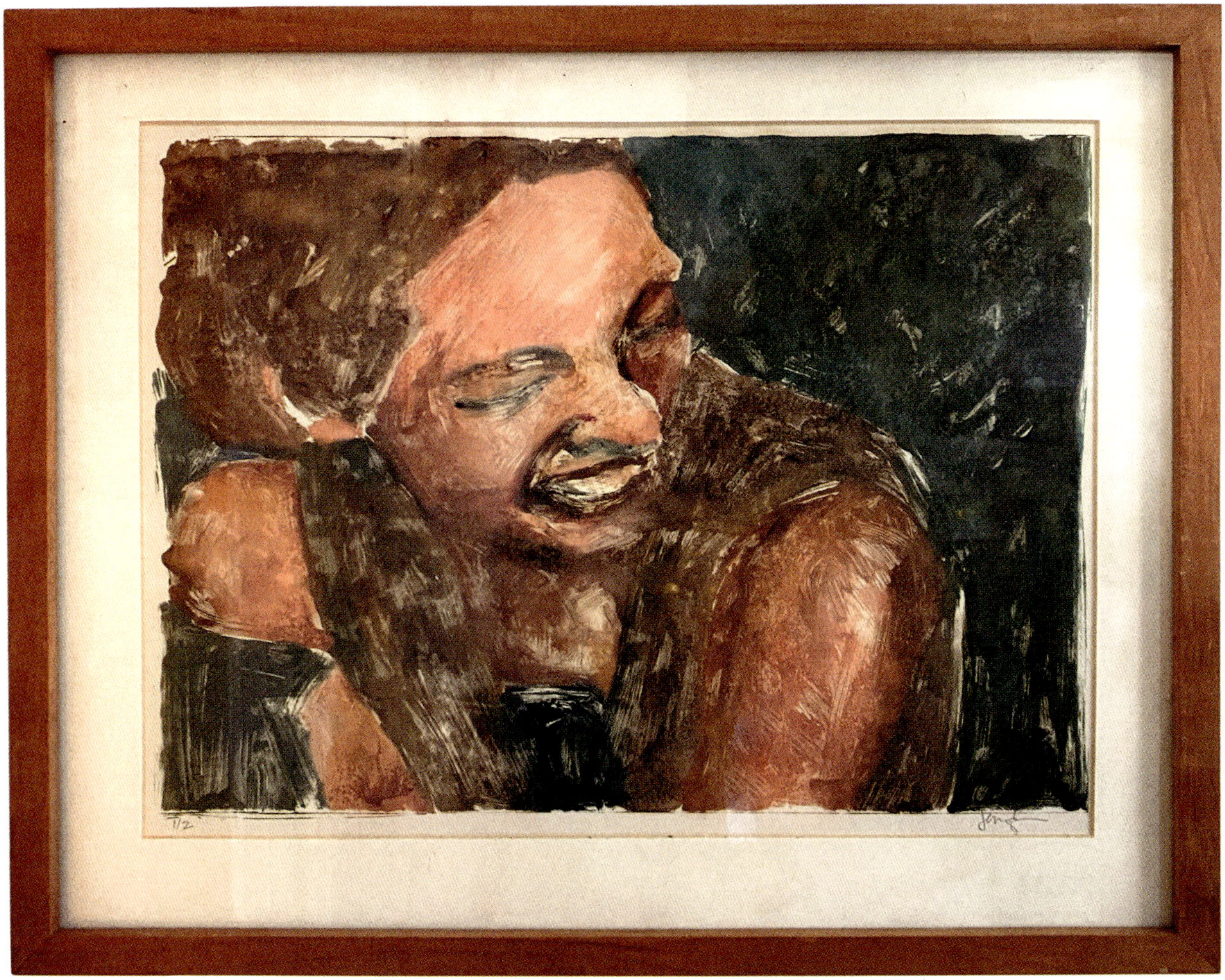

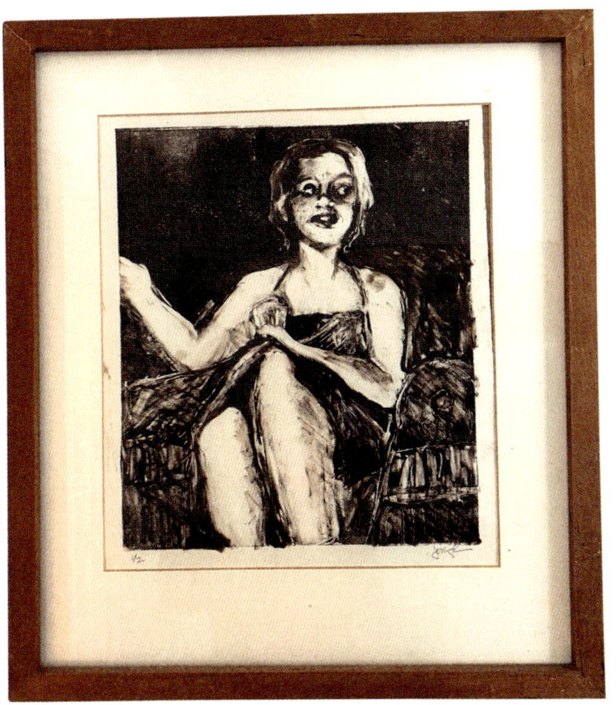 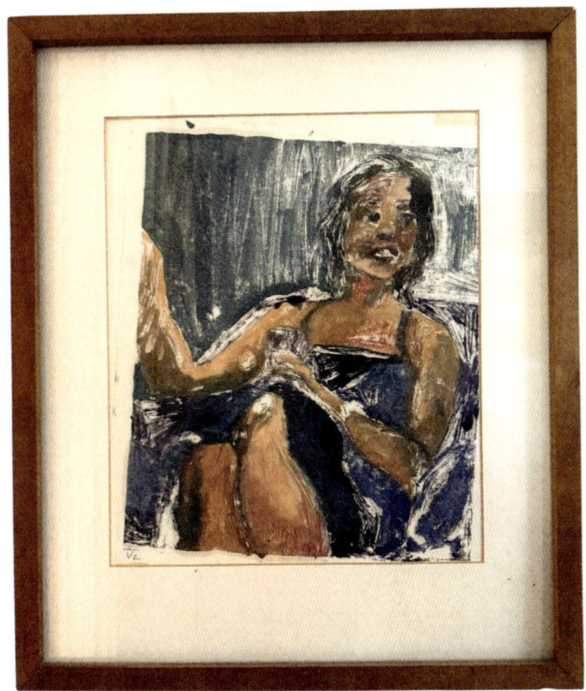

In a way, once you have a message that you're ready to translate into an image, the artmaking process is similar to that of freewriting. Freewriting, if you're unfamiliar, is when you sit down to write without thinking about what you're actually writing and instead simply keep your pen moving without stopping, writing whatever comes to mind. You don't edit or judge along the way; you just let your subconscious take over and get your thinking mind out of the way.

If your judging and thinking mind tends to get in your way as you're making art, try practicing this technique: As you create, just keep your hand moving—drawing, painting, collaging, or whatever. Don't try to guide your image in any direction at all; just make the next move that feels right. Intuitively choose the next color. Whatever comes to mind first is the right choice. Let the process unfold. Let it guide you instead of you trying to guide it. Loosen up. Let go of control. Pay attention to what's going on inside of you rather than what's happening on the page or on the canvas. Think of it all as a big experiment. Whatever happens externally doesn't matter. What matters is following your inner guidance.

Allow room for accidents as well. Remember, imperfections show you that you're human. They're a wonderful mark for yourself of where you've been and where you're going.

Earlier in the book I mentioned when my favorite painting professor in college taught me not to "get precious" with my work during a time when I was ruining every single painting I touched, overworking them and trying to make them perfect. He challenged me to try a technique that was brand new to me, called monoprinting. The monoprinting process involves painting on a plate of some kind with paint of some kind and then printing it onto paper. The version of this process that he taught me involved a plexiglass plate, oil paint thinned with linseed oil, inexpensive sketch paper, and a brayer to transfer the image from the plate to the paper. He encouraged me to paint quickly, not to get precious like I was used to, and not to overthink any of the paint strokes I was putting down on the plate. The reason was that in the last step—printing onto the paper—all of the soupy paint got squished and smeared around on the paper in weird and wonderful ways that I

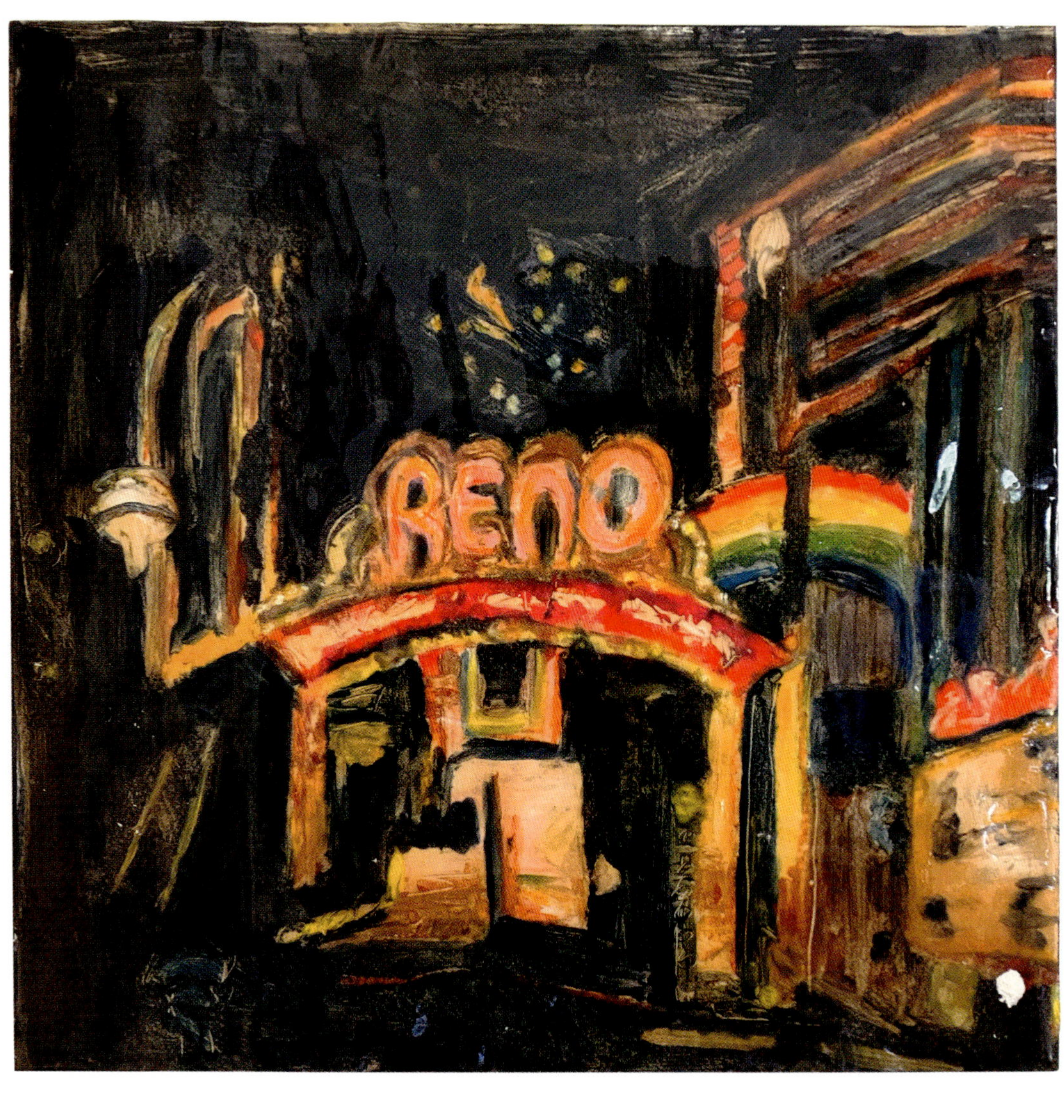

never would have been able to create on purpose. I had to get out of my own way and leave room for happy accidents and for some magic. I fell instantly in love with this process. It cured my tendency to get precious and ruin paintings, and the lessons I learned then are still impacting the way I make art to this day.

I don't make monoprints anymore, but even using different materials now I tend to work quickly, keep my hand moving, focus inward instead of judging what's happening on the surface, and let my intuition guide every move I make along the way. It's not usually a clear, linear process, but it always leads to interesting results!

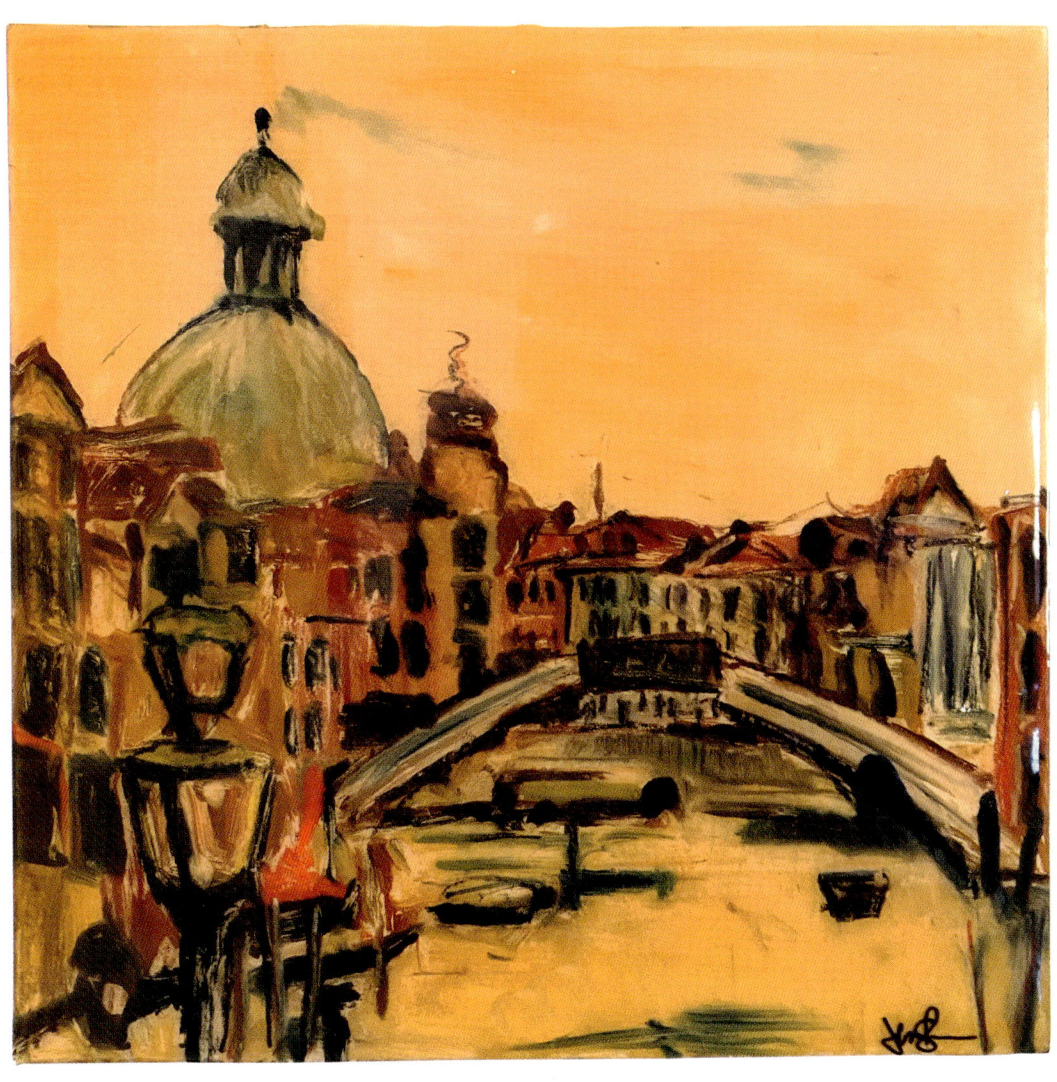

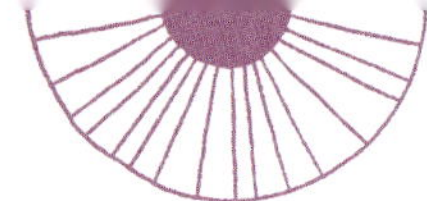

THE IMPORTANCE OF PRACTICE

IN HIS BOOK *Outliers*, Malcolm Gladwell famously shares a theory that it takes 10,000 hours to become masterful at something. Now, don't get me wrong—I'm definitely not suggesting that it will take you 10,000 hours to cultivate a strong relationship with your inner voice and to express it visually! But as with anything new and worthwhile, this is a process where the more time, effort, and practice you put into it, the more you'll get out of it.

On the one hand, it seems like it should perhaps be easy to listen inside yourself and hear the truth. I mean, you've been living inside your body and with your same mind since the moment you were born! You know yourself well. But on the other hand, the human mind is complex and vast, and all sorts of beliefs and thoughts and fears get piled on top of what's true over the course of a life, and most of us aren't taught to listen to our inner guidance above all else as the ultimate truth for ourselves. We learn that others know better, that we're not good enough, that we aren't safe, that we're bad or wrong or unlovable, and countless other false things that cause messages to get easily distorted, confused, and ignored.

Depending on what your life is like, carving out regular time to practice these techniques might be challenging. How can you make a commitment to yourself and make sure you keep it? It might be helpful to make a plan. For me, starting a 100-day project and then telling my public audience on social media that I was going to do it helped me stay accountable. Maybe this same kind of thing will work for you. Perhaps a friend or spouse or family member could help you stay on track so you keep your word to yourself. Or perhaps you're the kind of person who just says you're going to do something and then does it.

However you make it happen, practice, practice, practice! This might mean getting up earlier in the morning. Or staying up a little later at night. Or skipping your evening TV time. Or limiting the amount of time you spend scrolling on the internet. Or letting your kids watch a show while you create. There are lots of creative ways to carve out some time for yourself during your busy life. It's just a matter of making it a priority and then sticking to it.

However, this is not meant to have any pressure attached to it at all. Give yourself some space, and some grace. There's no need to rush and figure it all out as fast as you can! When I set out to do my 100-day projects, in the beginning I always tell myself that I intend to do it every day, but realistically it'll probably end up being more like five or so days a week, and I let that be okay. I give myself some space in order to take the pressure off and to make sure I don't get too rigid or judgmental with myself.

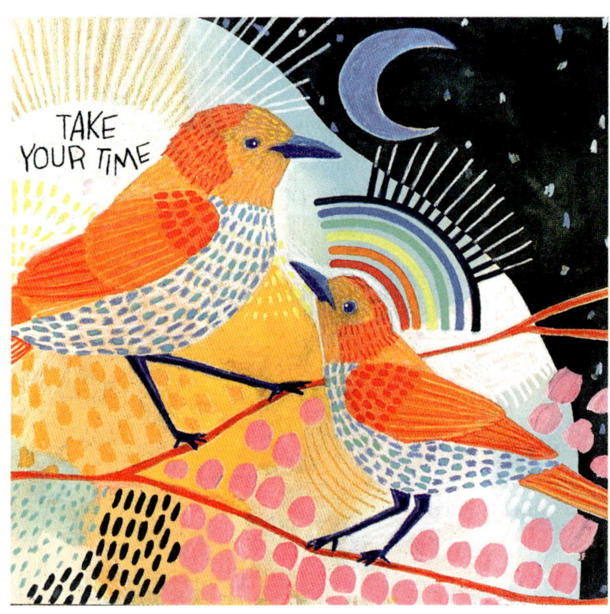

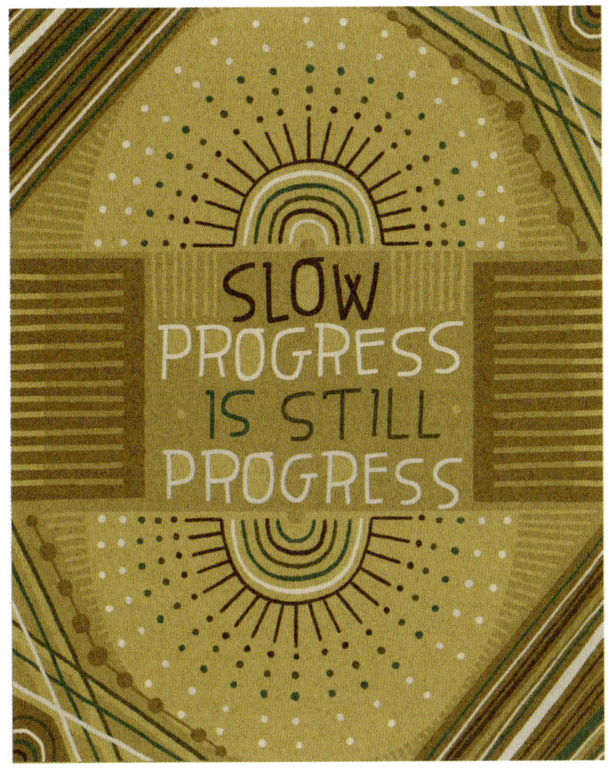

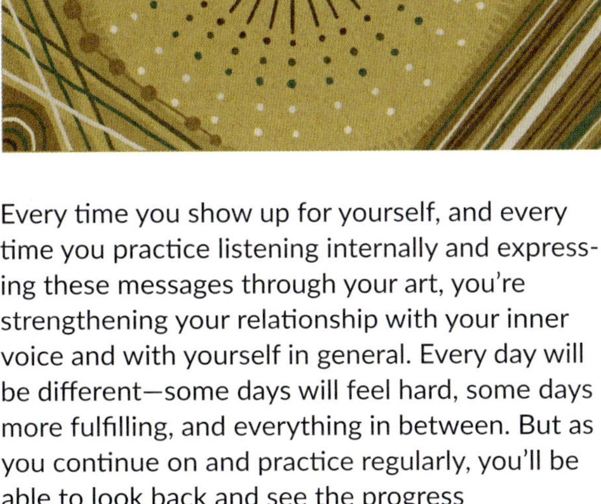

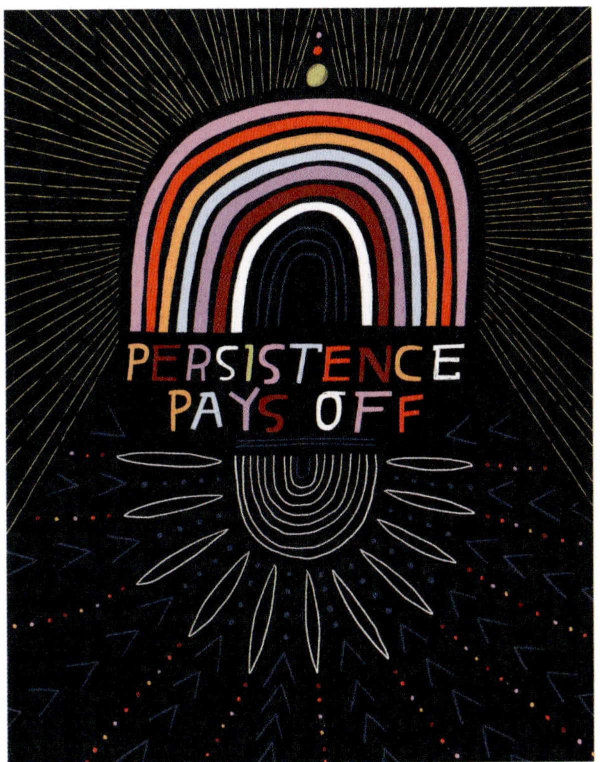

Every time you show up for yourself, and every time you practice listening internally and expressing these messages through your art, you're strengthening your relationship with your inner voice and with yourself in general. Every day will be different—some days will feel hard, some days more fulfilling, and everything in between. But as you continue on and practice regularly, you'll be able to look back and see the progress you've made:

- Your skills will have improved and your art will have changed.
- Your messages might feel deeper, richer, or more potent.
- It might not take as much intentional concentration to hear your inner voice.
- Your fear voice might not feel quite as powerful.
- You might have a little less resistance to the unknown.
- You might trust yourself more.
- You might not be able to explain it exactly, but you just *feel* better.

You'll still be the same you, of course, but you'll be different, too.

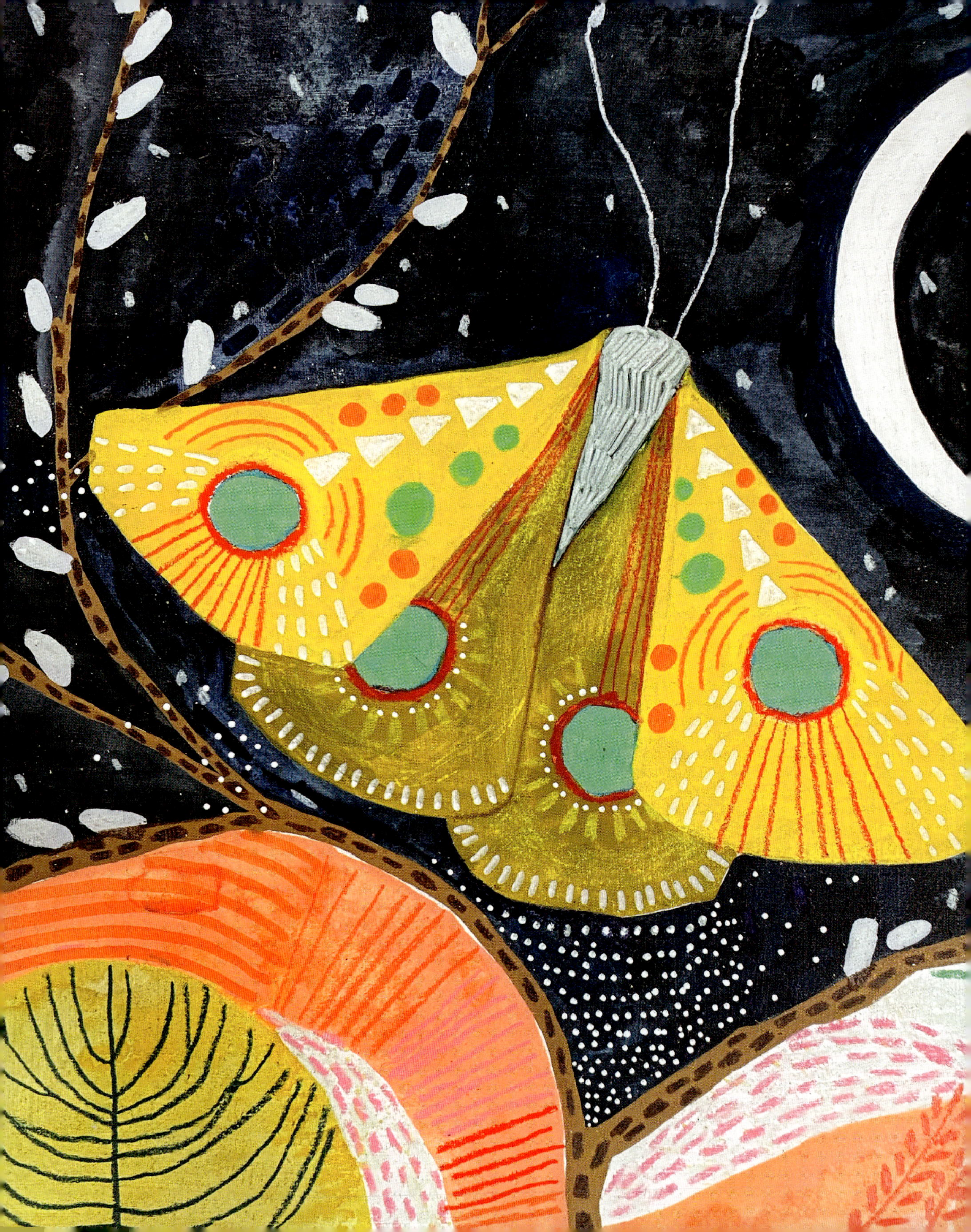

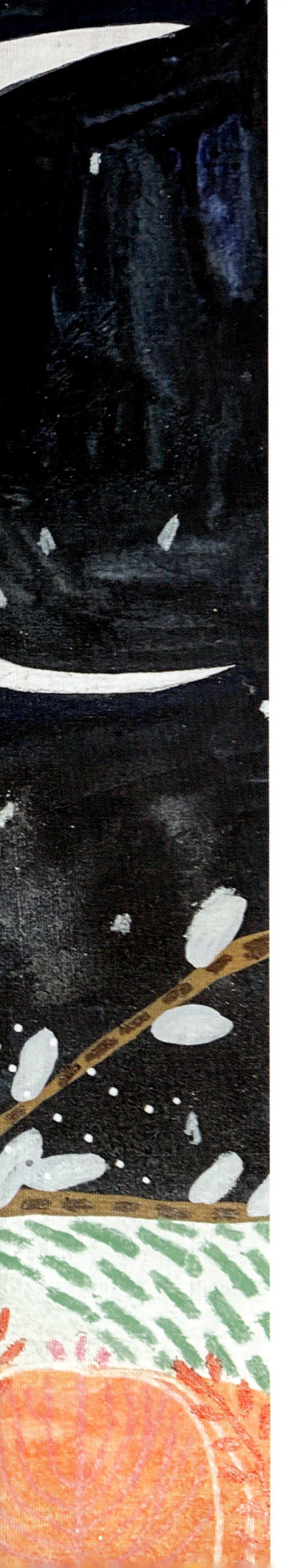

3

INTEGRATING + HONORING

TUNING IN TO YOUR inner world and remembering who you truly are in order to live as authentically as you can is powerful and important work, not only for yourself but also for the world. Each person who begins to awaken to their true inner power changes our planet for the better.

Hearing your intuitive messages and making your art are important steps in this process, but there's more to do once your images are complete in order to receive the full benefit of this practice. In this chapter, you'll discover why it's important to make time to honor, process, and integrate what you created so you can understand its full power and significance in your life.

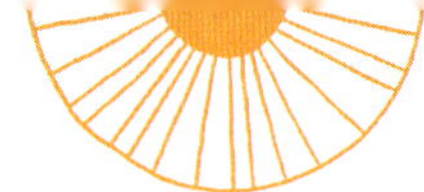

TRACKING YOUR FEELINGS

YOU MIGHT FIND it useful to note how you're feeling as you sit down to make your art and then how you feel afterward. It might help connect some dots or open your awareness to what's going on inside you. I've created a simple chart here that you're welcome to use, or you can create your own. Make it as basic or as beautiful as you'd like!

Learning to identify my feelings and emotions is one of the most useful and profound parts of my healing journey so far. Before Ryan died, I didn't know that conflicting feelings could live inside me at the same time. Feeling one feeling was hard enough! Once I began to pay close attention, I discover that conflicting emotions *almost always* live inside me at the same time! Emotions like:

- Gratitude and grief.
- Fear and excitement.
- Hope and despair.
- Joy and sadness.
- Anger and forgiveness.
- Hopelessness and possibility.
- Love and longing.

I also learned that feelings don't last forever. If I simply allow the physical sensations to move through me without attaching any story to them, the waves come and go and I am always there, centered and stable, when they subside. I've discovered that making art in this intuition-focused way helps me identify and name what I'm feeling and experiencing on the inside and the roots of those feelings. Then I can acknowledge

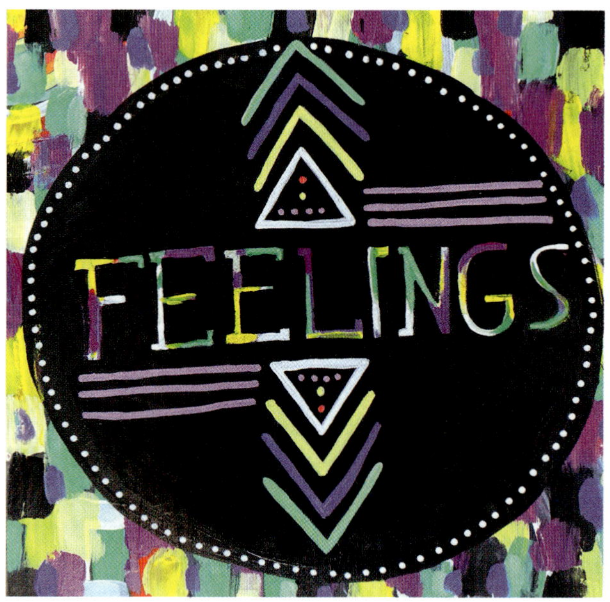

and move through them rather than keeping it all bottled up so no one (not even me!) will know what's going on inside. Bottled-up feelings are bad news.

What you resist persists.

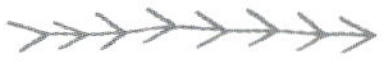

Learning to understand my feelings through the artmaking process has helped me identify what's going on inside in the other parts of my life as well. Tuning in while making art helps me tune in to my life in general. It's all related. Life is art, art is life.

On the following spread you'll find a big list of feelings that I hope will be useful as you're navigating your inner world. It's not an exhaustive list, so use this for inspiration and information and don't be shy about using different words when filling out your feelings tracker chart.

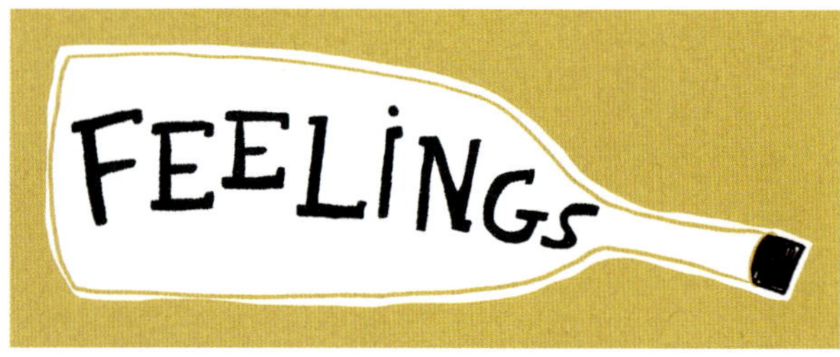

FEELINGS TRACKER

DAY	MESSAGE	HOW I FELT BEFORE	HOW I FELT DURING	HOW I FELT AFTER

LIST OF FEELINGS

FEAR	ANGER	SADNESS
HUMILIATED	HOSTILE	GUILTY
REJECTED	FURIOUS	ABANDONED
SUBMISSIVE	HURT	DESPAIRING
INSECURE	THREATENED	DEPRESSED
ANXIOUS	HATEFUL	LONELY
SCARED	MAD	BORED
RIDICULED	AGGRESSIVE	REMORSEFUL
DISRESPECTED	FRUSTRATED	ASHAMED
ALIENATED	CRITICAL	IGNORED
INADEQUATE	DISTANT	VICTIMIZED
INSIGNIFICANT	JEALOUS	POWERLESS
WORTHLESS	EMBARRASSED	VULNERABLE
INFERIOR	INSECURE	INFERIOR
WORRIED	DEVASTATED	EMPTY
OVERWHELMED	SEETHING	ISOLATED
FRIGHTENED	ENRAGED	APATHETIC
TERRIFIED	BETRAYED	INDIFFERENT
		HOPELESS

SURPRISE

STARTLED
CONFUSED
AMAZED
EXCITED
SHOCKED
DISMAYED
SPEECHLESS
PERPLEXED
ASTONISHED
AWED
EAGER
ENERGETIC
DISILLUSIONED
DISBELIEF

HAPPY

JOYFUL
INTERESTED
LOVING
ACCEPTED
POWERFUL
PEACEFUL
INTIMATE
OPTIMISTIC
LIBERATED
ECSTATIC
AMUSED
INQUISITIVE
IMPORTANT
CONFIDENT
RESPECTED
FULFILLED
COURAGEOUS
PROVOCATIVE
HOPEFUL
SENSITIVE
PLAYFUL
INSPIRED

DISGUST

DISAPPROVING
DISAPPOINTED
AWFUL
JUDGMENTAL
LOATHING
REPUGNANT
REVOLTED
DETESTABLE
AVERSION
HESITANT
AVOIDANT

HAPPY

RELIEVED
SATISFIED
ENTHUSED
CONTENT
OPEN
PROUD

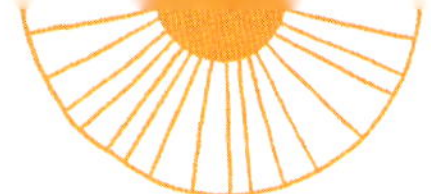

WHAT TO DO WHEN YOUR IMAGE IS COMPLETE

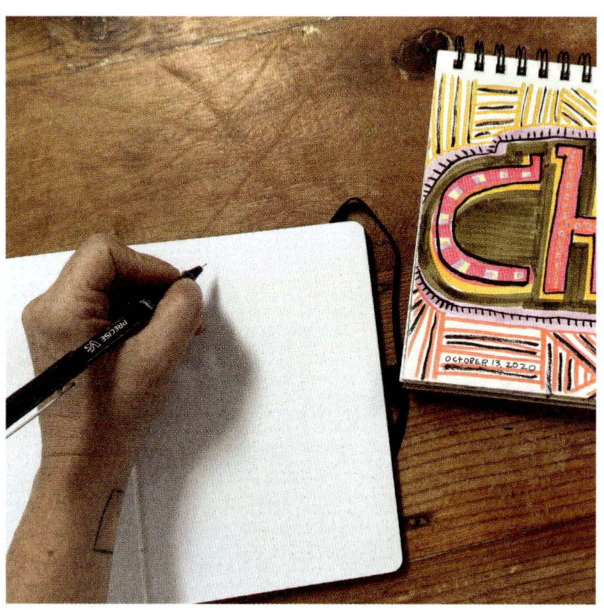

AS I MENTIONED in the beginning of the book, I first started making art in this way by doing a 100-day project called "100 Messages to Myself." I shared each image that I created on Instagram, and in the caption I wrote a bit about what I was experiencing that day, why that particular message came through, and how it was useful for me. I wrote whatever felt right, and I didn't overthink it.

What I discovered was that writing about the image was as important as hearing the message and creating the art. Writing about my relationship with my inner voice and the guidance it was giving me caused me to have new insights and to integrate the lessons and gifts in that message more than I would have without writing about and reflecting on it. This won't be appropriate or necessary with every single message you express visually, but the power of writing as the last step in this intuitive process has surprised me time and time again!

So when your image is complete, I encourage you to take a few minutes to sit and write about what you created and why. What was the message, why did you need to hear it, and what did you learn? What insights did you have? How did taking time to express this sacred message from your inner self make you feel? What did you discover about yourself? What else does your inner voice want you to know in order to fully integrate this message?

How you write about your image is up to you. Perhaps like me you want to share your images on social media. You could write about your image in the caption of your post like I did and share it with the world. Your process absolutely doesn't have to be public, though; remember, this process is ultimately for your own benefit!

You could write about your image in your sketchbook, right next to or on the back of where you created it. You could keep a journal, or you could use a Word or Google document on your computer. You could type on your phone using the Notes app. Maybe writing won't work for you, but speaking it into a voice memo on your phone feels more natural. There's no right or wrong way here! The idea is simply to reflect on what you created and what you learned from it.

The days that you don't like what you created (and believe me, you will have those days!) might be the most important days of all to reflect on your experience. Facing uncomfortable feelings about

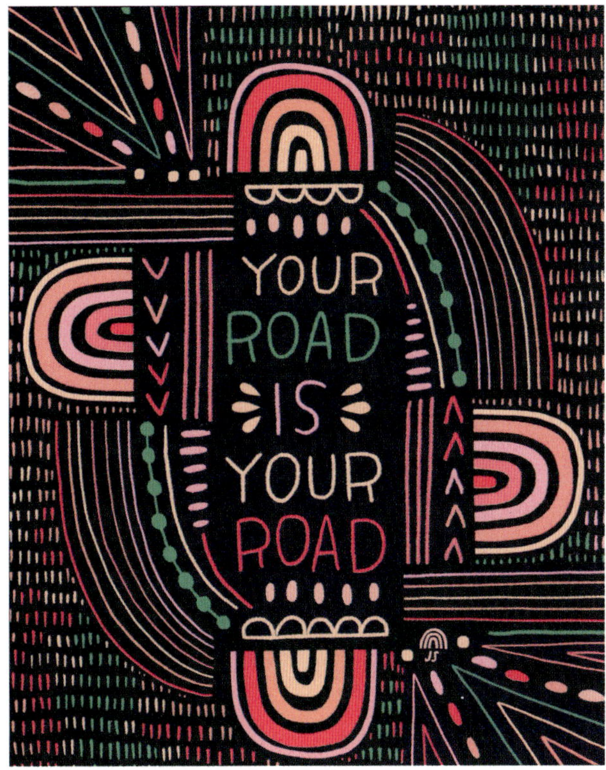

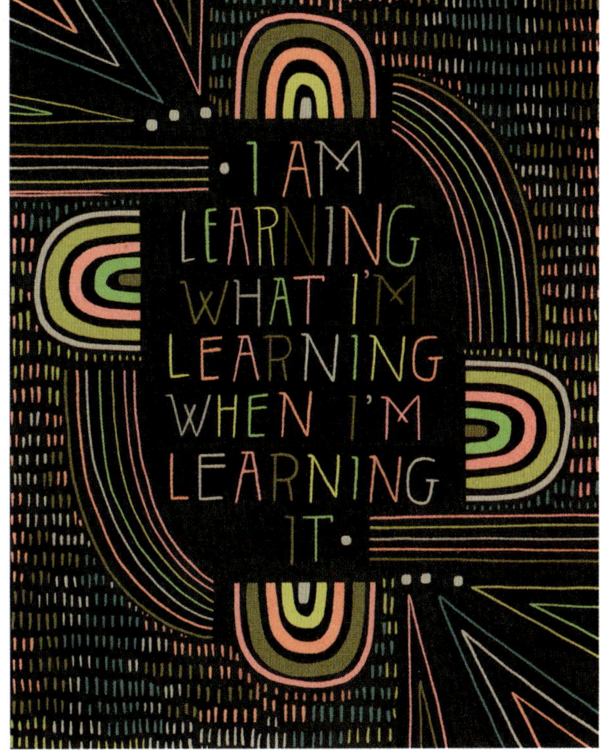

what you create—perhaps judgment, shame, or self-doubt—allows you the opportunity to practice radical acceptance.

To accept what is, without a story attached to it.

To remember that it's all part of the process and doesn't need to be taken so seriously.

To remember that tomorrow is a new day and you'll have a fresh new chance to try again.

To love yourself for not being perfect.

To laugh.

To fully feel what you feel, and then move forward.

To find all the riches and all the gifts in those uncomfortable feelings.

In making time to do this last step in the process, you'll start to feel the positive internal impact of paying attention to and valuing your own internal experience. By giving yourself the time and space to listen inwardly and then lovingly offering yourself exactly what you need, this practice has the potential to be an important way to help maintain your internal equilibrium and check in with yourself whenever you need to. You'll be reminding yourself over and over that you matter, that your experience matters, and this will radiate outward into the rest of your life.

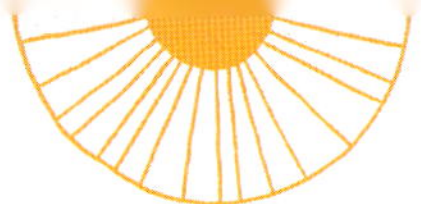

HONORING YOURSELF

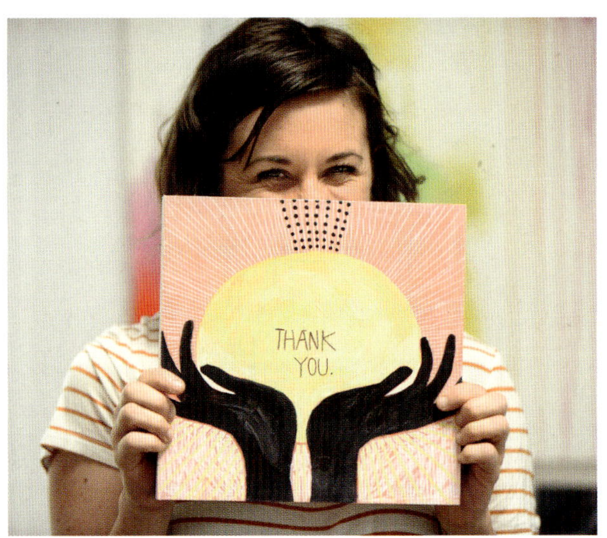

IN MY EXPERIENCE, we're not typically taught to follow our internal guidance or to trust ourselves fully in this modern world. (At least I wasn't!) Instead, throughout our lives, we start to believe that the answers we seek are outside of ourselves, and we pick up all sorts of false beliefs about the ways we're deficient.

Showing up to this way of making art can feel wildly uncomfortable if you're used to ignoring your own feelings, values, and inner knowing. You may be bumping up against years of unhelpful beliefs, stories, and judgments about yourself and the world around you!

But guess what? You're here, and you're doing it. And that is a *big deal*. Not everyone chooses to dive into their inner world to heal, change, and grow. Not everyone chooses to walk the path of the mysterious unknown. Not everyone chooses to live life and make art by their own design. Not everyone chooses to face what's in front of them with honesty and truth.

The fact that you're choosing these things is worth honoring and celebrating. You're not like everyone else. And that is a remarkable thing!

Each time you sit down to practice tuning in to your inner world, learning to listen more deeply to your inner voice, and making art that reflects its wisdom is a significant undertaking. No matter how it turns out. Every time you show up to face something difficult and make something meaning-ful out of it is a huge win. Showing up for yourself is pride-worthy. These things are not always easy! I hope you'll do your best to see that clearly and give yourself a lot of credit. Find gratitude for yourself. Say thank you to your inner voice for leading you back to yourself.

You are a changemaker.

You are a truth seeker.

You are a beacon of light.

You are a courageous soul.

You matter.

Let that sink in.

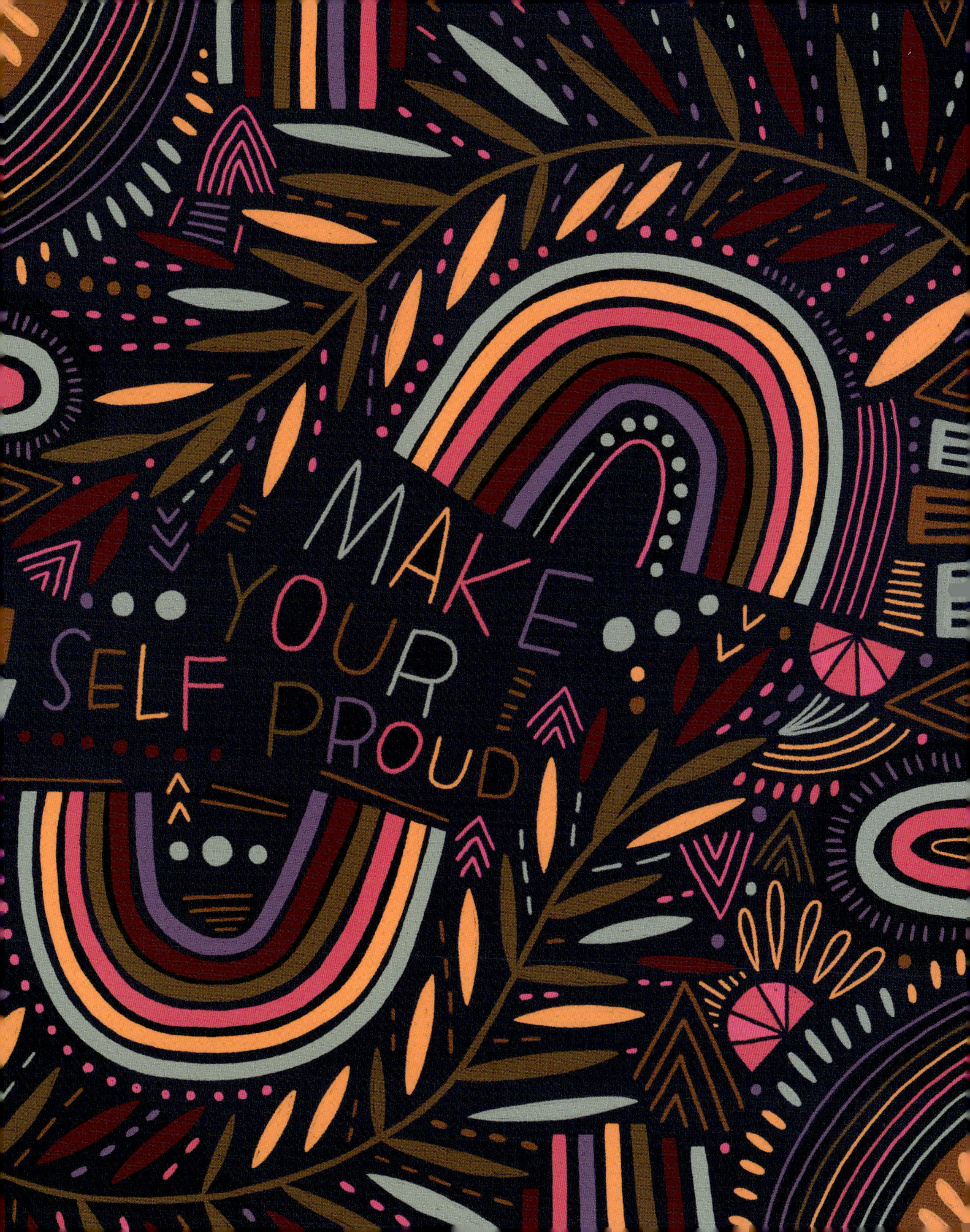

MAKE
YOUR
SELF PROUD

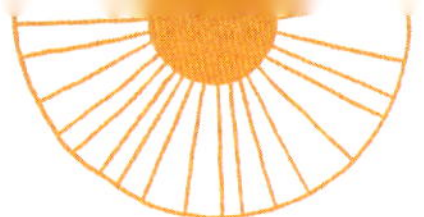

KEEP SHOWING UP

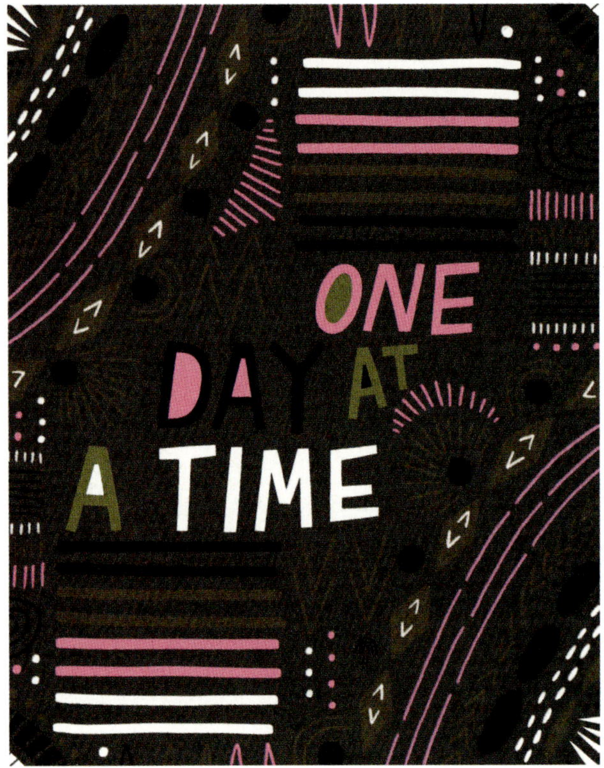

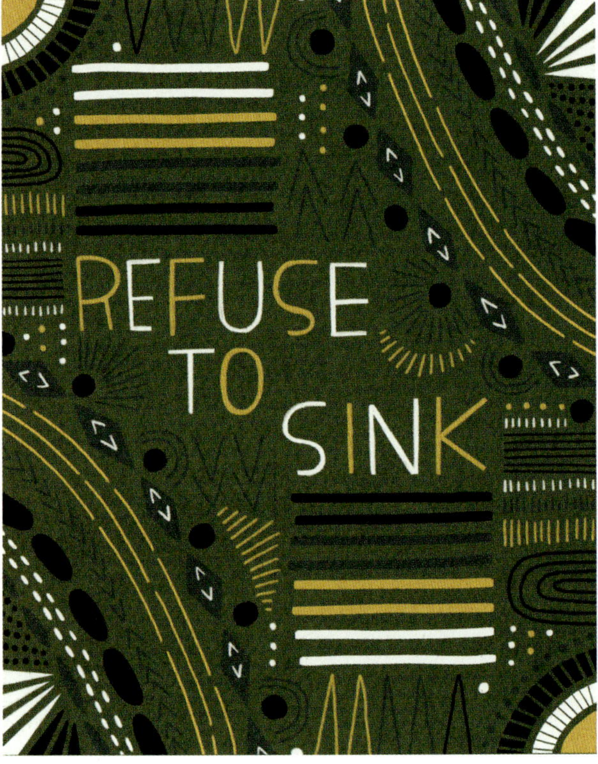

AS YOU CONTINUE to strengthen your relationship with your inner voice, you might notice that as your inner world changes, your outer world also starts to shift. It might be gradual and imperceptible as it happens, but you might look back one day and realize that you're different and that the way you see yourself and the world has changed.

When you keep showing up to make art in this way, you'll notice that it's easier to hear your inner voice in every part of your life and much harder to ignore it. You might start to notice when you're out of alignment with your inner truth and what that feels like. You might get to a point where your inner peace is your most important priority and that following the guidance from your inner self will lead you back to that lovely peace every single time.

Fear might continue to badger you, and your job as you continue along your path will be to acknowledge it, thank it for trying to help, and carry on your merry way with your inner voice in the lead.

As you practice and gain confidence in listening to your inner voice, you might find that you start making new choices.

You might start standing up for yourself in new ways.

You might tune out other people's opinions.

You might like what you create more, or at least appreciate it in a new way.

Your courage might grow.

You might be kinder to yourself and stop giving yourself such a hard time.

You might not care as much about what other people think.

You might change habits.

You might let go of things or people that are no longer serving you.

You might feel better!

Keep your heart open. Show up to your artmaking practice and to your life. Be vulnerable and take chances, even though you might be afraid that you'll make mistakes, embarrass yourself, or feel foolish. Showing up and potentially feeling big things (both the good and the difficult) and diving into life and art is worth all that, I believe.

Some days you won't want to keep showing up, and that's okay, too. Sometimes showing up for yourself looks like resting, and that's wonderful, too. The lovely thing is that you can check in with yourself later and show up over and over again when you're ready. You get endless chances in this practice. Remember, you make the rules.

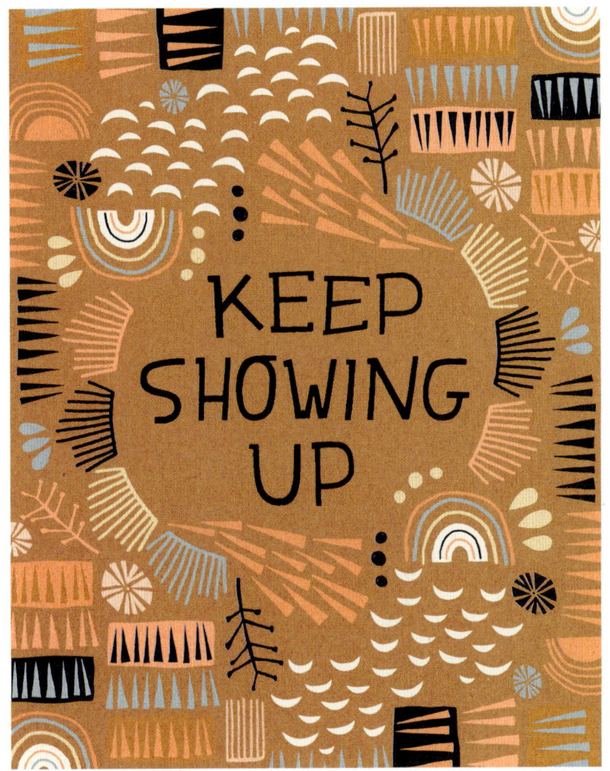

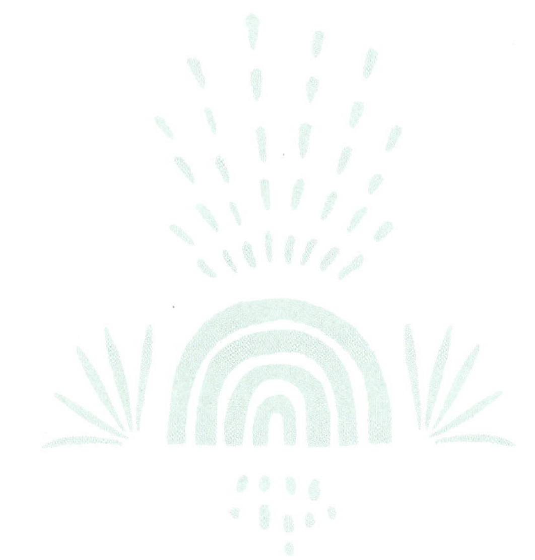

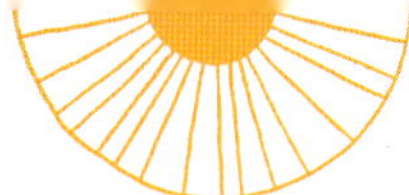

TRUST YOURSELF

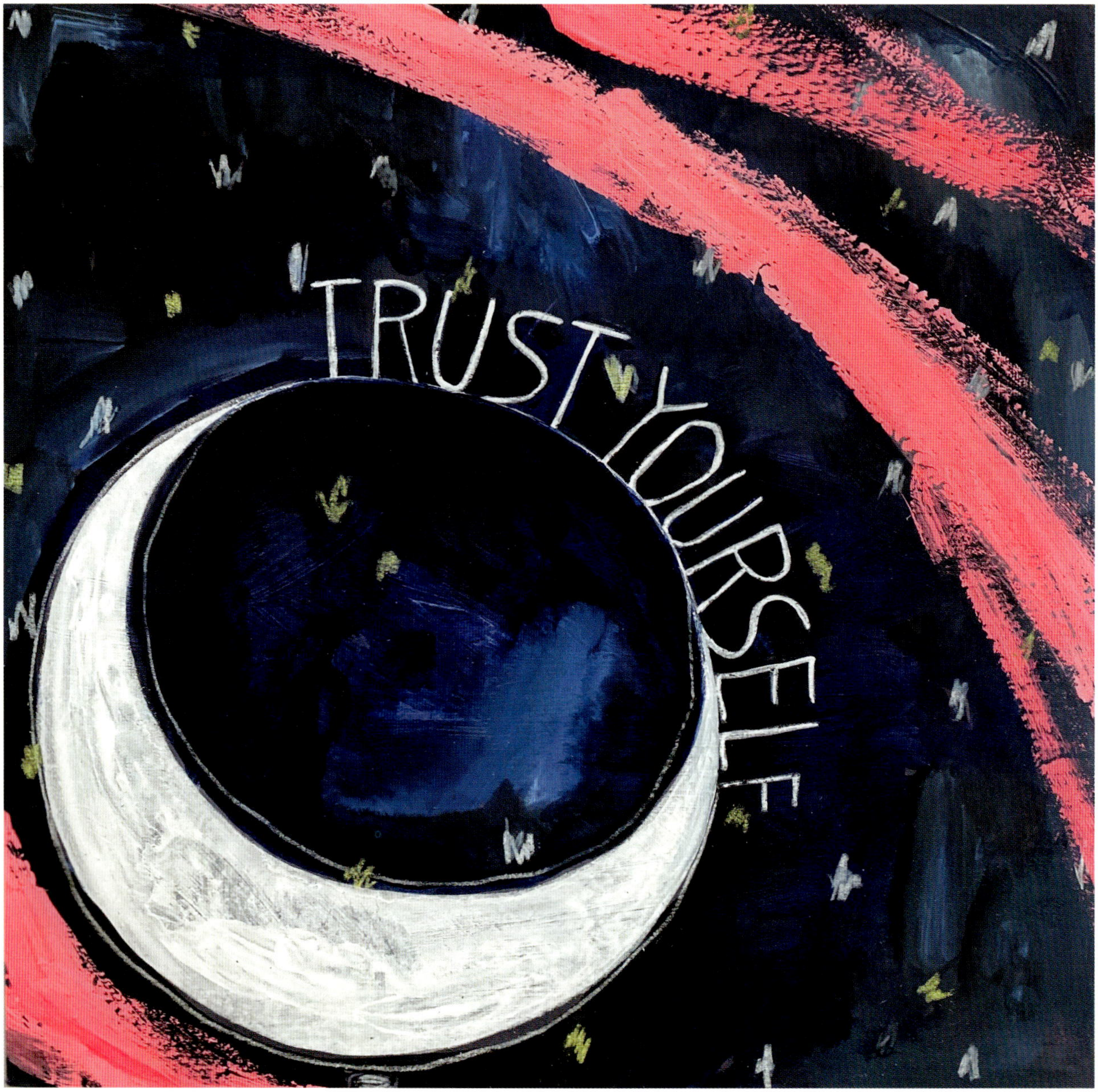

AS A CHILD, I was often told that I was too sensitive. I internalized that and carried that story with me for many, many years, believing I would be too much and not enough all at once, for others, for the world, for myself. Until one day my therapist asked me, "Do *you* think you're too sensitive? Are you too sensitive for yourself?" And the answer surprised me. I'd never considered

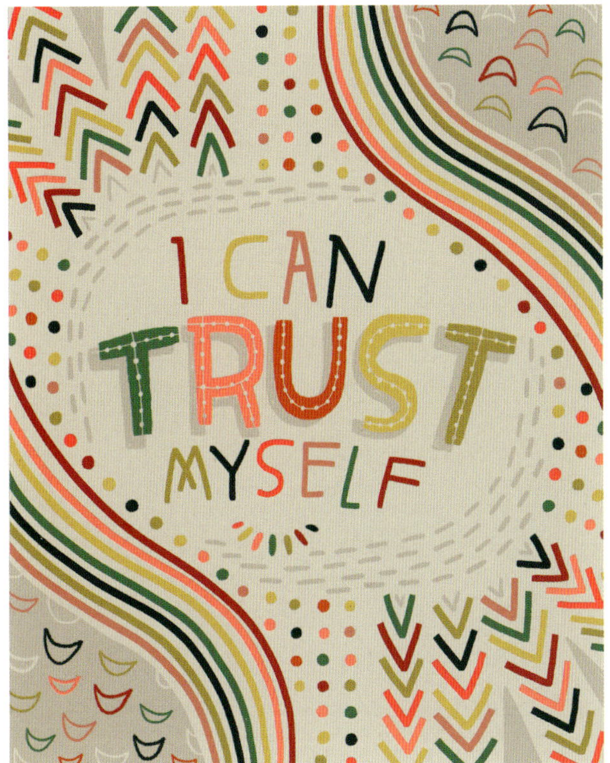

my own feelings on the matter. The answer was: "No. I love how sensitive I am. It's never felt like a problem for myself." And just like that, the story I didn't even realize was a story and was something I just thought was The Truth began to disintegrate and I got to start believing something new about myself. Something that came from deep within myself rather than from someone or something outside of me. Now I try to question as much as I can within myself, trying to discern where stories come from and the feelings contained in them, and then I choose to create new and better stories and beliefs.

What are all the unhelpful things you think about yourself?

What do you believe as The Truth but have never actually questioned where that truth came from?

What's getting in your way, stopping you, and holding you back?

Question everything. Ask your inner voice for the answers to your questions about yourself!

I promise, your truth is in there. And it's the most powerful truth for yourself that there is.

You can always trust what your wise inner self has to tell you. Always. No one else knows better for you than YOU. Get to the root of where your beliefs might have come from and then ask your inner voice what *it* believes. Remember this as you're making your art.

When you start to doubt yourself, or feel a judgmental voice, or wonder what other people will think about what you're creating or the choices you're making, pull all that outward energy back into yourself and direct it inward. Tune back in to yourself and focus on how *you* feel about it all. Nothing matters more than your own experience within yourself. Follow what feels good, what feels right for you, and what lights you up.

Trusting and following your inner guidance will never lead you down the wrong path. It will always lead you toward growth, light, and self-love. Your inner voice always knows the next right move and the next right step for you to take. Even when your mind is afraid, your inner self is solid within you, waiting to hold your hand and lead you forward. Trust it.

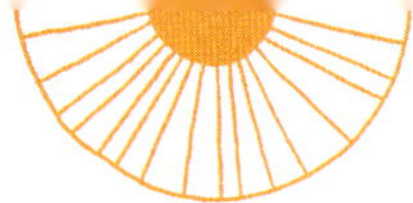

YOU ARE MAGIC

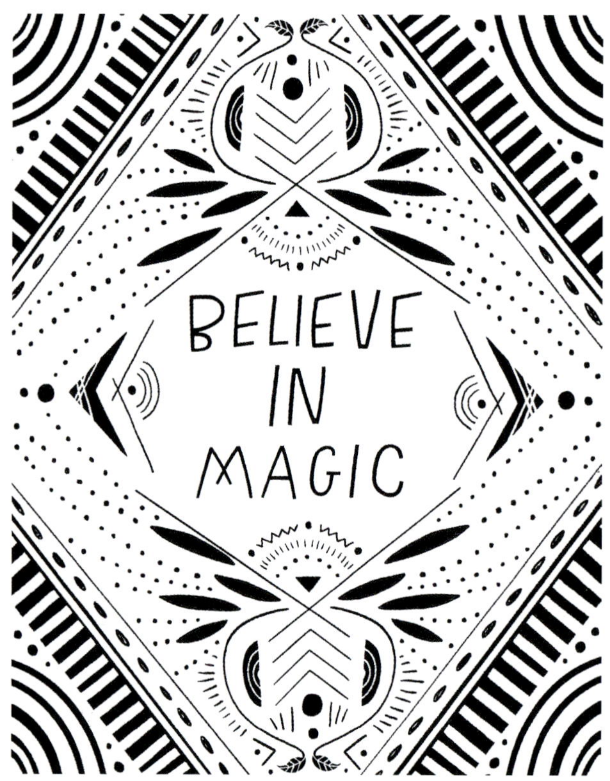

You are born from the unknowable, unnameable mystery.

You are powerful.

You are resilient.

You are capable.

You are creative.

You are made of stars.

You are an ocean, and you are a drop.

You are brightness and darkness and everything in between.

You are infinite possibility.

You are wild and you are free.

You belong here.

The world wouldn't be the same without you.

You are magic, darling.

Magic.

YOU'RE ETERNALLY TAPPED into the mysterious source of it all. Your inner voice is your direct line to it, and it's alive within you every moment of every day. You are an inextricable piece of the unexplainable magic of the universe.

You have the power to shape your thoughts and to move your life in whatever direction you choose, no matter your circumstances. You have the power of creativity in you—of creating something out of nothing—whether you believe you do or not. We all do. We're all part of the creative source; we're each a unique expression of it.

That includes you!

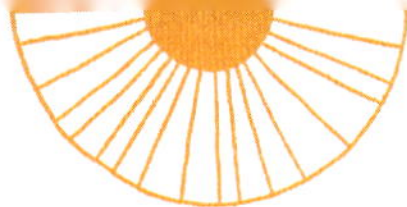

FINAL WORDS

THERE'S NO FINISH line when it comes to growth and expansion.

The good news (and maybe the bad news!) is that you can dive into this practice as deeply and as often as you like, and there'll always be more to learn and discover about yourself and your inner world. Intuitive artmaking is not a straight line, and that's part of the fun and excitement of it.

As someone who's always, relentlessly, looking for the silver linings and the lessons in my life, I've made it a practice to use art as a way to process my experience of being a human and to grow, change, and expand through it all. It's not always easy, but I'll tell you what—it's never boring, and it's totally worth it.

Everything that happens in your life is useful somehow. The hard stuff is fertilizer for your continued growth. The hot pain of life is part of your self-evolution. That's its purpose—to help you expand beyond where you are now and show yourself that you can rise, again, and again, and again. Higher and deeper each time. We all can.

I hope this way of making art will make a difference in your world. As you dive deeper into the wilds of your inner world and continue learning to swim in the glittering, intuitive oceans within you, these are my wishes for you:

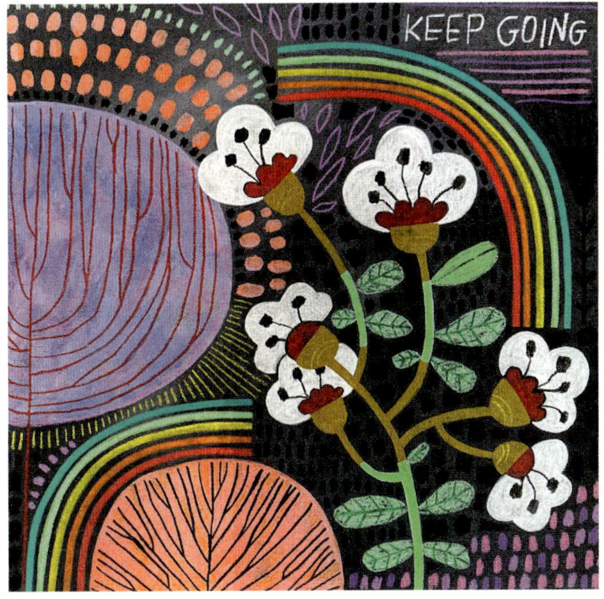

May you find freedom.

May you find peace.

May you be courageous and vulnerable.

May you create a home where you always belong, inside yourself.

May your artmaking be a sacred tool in taking exquisite care of your exquisite self.

May you walk through all the hard things you encounter with grace and truth.

And may you listen, deeply within, always.

xo,
Jessica

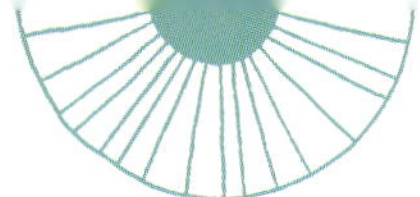

ACKNOWLEDGMENTS

So many people have made an impact on me along my path toward writing and creating this book. So many people have helped, held, hugged, loved, supported, and guided me as I've moved forward. Mom, Coen, Georgia, Jill, Britt, Marc, Bizzy, Taylor, Dani, Barbara, Bob, Tim, Jonathan, Monique, Yali, Donna, Anne-Marie, Charlie, Kari, Joe, Randy, Brad, Bill, Carolyn, Mary, Kelley, Elisabeth, Suzanne, Patricia, Rejina, Bill, Becca, Dan, Graham, Margo, Scootter, Jesse, Ashley, Ian, Atika, Merriah, Jaime, Gwyn, Jennie, Debbie, Susie, Sarah, Robin, Jack, Annie, everyone in my online community, and everyone else who's touched my life in some way: THANK YOU. Thank you! I am so deeply grateful for each of you and all you've contributed to who and how I am today.

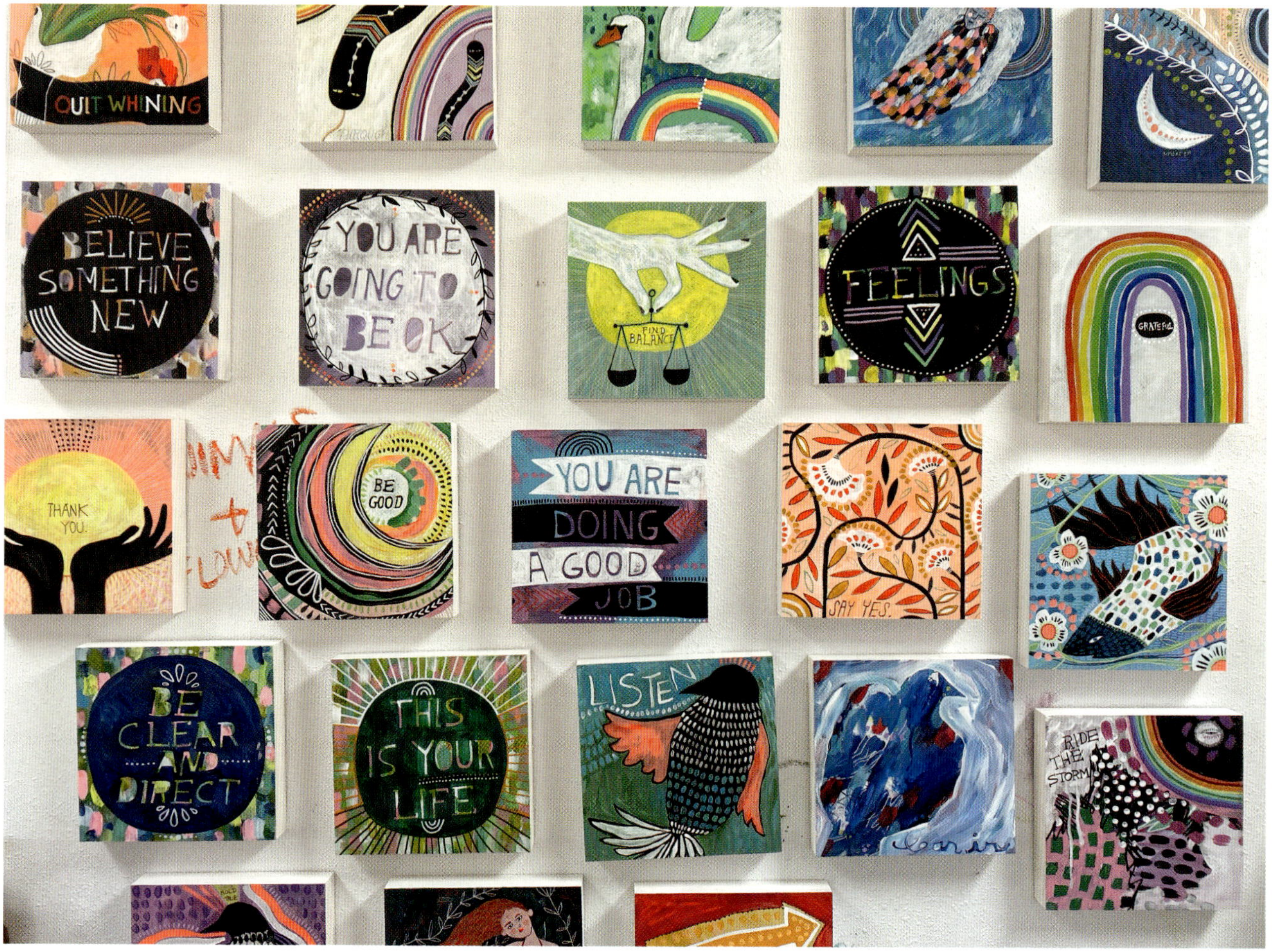

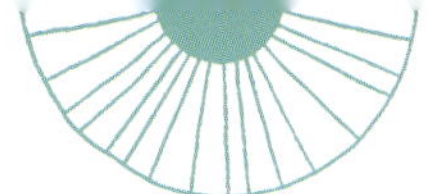

ABOUT THE AUTHOR

As a child, Jessica Swift sported a nearly permanent Crayola marker stain on her left arm, from pinky to elbow. She grew up and, naturally, became an artist. Jessica creates colorful, uplifting artwork and manufactures her own products in her studio in Portland, Oregon. She also collaborates with inspiring companies and publishers to create branded products such as fabric, stationery, puzzles, books, and more. Two rambunctious, creative young children call her mama. Jessica is the author of *The Crafter's Guide to Patterns* (2015) and *Radiant Rainbows: Messages of Hope, Healing, and Comfort* (2023). You can find Jessica on her website at www.jessicaswift.com and follow her on Instagram @jessicaswift

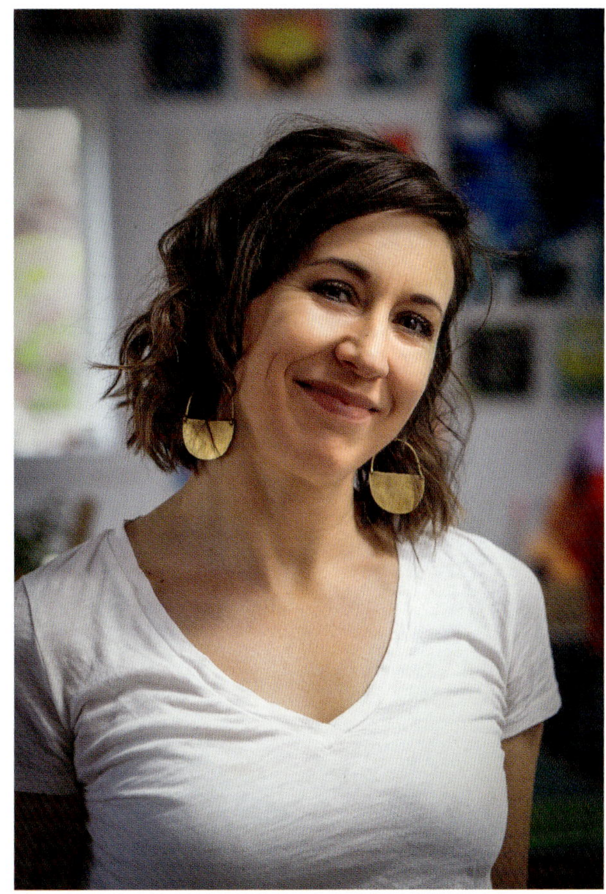

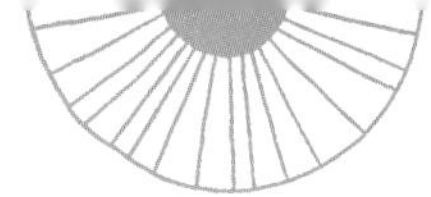

INDEX

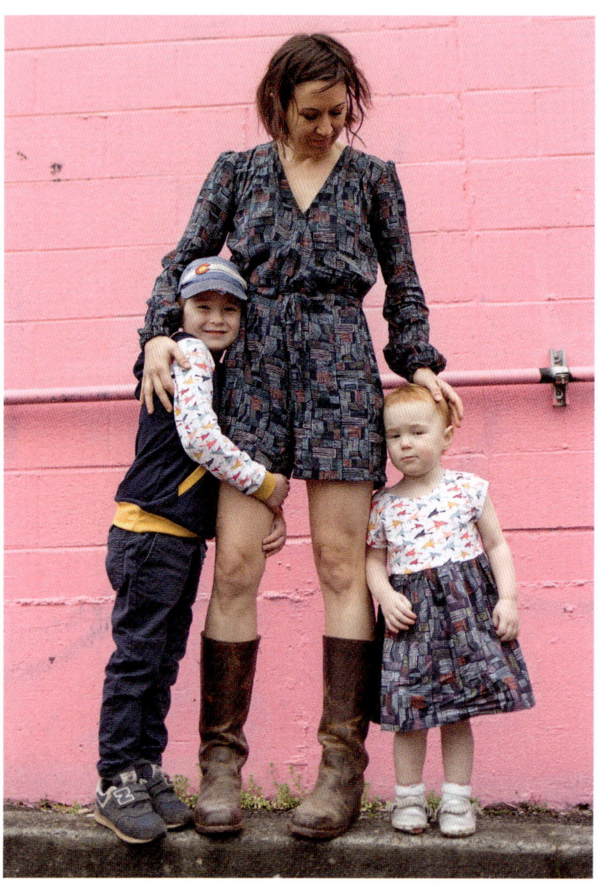

*For Coen and Georgia
—the loves and lights
of my world.*

*For little Jessi—at the
center of it all.*

*And for Ryan—this book
would not exist without him.*

Quarto.com

© 2023 Quarto Publishing Group USA Inc.
Text © 2023 Jessica Swift LLC

First Published in 2023 by Quarry Books,
an imprint of The Quarto Group,
100 Cummings Center, Suite 265-D,
Beverly, MA 01915, USA.
T (978) 282-9590 F (978) 283-2742

Quarry Books titles are also available at discount for retail,
wholesale, promotional, and bulk purchase. For details, contact
the Special Sales Manager by email at specialsales@quarto.com
or by mail at The Quarto Group,
Attn: Special Sales Manager, 100 Cummings Center,
Suite 265-D, Beverly, MA 01915, USA.

10 9 8 7 6 5 4 3 2 1

ISBN: 978-0-7603-8259-2

Digital edition published in 2023
eISBN: 978-0-7603-8260-8

Library of Congress Cataloging-in-Publication Data available

Design and Page Layout: Samantha J. Bednarek,
    samanthabednarek.com
Photography: Jessica Swift; except pages 132 and 144,
    Gwyn LaSpina; 106–107, 109, and 141; Shutterstock.com;
    8 (right), 17 (left), 33 and 112, Michael Tewfik
Illustration: Jessica Swift

Printed in China